THE IDEA OF THE BEING

AN EXPOSITION OF

ITS INCARNATION AND REVELATION
and
THE PRIMARY LAW OF THE SPIRIT

by

S. D. PHILARETOS

«I am the way, and the truth, and the life»
(John 14,6)
«The LOGOS became flesh, and dwelt among us»
(John 1,14)

Translated from the Greek original
By
D. CUMMINGS

Published by

THE ORTHODOX CHRISTIAN EDUCATIONAL SOCIETY
1956 HENDERSON STREET — CHICAGO 13, ILLINOIS, U.S.A.
1963

TO

APOSTOLOS MAKRAKIS

A LEARNED AND VIRTUOUS MAN

PRIVY TO THE TRUTH,

AND

A VALIANT CHAMPION THEREOF,

WHO AS MY TEACHER

GUIDED ME SAGELY

IN RELIGION AND PHILOSOPHY,

THE PRESENT BOOK IS

GRATEFULLY DEDICATED

BY

THE AUTHOR

S. D. PHILARETOS

EDITORS' PREFACE

This book deals with the loftiest objects of the human spirit, and especially with the self - subsistent Idea of the Being, the principle law of the Spirit. It aspires to demonstrate the necessity for the existence of God's absolute Idea, and Its revelation by means of the creation of the physical world, and the incarnation in the person of our Lord Jesus Christ, who is the Idea of the Being, the Logos and the wisdom of God, and the rational and ethical and social Principle whereof springs every rational and ethical and social law. Such then is the intent of this book. It is especially written for the information of those who disbelieve in Christ, and who are not willing to acknowledge His Divinity without demonstrational means, and to confess Christ as the Son of the living God.

This book proves scientifically that Jesus Christ is the Logos of God, the absolute and principle Idea. That the Godman is the absolute law of the spirit and the social principle WHICH PROMISES PROSPERITY UNTO MANKIND, IF EVER THIS PRINCIPIE BE PREACHED AND PROMULGATED EVERYWHERE. But in order to put this idea of (CHRISTOCRACY) into action it is necessary that much and great labor should follow. To this end, therefore, we had to translate and publish it from the Greek original into English, hoping that, God working with us (Mark 16. 20), it might open up the eyes of many, that they might learn the truth scientifically, and the truth might emancipate the leaders of the various systems of delusion along with the people which they guide, and that they might forsake the way which leads to social damnation.

If by some logical and inviolate law and rule the absolute Idea was removed from the absolute Being, and had the absolute Being not pre - existed, we would not have possessed Its IDEA. If the ideas of all relative beings, of both visible and invisible, had been received from the beings, and we did possess them, yet had not the beings pre - existed, we would not have had any idea.

Now we possess the idea of God's absolute Truth, that it is Received from the being. We also possess the ideas of all absolute truths, that they have been received from the relative beings. Moreover we possess the idea of falsehood, that it has been received from the being whereof it was begotten. It is impossible for the absolute falsehood to be perceived and to exist, for it is impossible for two absolute beings to co - exist. Accordingly, then, God, the absolute Truth, precedes the posthumous falsehood, whose father is Satan. Falsehood lives, moves, and acts independently due to the forbearance of Truth, because of the law of justice, but when departing from its limitations, it is bound, for it suffers inactivity.

Since we have numerous contradictory and heretical religions and philosophies, we have also, by necessity, the true religion and philosophy. Now the founder of the numerous false religions and philosophies is invisible, he is the father of falsehood through his ministers and servants. As for the true religion, the founder and establisher thereof is God, through his absolute Idea, by means of His ministers, and servants, the TWELVE APOSTLES. The absolute Idea is also the founder of the Philosophy through one of His servants, APOSTOLOS MAKRAKIS. AND IF YOU doubt, come and receive Instruction therefrom, and you will see its source.

The author of the present volume is Professor Sotirios Philaretos. Being one of the first disciples of the great philosopher Apostolos Makrakis, and having been instructed by him, as the same confesses in the preface of the present volume, he worked together with his tutor up until the end of his life in this world, he was Makrakis assistant editor of two weekly papers «THE LOGOS», AND «THE KIRYGMA», for thirty two years, professor Philaretos taught the most important philosophical subjects at the «School of the Logos», and was the Author of multitudinous works, such as: 1) The Future of Mankind, 2) Three Universal Questions, 3) Human Nature, 4) The Ethical Law, 5) An Orthodox Debate On Catechism, 6) The Ten Commandments, And The New Testament, 7) Refutation of Darwin, 8) The Moral Fight Between Two Opposite Parties in Greece, 9) The Constitution of The Logos to The Christians, 10) Homily Ecclesiastics, 11) The One And Triune Bible, 12) Sermons Referring To The Resurrection, e. t. c ... With creating genius Philaretos elaborated and developed the principles of Makrakis in all his writings, the most important of which is the present volume, «The Idea of the Being».

The Law of God is in the Scriptures and in the Dogmatic truths of the Scriptures that they might regulate the will of the members of the Church in accordance with the will of the Lawgiver. The Law is the expressed and the stated will of Christ therein. No one is superior to the law. The law must govern the will of those under the law, and the transgressors ought to be punished in accordance therewith. Clergy or laymen, and all people, ought to study the law and keep it. «No man in this country is so high that he is above the law. No officer of the law may set the law in defence with impunity. All the officers of the Government, from highest to the lowest, are creatures of the law and are bound to obey it». (U. S. Supreme Court 106 U. S. 220, 1882). Behold, therefore, just as the officers of our country are bound to obey the law, even so are the officers of the Church, the clergy, bound to obey the law and the dogmas of Christ's Church. The law and the dogmas of the Ecumemcal Councils are the ideas of Christ expressed and stated therein. The Dogmas are the manifested truths, but have been misinterpreted by the heretics as do in our times the Jehovah Witnesses.

The Jehovah Witnesses, although they believe that Christ is the Son of the Living God (Matt. 16. 16), yet they strangely believe not that He is God - for the Son is an offspring, God begets God. They believe that He is a creature. But if He is a creature He is not a Son, because the son is not created but born. They confess that Christ is the Son of God, yet they deny that He was born, and believe that He was created, but the Son is an offspring and not a creature. If He is a creature He is not a Son. If He is a Son He is not a creature. The son of man is the offspring of man and consequently a man of men, and is not a creature. Behold, then, the authors of heresy to the Dogmas of the orthodox Church.

Though the Jehovah Witnesses, the self - called Students of the Scriptures, do believe that Christ is the Son, yet they will not believe that He was born, this signifies that they are inconsitent in regards to their confession. Behold, therefore, the authors of heresy to the Dogma concerning the Holy and adorable Trinity. For Christ is «Light of light, true God from the true God, begotten and not created, consubstantial with the Father, through Whom were all things made». Behold the symbol of the Orthodox faith refuting the heresies of those that believe not correctly.

Man' s word (logos) is the offspring of his mind, and he could not be perfect had he not a mind (nous), word (logos) and spirit. From God's image, man (Gen. 1. 27), we advance to the knowledge of God, the Holy Trinity, NOUS, LOGOS, SPIRIT The NOUS begets the LOGOS and emits the HOLY SPIRIT, Where there is a self-acting MIND (NOUS) there coexist also the LOGOS and the SPIRIT, because these attributes constitute the NOUS OR MIND. This truth is being scientifically proven in the present work.

All liberty is under the law and remains free as long as it keeps the law. He that subjects his will to that of the law freely and independently, the same remains free. «Whosoever committeth sin is the servant thereof. And the servant abideth not in the house for ever (John 8. 34)». Sin is the transgression of the law, and it is healed through penitence. Penitence is the acknowledging of sin through confession and the returning to the truth, to the spirit of the law. Christ' s grace does not destroy the law (Matt. 5. 17), but forgives the sins only unto those who repent and return to the will and the spirit of the law, according to, «Shall I at all desire the death of the sinner saith the Lord, as I desire that he should turn from his evil way and live. (Ezek. 18. 23)»? But they who do not return are under the law. «For as many as have sinned without law shall also perish without law: and as many as have sinned in the law shall be judged by the law; for not the hearers of the law are just before God, but the doers of the law shall be justified (Rom. 2. 12, 13)». Accordingly, then, the violators shall be condemned, and Christ's grace shall in no way profit them which rely on it.

The road to unity amongst the Churches is one: the return to the truth amongst those who are guilty and misled. Behold, therefore, the present work, as also the Philosophical System of Apostolos Makrakis, which are written with the intent of helping those which have gone astray to return to the faith in the True God.

The Editors

MY RESPECTED TEACHER!

Long ago I became firmly convinced of your scientific and moral worth, after perceiving that you have worthily exercised the calling of learned and virtuous teacher, that both in words and in deeds you have been teaching and advocating knowledge and cognizance of the Truth Itself, and the achievement of evangelical virtue. By you and you alone I was taught precisely that which all the seemingly learned and scientific men on earth are ignorant of and for want of method are vainly attempting to learn, though it must be added that they are mostly conceited egoists. That is the absolute truth in Christ, whereby both God and world and man can be known and comprehended, and the mysterious problem of science, namely, what is the Universe?, can be solved for the good of society, and for the fulfillment of our philosophical yearning. After becoming personally aware of the God-man Christ and after being by Him instructed and educated in His divine doctrine, whereof He is the Chief Professor and Chief Teacher, you were the first to recognize the fact that Christ is the object (or, as we usually say in English, the subject) not only of religion, but also of philosophy, and of the political state; that He is the one who is really Holy, really Wise, really Righteous, the Truth Itself and the absolute Logos (or Reason) of the Universe, the substantiated Idea of the Being, and the primary and ontological Law of the perfect Spirit, the social object out of which arises every law, and the absolute social principle, the Principle which regulates the social relations of life by means of religion, science, political state, and art. Having been taught this truth by you thoroughly and for a sufficient length of time, and having become devoted to it, I consider it my duty, so far as it lies in my power, to impart this great truth to others, and to confide this exceedingly valuable treasure and social weal to others, and to acknowledge the gratitude I owe you, who became and are my teacher in the matter of the scientific proof of this great truth, of this cornerstone of the social edifice, anyone falling against it is bound to be crushed to pieces, and which will winnow whomsoever it falls upon. Even though the unlearned and uneducated and unscientific have failed to appreciate your scientific and moral worth, and for want of learning and education have enviously and maliciously calumniated and slandered you, and have disseminated and trumpeted as many charges against you everywhere as the cunning and deceitful tongue of the Scribes, Chief Priests, and Pharisees disseminated and droned against the divine Savior, yet they have not been able to sully and dim your real worth, which never fails to shine forth more brightly than the sun to those who have even once listened to your scientific and pious teaching and have reflectively perused your important writings, theological, philosophical, and educational, and have learned your political principles and ideas. To you therefore by dedicating this work of mine as a token of my deep gratitude to you for having piloted me into the unruffled haven of the truth unerringly with reason and right reflection, I deem that I am performing a duty, and no one can reprehend this act of mine as improper and unreasonable. I am sensible of the duty, in dedicating to you my present work, to express outspoken praise of your true and unerring doctrine, which is in all respects consonant and consistent with the spirit of Christianity, with the sound doctrine of the Gospel, but which is strongly opposed to the prejudices and Jewish and Godmongering Christianity of the rhasophores of the Synod (of Greese), and to the imaginary and injudicious and euphemistically so - called science of the schools of the West, and particularly to the school of our Greek university which is a child of theirs, and to the egoistic and deceitful - minded and selfish policy of our politicians. I feel it to be my duty to praise your virtue, your great faith which you have in Christ, and your great self - abnegation as you are working without a view to profit for the dissemination of the Christian and Evangelical truth, for the establishment of Christicracy, and for the liberation of humanity from the internal enemy called sin and from the external tyranny of Kaisers, and from the misteaching and viciousness of those falsely called chief priests and teachers. While praising your worth and ability in Christ, I strenuously reproach and pity those who foolishly assail you by words and deeds, on the ground that they know not what they are doing. Accordingly, I wish and entreat them to be enlightened and to show regret for their action, if there is any strength for repentance in them; for it is hard to have them kick against the pricks, to have them wage war upon the evangelical doctrine, and to have them traduce it multifariously in the person of its workers and disseminators who are doing and teaching it.

A grateful pupil of your Eruditeness,

S. D. Philaretos

PROLEGOMENA

To philosophize means to yearn after the truth, to search and seek for the truth, to be attracted by reason towards the truth. The yearning, the search, and the seeking for the truth are the thermometer of spiritual life. That is why philosophizing is living spiritually. Wherever philosophical activity is in evidence, there spiritual life is to be observed; but wherever it is absent, there spiritual deadness is manifest. Spiritual life demands contact of the cognitive spirit with the eternal truth; and in order that it may be perfect life, the contact of the spirit with the truth must also be perfect: or, in other words, the contact and union of the philosophizing spirit with the perfect and eternal truth must be complete. For this spirit yearns for the eternal and absolute Truth. God, who implanted in man a yearning to know everything, a yearning for the eternal Truth, implanted in him a desire for Him, the fulfillment whereof cannot be achieved by any other means than through God. On this account·the end and object of the yearning to know in the philosophical spirit is knowledge of God, knowledge of the eternal truth concerning Him, toward which he is irresistibly and anxiously drawn. Beginning with a yearning for the truth, and ending by discovering and apprehending it through search and inquiry, it succeeds in fulfilling its yearning, and reposes in the truth which it has become acquainted with and by means of which all knowledge and truth can be discerned and comprehended, and everything that is knowable can be fully known. This cognoscitive procedure of man for the discovery and apprehension of the truth which corresponds to his philosophical yearning has for its end a theoretical knowledge of the eternal truth, an exaltation of the spirit in the existence of the idea of the Being and of the eternal ideas principles, and laws of the spirit, the contemplation of the Being through His eternal idea. But this cognoscitive procedure of the intellect is accompanied by the active and practical procedure of the will and of the feelings of the philosophizing soul, the end and purpose of which procedure is the actualization and realization of the moral weal, the experimental and practical ascertainment of the truth, the fulfillment of the philosophizing soul's interminable and everlasting joy, which results from the apprehension of the truth and the actualization of man's moral purpose. When both these procedures, the theoretical and the practical, of the philosophizing spirit progress in parallel, the philosophical spirit achieves its destiny by means of philosophy, cognizes the eternal truth, and actualizes the good within it, and feels an ineffable and interminable joy. One philosophizes soundly when he pursues the truth for the sake of the good, and not for the sake of egoism and vainglory — when he applies the truth apprehended in life, it thereby becomes of benefit to himself and to society as a whole. For the purpose of philosophy is the most beneficial of all. Through philosophy prejudices and erroneous impressions are expelled and eliminated from men, and everywhere the truth is made to appear as a result of reason and proof, and enlightens and adjusts and regulates social life. The philosophical light penetrating everywhere dissolves myths and prejudices like so many cobwebs, exposes falsehoods and errors, safeguards the religion from being adulterated and debased by heresies, distinguishes and separates what is divine from what is human, safeguards the political state from tyranny and slavery, detects and exposes the laws that are inconsistent and conflict with what is right and just, points out the nature of what is right and just, attacks false political systems, and illuminates the social aim.

God, who revealed the religion to us through His Son and our Savior, and invested it with authoritativeness, was the one who implanted in us the yearning to know, and gave us the law of seeking and searching for the truth, so that we might seek it freely and under the sway of observation and right reason. Hence it is that the true religion and the true philosophy, though differing in respect of their aim, agree as to their object of pursuit, which is the eternal Truth, which through religion and faith is imposed upon us authoritatively, while through philosophy it can be sought by us freely and under the sway of the right philosophical method. Religion springs directly from God. Philosophy springs from man, because of its being a free search and consideration and quest of the truth. But truth is the basis of both, of religion and philosophy, and it springs from God. God, being the source of truth. Man o b t a i n s the truth dogmatically by means of religion, and demonstratively by means of philosophy and logical search and inquiry. The true religion and the true philosophy agree with each other in respect of their basis and of their object of pursuit, and with the true political state too, though they differ in respect of their nature, means, and final purpose. The political state, being a free society and association with our fellows and with God, as a rational and moral being, joins the moral and free persons by means of the truth and what is right, and regulates their moral relations in accordance with their destiny. Thus the one and eternal and immutable truth in God is proved to be the basis and the object (or what we usually call the subject in English) of religion, of philosophy, and of the political state, in accordance with which the religious, and the philosophical, and the political aim of life is carried out. If it is true that the Christian religion is the true and divine religion, is it not plain that its basis and object is the eternal Truth? But the Truth of the religion is Jesus Christ. But since the Truth, being one, eternal, absolute and ever the same, is the basis and object, as has been said, of religion, philosophy, and political state, and is in fact Jesus Christ, it may be logically inferred that Jesus Christ is the basis and object of philosophy and of the political state. For if Christ is not the object of philosophy and of the political state, then neither is He the object of religion. Thus the Christian religion would be proved to be false, and to be a human invention, instead of being true and divine. Either then confessing the divinity of the Christian religion, we ought necessarily also to confess together therewith that Christ is the absolute Truth, and consequently the object and basis of philosophy and of political state, or, denying that Christ is the object of philosophy and of the political state, we necessarily ought also to deny the divinity of the Christian religion. There is no middle road. But if it is indisputable that Christ is the Truth Itself, the foundation of religion, philosophy, and political state, and the object whereby man's religious and moral and political aim may be achieved and actualized, is it not plain that the society which recognizes Christ as the object fulfilling its three infinite yearnings - that of knowing everything, that of being able to do everything, and that of living forever is based upon the Truth Itself, Life Itself, and Power Itself, having a basis which is everlasting and cannot be displaced, and being itself everlasting and permanently fixed in place; It being granted that the God - man is the Truth Itself, society as aiming at the Truth, necessarily ought to aim at the God - man. It ought to pursue religion in accordance with His example, becoming religiously refined; it ougt to get educated and philosophize in accordance with His principles and logical laws, to be brought up and to be provided with a schooling in accordance with His moral laws and His commandments; and it ought to conduct itself in accordance with His everlasting and immutable civil laws of justice and of equality, in accordance with the laws of moral and civil freedom. Society ought, in a word, to conduct itself in all of its aspects Christocratically, and evangelicaly, recognizing Christ as its absolute Principle, and His Gospel as the Supreme Law and as the criterion of every law. We ought to be consistent with both our theoretical and our practical life, walking logically and morally in accordance with the principle of the eternal truth, of the moral, weal and of what is right. If Christ is the Truth Itself, as He was previously proved to be, both in religion and in philosophy and in the political state; if He is the first theoretical and absolute social principle, He is necessarily also a practical principle: for our single and triple social nature demands a single truth and principle that corresponds to it, having likewise a triple aspect. The theoretical life of society is not any other than the practical life; nor is the practical life any other than the theoretical life; life being manifested under two aspects, the theoretical and the practical. Thus neither is the truth any other thing than the moral and social weal, but, on the contrary, both are essentially one and the same thing, being manifested under a different aspect in life. Jesus Christ is the center of society and of the social circle, the great Sun in the spiritual firmament of society, the beginning, or Principle, and the end, or goal, of social life. The religion has regard to Him; the philosophy has regard to Him; and the political state has regard to Him; the philosophy has regard to Him; and the political state has regard to Him. Both the theoretical and the practical life of society have regard to Him. Everything begins through Him as the one who is the creative, or efficient, Logos of the universe, and everything trnds towards Him as the end because He is the final Logos, or Reason, of the universe.

Apprising mankind of Christ as the efficient and final Logos of beings, as the social principle whereby all the needs of society can be supplied, is the greatest of benefactions, because it saves man from everlasting death, from everlasting perdition and deprivation of what is good, and brings him into propinquity to the Absolute Good, i. e., to God, whom we can in no other wise approach than through the eternal Truth, through Christ. Those who bear witness to Christ, and who confess Him even at the sacrifice of their lives as the absolute Truth and the catholic Logos of God, are the ones that are the great benefactors of mankind, the ones who confer great benefits upon it. But the men of today, with few exceptions, are ignorant of the social worth of the God-man, and on this account they are nowise benefited by His social power and His boons and blessings, be cause they are not seeking them. It is on this account that they are unhappy too, and are suffering countless woes, undergoing extreme hardships, involved in conflicts with one another, and coming to blows with one another, and going astray in their theoretical lives, and clashing with one another in their practical lives. But the voice of the eternal Truth, the divine voice of the Savior, is calling upon the rebel society to repent and regret and return after straying from the way of truth because of its ignorance and infancy and because of its yielding to a deceitful suggestion made by the

Evil One. In the words «Repent : for the kingdom of heaven is at hand» (Matt. 4 : 17) the divine voice of the Savior interrupts the further excursion of mankind into sin, and recalls it to its proper status by saying:.«Come unto me, all ye who are troubled and are burdened; and I will give you rest. Take my yoke upon you, and learn from me; for I am meek and humble - hearted; and ye shall find rest for your souls. For my yoke is easy, and my burden is light» Matt. 11. 28-30).

Yea, turn quickly, O mankind, in the direction pointed out by the voice of the God - man, and hearken to His saving voice; and repent quickly, and return ftom the way of error, of falsehood and of sin, of prejudices and of thy ancient habits, which are the heritage of thy ignorance. Behold, the divine light is here shining upon thee, and the brilliant Sun of the spiritual world has already dawned upon thee, and has effused its golden rays, imparting to thee by means thereof the light of knowledge and of science, the light which guides thee to all the truth and to a life of virtue, to progress and to the achievement of thy social aim, to the effectuation of thy everlasting contact with God, the Absolute Good, and thy perfect and everlasting association with Him in a logical and moral relationship by virtue of the Spirit. So be it !

INTRODUCTION

«But as for a lover of science, he
must seek after the first causes of
intelligent nature».
(Plato in Timaeus)

A search for the First Idea and the first principles of Philosophy, the highest of all sciences, presupposes their existence and the existence in our spirit of an ability to seek and find them. For if they did not exist, neither should we be able to seek and to attempt to find them. We seek the being, or reality, even though it eludes our superficial observation in the very beginning. But we can discover it when we delve after it with due care and methodically, confident of its existence. Being, therefore, convinced of the existence of the First Idea and of the first principles, we are convinced of the existence of the f i r s t s c i e n c e, which otherwise could not exist if the First Idea and the first principles did not exist. There are many and various ideas and principles and each science is a systematic survey of the ideas and principles of which it is the science. Thus the science of sciences is the systematic survey of the First Idea and first principles, and knowledge of these is knowledge of the science, the name whereof is P h i l o s o p h y. Philosophy is the first and chief science which has governing authority over all the other sciences, having and exercising supervision to see that they examine and investigate their own object (or, as we usually say in English, their own subject · matter) methodically, and coordinating and correlating them to the catholic purpose of science, both theoretical and practical. For just as all ideas and principles are connected and associated with the First Idea and the first principles, so and in like manner are all sciences connected and associated with the first and chief science. Philosophy, in much the same way as servant - maids are connected and associated with their mistress; in much the same way as consequences are connected and associated with their premises, and as the links of a chain are connected and associated with the first and chief link upon which they depend. Such a relational association and such a conjunctive connection exist between the chain of the sciences and Philosophy as the first and chief science.

The science of the First Cause and first principles is the highest step in the ladder of man's intellactual development, the highest mountain of the intellect (mind), upon which when the latter ascends it can reconnoiter all the ideas of beings, and learn thoroughly and succeed in knowing and comprehending the general laws in accordance with which the universe is governed and administered, and in accordance with which all things concur harmoniously in assisting the general and catholic purpose of creation. If we conceive the science of the First Idea and first principles as a high mountain and the rest of sciences as hills surrounding the bottom of it, we may conceive the ascent of the human spirit up this mountain as the product of a proportionate yearning and power, as, in a word, a gigantic achievement. In order to ascend to the top of a high mountain one must have a yearning and a power proportionate to the accomplishment of the task. He must be of mature age and must have healthy legs. He must also be familiar with the way of ascent up the mountain. The ascent of the human intellect up the metaphorical mountain of Philosophy is the comprehension of the First Idea and first principles of science, knowledge and apprehension of the first and absolute scibile, of the first and absolute Idea of the Being. The ascent of the human spirit up the metaphorical mountain of Philosophy cannot be effected without the prerequisite conditions and terms. For just as one must first have healthy legs trained in climbing and sufficient knowledge of the way in order to ascend to the top of a mountain, so and in like manner one must first receive preliminary instruction in knowledge of the other sciences that constitute the foot of, or the bottom surrounding, the mountain of Philosophy, and learn securely the philosophical method whereby the ascent up the mountain of the first and chief science can be accomplished. So let us turn our attention to.

Yearning. Power. Knowledge of Method.

These three are the elements of the philosophical spirit of the man who is ascending to the top of the first and absolute scibile, and is gaining a comprehension of the First Idea and of the First Principle of beings, and is organizing within him the first and chief science. The cause of the yearning which the human spirit conceives for the discovery and comprehension of the First Idea and first principles is their existence. If no First Idea and first principles existed, neither would any passionate love of them be engendered in our spirit. This yearning in our spirit is characterized as the first and highest, as a yearning after the Absolute, urging and impelling us to seek the Absolute. It is aroused within us after we first acquire a consciousness of our existence, and a perception of the world outside of us. Being nowise content with this elementary knowledge of the ego and of

the world, we ascend higher in search of knowledge of the efficient, or creative, cause of the universe, and thus conceive the
Idea of the Absolute. Being conscious that I exist and that the
other beings exist together with me, and yearning intently to
learn whether I exist of myself and the world roundabout me
exists of itself, or whether it is as a result of something else that
I have received my existence, I begin climbing by the law of
a n a g o g e, or logical process of ascending reduction, to a
conception of the absolute Idea of the Being who created me and
the visible world roundabout me. Thus the human spirit ascends
and gradually climbs up to a conception of the First Idea of the
Absolute Being, and lays the foundation and basis of the first
and chief science, the concept of the absolute scibile.

The yearning after the absolute is called also an absolute
yearning : 1) Because it is the first and highest and governing
one among the many and various yearnings of man ; 2) because
it leads the soul to the absolute. It corresponds to the nature of
the First Idea and first principles, and to the nature of the first
and chief science. None of the schools were able to deny the existence in man of a yearning after the absolute, but, on the contrary, all of them accepted and admitted it. Yet they belied themselves by denying the truth in the consequences of it. And this is
the self-contradictory doctrine of the schools, which roundly
exposes them as being self-contradictory and self-inconsistent.
Thus the school of the ideologists at times acknowledged the Idea
of the Absolute through Kant to be something unattainable ; while
at other times through Hegel it represented it to be identical with
the abstract and general idea of humanity and of the universe,
which it even called the absolute idea of cognition. At other times
again it confused it with the idea of the ego through Fichte and
the school of the panegoists. Thus it represented the universe and
the ego as the absolute by means of the system of pantheism and
of panegoism, while on the other hand by means of the system of
criticism it proclaimed it to be altogether unattainable. The school
of the materialists, on the opposite side of the picture, identified
the Idea of the Absolute with the idea of the finite material world,
and accepted and admitted matter as the absolute. Kant, though
acknowledging the existence of the absolute outside of matter and
the senses, as well as the yearning in man after the absolute,
denied, for want of judgment and owing to inconsistent reasoning,
the ability and power of the human spirit to conceive the absolute by means of right reason, having in mind as he did the numerous self-contradictions of the men who had been philosophizing
before him in regard to the Idea of the Absolute. But if this is
true, how did Kant, we ask, ascend to a conception of the Idea of

the Absolute? By means of what law, we wonder, did he prove and confirm the simple existence of the Absolute? Was it not by means of right reason? But if right reason can conceive and reveal within us the Idea of the Absolute Being, why can it not conceive and reveal to us also all the properties, or peculiar attributes, of the Being, and the totality of the Idea of Him? Kant thus commits the greatest absurdity and falls into a terrible self-contradiction by predicating two self-contradictory peculiarities, of right reason, by asserting that right reason c a n   a n d   a t   t h e s a m e   t i m e   c a n n o t   c o n c e i v e   t h e   A b s o l u t e. For, if right reason can conceive the existence of the Absolute, it necessarily must also be able to conceive the Idea of Him. It can even elevate us to the conception and comprehension of the First Idea and first principles, and establish thereupon the first and chief science. But if it cannot conceive the Idea of the Absolute, neither can it apprehend it. The conception of the Idea is the premise, or principle; the apprehension of it is the consequence, or development. If the ego usually errs, its error is due to illogical thinking. Reason itself, however, never errs; for it is an eternal law in our spirit, an infallible rule, a true and right compass which shows the truth as it verily is. But Kant after confusing right reason with the nature of the finite ego, and mistaking the cognitive faculty of the soul for right reason, after confusing the law with the object it was laid down to govern, and wrongly identifying them with each other, it was to be expected that Kant would wind up by drawing such false conclusions and falling into a terrible self-contradiction which opened wide a chasm into which the school of criticism, ineptly called rationalism, was hurled headlong.

The modern school of criticism and of idealism, following in the footsteps of the Kantian school, and philosophizing by the same method, and predicating at times all and at times some of the errors and self-contradictions of the ego of right reason, without any proof to sustain this view, became a likely prey of materialism, being unable to leave the confines of the finite and to conceive the Absolute and His relation to finite matter. Thus it too involuntarily and against its own inclination and intention trends either to positive skepticism, which in no way attempts an examination of the Absolute, or to negative skepticism, which entertains doubts as to the existence of a nonego and of any other objective essence, or extra-mental entity. The ego, together with its finite ideas, of the school of the ideologists, and cognitive matter, together with its ideas derived from experience, of the school of the materialists, are two cogitative results of the same nature which can be considered identical, notwithstanding that they have a different form. Neither the criticism of Kant nor the pantheism of Hegel nor the panegoism of Fichte ascended to an apprehension and comprehension of the First Idea and first principles, nor were they able to establish the first and chief science and make it independent of the other sciences; but, on the contrary, they took it to be identical with them and confused it with the anthropological and the cosmological sciences. By deifying the universe, pantheism assumes the universe as the first Idea and First Principle; consequently the philosophy proposed by the school of pantheism was the science of the universe, or universology. By deifying the ego, panegoism assumes the ego as the First Idea and First Principle; consequently the philosophy proposed by the school of the panegoists was a science of the ego. In pantheism philosophy became identified with the finite and the fact (i.e., the sum-total of everything made). In panegoism it became identified with the finite ego, and was taken to be a science of the finite, thus being subsumed in the same category as the other sciences of the finite. This absurd and improper identification with the other sciences of the finite was due to the identification of the First Idea and first principles with the ideas of the finite and of the fact. But if these schools of pantheism and of panegoism had distinguished the First Idea and the first principles from the ideas of the fact, they would also have distinguished Philosophy from the other sciences of the fact, as the first and chief and highest science.

The school of materialism, though far from solving the problem propounded by pantheism and panegoism, yet succeded in treating it in a simpler fashion, more practically, and without making any noise about it. Acknowledging matter and the objects of the senses as the absolute, it identified philosophy with the cosmological sciences, identifying the science of the First Idea and first principles with the ideas of the fact and of the finite. As respecting the Absolute Being the school of materialism conceitedly asserted that that was matter, which organizes itself and produces by its own activity the variety of forms which we behold in the universe. Consequently the idea of matter is to be considered the first and chief and primary idea, while the laws of nature become the first principles. The science which is occupied with comprehension of the first idea of matter and of the laws of nature is the science of philosophy. Thus the first and chief science in materialism turns out to be a science of the fact and of the finite, and not of the Infinite and of the Absolute. What we are now interested in learning, however, while investigating the schools of criticism, of pantheism, of panegoism, and of materialism, is this, that all the doctrines of the schools, no matter under what principle and mien and form they have been represented in the scientific world, have acknowledged that there is something that is absolute, and that consequently the First Idea and first principles do exist, as well as a science whose function is to discover and comprehend them. Their disagreement did not pertain to the question concerning the existence of the Absolute, as to whether It exists, nor that concerning the yearning to investigate and comprehend It, but concerning the qualification comprised in the question, what is the Absolute? Criticism looked for the Absolute outside of the world and outside of the ego, in some particular and individual personality. Pantheism sought It in the universe, in the world and in the ego, or in general and abstract ideas, as a general abstract conception, as a being not to be distinguished from the world and from the ego. Panegoism sought It in the ego, in man, denying any distinct existence of the Absolute Being. Materialism sought the Absolute in matter, and in the sensible world, refusing to admit any existence of an absolute being apart from matter. But the Absolute of criticism is unattainable, a view, however, which obviously contradicts the Idea of the Absolute, which Idea can nevertheless be apprehended by the intellect through right reason. The absolute of pantheism, and of panegoism, and of materialism contradicts the nature of the yearning after the absoloute in man; moreover, it wholly contradicts human nature, which cannot identify the fact with the absolute cause, nor confuse the absolute cause with the fact. But as concerning these matters, the discussion of them will be undertaken in the proper place.

Philosophy being the science of the First Idea and first principles, and consequently the first and chief science, it may be said to be the science proper of the Logos. All the other sciences are sciences either of consciousness or of perception (by which term is meant cognition through — p e r — the senses). The first idea of the Absolute that the human spirit can conceive is a product of r i g h t r e a s o n (and consequently a concept, and not a percept); and unless the human spirit possessed the power to ascend mentally from particular and relative ideas to the first primary idea, to conception of the Idea of the Absolute, the word a b s o l u t e itself could not have existed, nor could any distinction of it from the relative have been arrived at by man. The correlative term corresponding to the term a b s o l u t e is the term r e l a t i v e. In conceiving and expressing by means of a term analogous to the actuality, or thing itself, and usual to language, the Idea of the Absolute, the human spirit cognizes Its necessary existence, corresponding to the idea of the existence of the relative and of the finite, which it apprehends before the Idea of the Absolute. He who cognizes the existence of the Absolute cognizes it as related to the existence of the relative. But the Idea of the Absolute cannot be conceived unless the idea of the relative is conceived first. From the idea of the relative the intellect proceeds to apprehension of the Idea of the Absolute, in accordance with right reason; and before conceiving the idea of the relative it cannot conceive the Idea of the Absolute. It is for this reason and on this account that we say; «There exist relative causes. There exists an absolute cause to which these owe their existence and on which they depend as its effects.». While in their existence the Absolute Cause precedes ontologically, being eternally and necessarily existent, yet nevertheless in cognition and the logical order of ideas the idea of the relative precedes logically, and the Idea of the Absolute necessarily follows. The existence of the Absolute is not necessarily the cause of the existence of the relative, for the Absolute can exist even without the existence of the relative, as a necessary being. The existence of the relative, however, presupposes the existence of the Absolute; for the relative cannot come into being and continue existing of itself. (Note of Translator.— By this the author means to say that nothing relative can come into existence spontaneously, but that everything relative must have a cause whereby it was brought into existence out of nonbeinghood). The school of pantheism. of panegoism, and of materialism, being deluded, mistook the Absolute Idea to be a product of consciousness and perception, because they identified the world, the ego, matter, and physical forces wrongly with the absolute cause; they mistook creation to be the creator, the world built to be the builder and maker of it. Accordingly, the school of the pantheists conceitedly proclaimed the universe to be God. The school of the panegoists proudly declared the ego to be God. The school of the materialists deified the world and sensible beings.

Pantheism	says :	The universe is a God
Panegoism	»	The ego is a God
Materialism	»	Matter is a God

But if the universe is a God, matter, being a part of the universe, is therefore a part of God. Consequently God is divisible, and not indivisible, according to the pantheists. But in the universe are to be observed both good things and bad things. If the universe is a God, and God is the universe, then God is both good and bad, it may be logically inferred. Hence it is evident that pantheism is not only logically false, but also morally. Consequently pantheism is the cause of every paralogism and of every error in scientific life. But in practical life it is the cause of moral disorder and of licentiousness. The universe, according to the pantheists, is the absolute. But how did these men succeed in ascending to the Idea of the Absolute? By employing what method? What sort of relative is that from the idea of which by a law of anagogical (or ascending reductive) cognition they conceived the idea of the absolute? But if the universe is the absolute, then the parts of the universe must be admitted to be parts of the absolute. That being so, what sort of relative is opposed to the absolute? we wonder. If, again, the parts of the universe, or, more expressly speaking, of the absolute, are also relative causes, is not the relative thus being confused and identified with the absolute, and the relative itself being made to appear to be both relative and absolute at the same time, and the absolute to be at the same time also relative? But according to the universally valid principle of contradiction, the same thing cannot be at the same time both relative and absolute. It may only be either relative or absolute. For these two ideas of absolute and relative are logically distinguishable and distinct in thought, just as the existence of the absolute and the existence of the relative are distinguished ontologically. That which we distinguish logically in accordance with the principle of contradiction is something that preexists ontologically in the order of beings as something distinct. And just as we cannot confuse the existence of the relative with the existence of the absolute in the order of beings, so and in like manner may it be said that we cannot make any confusion of the ideas of them that are distinct from each other, even in the logical order of ideas. But pantheism, though unable to confuse things distinct in the order of beings, confused them nevertheless in the logical order, and did so for want of method and want of logicality, because it philosophized outside of right reason. No one who philosophizes in accordance with right reason can confuse things that are distinct, or distinguish things that are not distinct by nature. Anyone cognizing and thinking in accordance with right reason will cognize and consider the ideas in accordance with the order of beings and will build a science in accordance with the nature and order of things as they actually occur. For this reason and on this account when pantheism philosophizes outside of right reason, it manifestly presents no charm no attractive feature. Being false in the premises, it is false also in the consequences: a system that is unorganized as such, having neither a beginning nor an end. The denial is of freedom, of personality, of morality, of reality, and of moral order, as presented through Hegel and Spinoza; and it is a most hideous monster. Pantheism is in effect materialism, though wearing a certain form of fictitious spirituality,

Panegoism says: God is the ego, man. But if God is the ego, man, there being many men, and therefore many ego, there are many parts of God, inasmuch as they are distinquishable from each other. Hence it follows logicaly that the absolute cause is divisible, and not indivisible, in panegoism, precisely as in pantheism. But if the absolute is divisible, it follows logically that it is not one, but many. But many absolutes cannot be conceived in accordance with reason, but one and only one being conceivable. Hence it follows as a logical conclusion that pantheism does not think in accordance with right reason, but outside of reason; and on this account it is false in its premise. Every human being is conscious within him that he is an effect of a relative cause, a product of his father and mother. This consiousness is common and is to be found in all men and women who are sane. All mankind is conscious that it is an effect of some relative cause, of the same race and of the same nature, of a first man and of a first woman, who were molded immediately and directly by the absolute efficient Cause, by God Himself. Human consciousness rejects and repels the doctrine of panegoism, just as it rejects and repels the doctrine of subjective and of objective pantheism on the ground that it is opposed to the nature of things and false. Panegoism, which deifies the ego, deifies nothing else than the finite essence of man, the human will, from which spring both good and bad things. For there are human beings who do what is good, and others who do what is bad or evil. Deification of the ego, therefore, means deification of the good and of the bad on the same footing and on a basis of equality; while the essence of the absolute resolves itself into a mixture of the good and of the bad, or the absolute out of which spring at the same time both what is good and what is bad. Hence it is evident that just as panegoism is false logically, it is false also morally, and is opposed to the logical and moral order. Right reason is an implacable enemy of the errors of panegoism, just as it is of the errors of pantheism. Accordingly, the doctrines of these unorganized systems, being outside of right reason, cannot come within its consideration. In vain they try to make it appear that they are performing their task in accordance with reason. No reasonable human being can become a pantheist so long as he is his right mind and makes right use of right reason. Such false doctrines, which contradict themselves and the facts and are conflicting, are products of imaginative cognition and not of logical cognition, of impressional thinking that cognizes contrary to reason and outside of the terms and conditions of rational cognition. The w h y and the b e c a u s e are the reefs upon which these false philosophemes are dashed to pieces and wrecked, and they sink in the open sea of obscurity and go to their perdition. When reason is idle or kept in abeyance, then it is that these systems exercise an influence over thought. But when reason exercises an influence over thought, then it is that these systems hide themselves in the deep darkness of obscurity, fearing the rise of the metaphorical sun, right reason, upon the firmament of cognition and dreading its vivid briliance.

Materialism, with its usual light - mindedness and haughtiness contends that m a t t e r i s a G o d, o r G o d i s m a t t e r, t h a t n o t h i n g h i g h e r t h a n m a t - t e r e x i s t s. This testimony is false, however, since it is not given by either consciousness or perception or right reason, nor does it agree with the nature of things. Now, being based on perception, materialism assimilates consciousness and right reason to this ability of the spirit, and abolishes the two abilities to cognize. Materialism is h y p e r t r o p h y of perception, an objective and subjective disorder and confusion. For just as is confuses the abilities to cognize, which are clearly distinguishable from each other in the process of cognition, so and likewise also in the order of ideas it confuses the logical order, and in the idea of matter it confuses the idea of the ego and that of the absolute. For, if matter is a God, the ego, inasmuch as it is identifiable with matter, is therefore a God. Hence it logically follows that the universe is a God, or that God is the universe. Thus materialism attains to identification with Pantheism and panegoism, though under a different form. The end and aim of these systems is one and the same, the deification of matter and its forces, the deification of the fact and of the finite. The materialists teach that they are Gods, and that there is no God above them and matter. Everything is derived from matter, and came to be through the action of matter, and everything returns and comes back to the state of matter. Hence it is logically evident that matter is a God. But if matter is the absolute, while the ego and the universe are included and comprised in matter, what are the relatives from the idea of which the intellect is led to conceive the idea of the absolute? The Absolute, as we showed hereinabove, is something which we cannot cognize until we have cognized the relative. But materialism presumptuously thinks that it can cognize the Absolute before cognizing the relative things, apart from the existence of the Absolute. Hence it logically follows that materialism is attempting what is naturally impossible, and is proceeding contrary to the terms of cognition. Matter is the absolute of materialism, and the idea of matter is the idea of the absolute. But inasmuch as the universe, according to materialism, is matter, both man, the world, and God, the universe itself, is consequently an absolute, conceived i n t o t o and i n p a r t i b u s . Hence it follows in accordance with the laws of logic that there is no such thing as anything relative. How, then, did materialism conceive the Idea of the Absolute, after denying the idea of the relative? How did it manage to lift itself up to the Idea of the Absolute without the idea of the relative, serving as basis in the process of thought? Hence it is logically evident that it did so unmethodically, and contrary to the conditions imposed upon the processes of thought, and after wrongly confounding in cognition the very things which in the natural order of beings are distinct, after confounding, that is to say, the idea of the relative with the idea of the Absolute. And right here is where occurred the great wreck of materialism, and the deep chasm into which it has fallen, never to come back out of it. In the contention of materialism that the Absolute exists lies the admission which involuntarily by the perspicuity of the actual facts it is forced to utter, to the effect that logically the relative precedes it in existence, since without the relative the absolute cannot by the nature of the case be conceived. This admission being an inner conviction of the spirit, though not outwardly expressed by the tongue owing to Luciferian pride and conceit, is an admission of the spirit reflecting in accordance with reason, and is a testimony of right reason, which exhibits the idea of the relative as distinct and separate in the spirit from the Idea of the Absolute.

Materialism being logically false, it is also morally bad. For it destroys the logical order and disturbs the moral order, and militates against the catholic order of things itself. Being false in the premises, it is false also in the consequences; and on this account and for this reason it ought to be frowned upon by society as the most ruinous error and delusion, tending to the moral depravation of society, and ought to be utterly discarded. Right reason is an implacable enemy of materialism; and materialism cannot stand up in front of it: but neither can any of the systems of error conceived and gestated and born outside of reason. Materialism, acknowledging as the First Idea the idea of matter, and avouching the forces of natures to be the first principles, accepts the view that Physics and Physiology (or, as we used to say in English, as late as the last century, Natural Philosophy) in general is a main and chief science; and accordingly it holds all scientific knowledge and ideas to depend on that science. M a t - t e r and F o r c e , these are the objects (or, as we more usu-

ally say in English, the subject - matter or subjects) of the philosophy of materialism; accordingly, the ideas thereof are the first
principles and ideas of this system of a most vulgar error and delusion. Thus, in pantheism the idea of the universe—of the ego,
of the world, and of God, these being conceived to be identical—
is posited as the First Idea—a grotesque, composite idea. In panegoism what is posited as the First Idea is the idea of ego,
which is wrongly amalgamated with the idea of the nonego and
of the Absolute Being—a grotesque combination. In materialism
what is posited as the First Idea is the idea of matter, the idea
of the material world organized in accordance with physical laws,
and amalgamated with man and God—an idea that is no less
grotesque and composite. Hence it may be said that the science
proper of pantheism is the science of the universe, confused and
confounded with the other sciences. The science proper of panegoism is the science of the ego, confused and confounded with
the other sciences. The science proper of materialism is the science of the physical world, confused and confounded with the
other sciences. Hence it is logically evident that philosophy was
not born in any of these systems, because not one of them conceived the truly First Idea and principle of science. In these systems the human spirit (or, as we more usually say in English,
the human mind—the meaning of the word «spirit» here being a
Gallicism introduced into modern Greek through translations
from the French) seeking to discover and comprehend the first
causes, for want of a true method, accepted the view at times
that m a t t e r and the e l e m e n t s of nature are to be
considered the first cause and first principle, and at other times
that g e n e r a l and a b s t r a c t n o t i o n s, the u n i-
v e r s e, and at still other times the e g o, and in general the
f i n i t e and the f a c t ought to be posited as such. On this
account and for this reason what was called philosophy by these
systems was a science of the fact and of the finite, unable to
fulfill the infinite yearning in man t o k n o w. Hence it is
evident that it would be seeking in vain were we to seek a system
of philosophy consonant both with the nature of man and with
the nature of things, in these systems, and further even in the
system of criticism itself, which, though admitting the existence
of an absolute outside of the world and of the ego, fails to undertake to comprehend it, for want of cognitive ability, or thinking
capacity, and for fear of being led astray, a contingency which,
as it contends, is evolved from right reason itself, which it wrongly and absurdly confuses and confounds with the cognoscitive
faculty of the soul. Philosophy, being the science of the Idea of
the Absolute, is the science of Right Reason; accordingly, we

ought to look for it in Reason, or the Logos, and through the Logos, taking care to distinguish the Being from the fact, the absolute from the relative, the infinite from the finite. We ought not to confuse things that are distinct, nor distinguish things that are not distinguished by their nature, in order to escape the possibility of erring. The desire to know implies an ability to do this. Had we not the ability to comprehend the First Idea and first principles, neither should we have had the yearning to know everything. Hence it may be logically inferred that inasmuch as we have the yearning to know, we must possess likewise the ability to do so. Nevertheless, we ought to regulate the ability to know in accordance with reason, and to restrict it within the conditions and legitimate bounds of cognition. In the matter of knowing we ought to follow reason, guided by the testimony of consciousness and perception, and to ascend mentally from the idea of the fact to the Idea of the Being, and from the idea of the effect to the idea of the cause. By observing and reasoning in this fashion we are enabled to build up a system of philosophy consonant with the nature of things and with the philisophical nature of man. This system, moreover, is the true Philosophy, the one which our Philosophical school of Christianity has and possesses, which school philosophizes in accordance with consciousness, perception, and logical thought, in accordance with a sound method of observing and reasoning, which method, however, the would - be wise men of the age have overlooked and ignored, and which indeed the schools in the West have missed entirely which hitherto have been philosophizing outside of the Logos and contrary to right reason, and which are therefore called philosophical schools improperly, by abuse of the word p h i l o s o p h i c a l, since they are standing aloof and remote from the system of the true science of Philosophy, and possess error and falsehood instead of the right method and the eternal Truth.

CONCERNING IDEAS

Before asking any other question we ought to ask the question, what is an idea? and what is its nature and power? The term idea (in the original sense of the word in Greek) denotes the image, picture, or form and shape of a being, whereby we recognize and distinguish it from every other being. For this reason it is that when the word i d e a is examined etymologically (in Greek), it is found to be derived from the (Greek) verb i d o, which signifies to see, to behold, to look at, to perceive something as existing in one's mind (or, as the Greek text has it, in one's spirit),

An idea in our mind is like the light in our eye. Just as light shows objects in our eye and by means thereof the eye perceives them, so and likewise an idea, being a mental and incorporeal light in the spiritual mental eye of our soul, shows us the objects and the soul thereby perceives them and obtains knowledge of them. Hence it is evident that just as it is impossible for the eye to see things without a light, the soul too is unable to see objects and to obtain knowledge of them without an idea. The mind has need of ideas for the purpose of contemplating beings, just as the eye has to have light in order to see objects. If we deprive the eye of light, we deprive it of the means of seeing and thus sever its connection with visible object. By illuminating the eye we connect in a way, with visible beings, and are thus enabled to utilize it. Thus also if it be supposed that we deprive the cognitive mind of the idea, we thereby disconnect it from the beings, because we remove from it the means by which it is enabled to see them. By illumining the mind with an idea we connect it with objects and are enabled to utilize it. So that an idea in the mind showing the object which it represents and of which it is an image, affords evidence at the same time of the connection which exists between the cognizing mind and the object cognized by means of the idea. Hence it is manifest that an idea is not only an image of an object, but also a bond, or nexus, between the mind (or spirit) and the being, or reality, therein imaged. An idea in the cognitive faculty is the revelation and manifestation therein of a being, i. e., of the reality which it represents. We gain knowledge of beings by means of the ideas of them. Without the presentation of any idea in our mind (or spirit) we are completely ignorant of beings. Our ignorance respecting the nature and essence of beings presupposes the absence of any idea of them in our mind. The knowledge which we have of beings presupposes the presence of an idea of them in our mind, the manifestation of beings by means of the idea of them. When I say that I have knowledge of this or that object, I am saying nothing else than that in my mind I have a picture of it, the idea. When I say that I have no knowledge of it, I say this because I mean that I have no idea of the object in question in my mind.

An idea as an image of a being is also the truth of it when the image in my mind presents a faithful and exact picture of the being in question. A faithful and accurate picture and representation of a being is the truth. But in order to learn the truth of some idea that is being presented in our spirit it is necessary that we compare it with the being of which it is a representation. This comparison will serve to apprise us of the agreement or disagreement of the idea with the object represented by it. If

I compare the idea of a sheep with the sheep, and the idea of an ox with the ox, I shall learm from their agreement the truth idea of the sheep and of the idea of the ox. But if, by comparing the idea of an ox with the ox, I do not find it in complete agrement with the ox, I say that the idea of the ox in my mind is imperfect, defective, or incomplete, as the case may be, and that it is on the order of an impression rather tham of an idea. But if the idea I have of the ox be compared with a sheep, which it does not depict, it will be shown to be an idea that is not false in itself, for no idea is false in itelf, since it really possesses the requirement of trueness, namely, reality but only in relation and comparison with the being which it does not depict or even represent. Hence we may draw the following logical conclusions.

1) That every idea in our spirit is an image of some being, of some reality, and is a bond, or nexus, of the cognitive spirit with the object cognized, the existence of the being in question being taken for granted, seeing that it is revealed in our mind ; 2) that the measure, or standard, of every idea is the being which it represents in our mind, while the measure of our knowledge of the being is our idea of the being ; 3) that we cannot have any idea of anything that is not a being, but can have ideas only of real beings.

An idea as an image of a being necessarily presupposes the existence of the being in question ; accordingly it may be said that if there were no beings, neither would there be any ideas in our spirit. Hence it is logically evident that every idea depends on the existence of a being of which it is the idea. The spirit acquires ideas from its relation and connection with the objects, and there is nothing else that is receptive of ideas but the mind, or spirit. The spirit possesses the power and the ability to conceive in itself ideas resulting from its relation to beings ; and first of all the idea of itself, in which case it becomes by itself both the subject and the object of cognition at the same time. Nevertheless, the idea conceived in the spirit mind in the beginning is a faint or dim image ; it is an imperfect depiction of the being and is subject to the law of perfection. A complete and perfect idea is presented to the mind by complete and perfect knowledge. The measure of complete and perfect knowledge, however, is a complete and perfect idea ; and the measure of the latter is the being which it manifests and depicts in the mind. The knowledge is the product of the idea, precisely as the latter is a product of the being. Knowledge without a knowing mind is impossible. Moreover, an idea without a preexistent being is also impossible. An idea is born of the contact of the cognitive mind and the object cognized. If we imagine these two conditions for the generation of ideas, namely, a cognizing subject and a cognizing object, to be removed and done away with, we have no idea. Hence it is logically evident that no idea can exist in us of itself. An idea can be present only where there is a cognitive mind, or cognitive spirit, as a bond, or nexus, between the subject and the object, as a manifestation of the being in the (Spirit), as a mental visiom.

Cognizing Object	Vertical lines	IDEA	Vertical lines	Cognizing Subject

An idea as an image of a being must represent the being as it actually is in the mind, which must know the being as the idea presents it, accurately and truly. Since, however, the conception of an idea is a result of an operation of our (Spirit) which is imperfect, though subject to perfection, and the idea is imperfectly formed, therefore our knowledge of objects is also imperfect, and we know the beings imperfectly, including ourselves. This imperfect knowledge imperfectly, including ourselves. This imperfect knowledge of ours, however, will retreat in time in the face of the dawn of perfect knowlege, and complete development of our mind, when we shall know the beings by means of the ideas of them as they really are. A perfect spirit has perfect knowledge of beings, because it possesses in itself the ideas of the beings and can see them in itself perfectly. A perfect spirit knows itself perfectly, because it has in itself a perfect idea of itself. An imperfect spirit on the other hand, knows itself imperfectly, because its idea of itself is imperfect. As long as we exist on the earth we are mentally imperfect beings, though destined to perfectness. Hence it is logically evident that we also cognize beings imperfectly and know the nature of them imperfectly, because our ideas of them are imperfect. We naturally aim at perfect knowledge of everything through acquisition and perfect possession of the ideas of all beings, and especially of the Idea of the Absolute Being, through which idea our philosophical yearning is fulfilled and our spiritual nature is perfected. Whatever we now possess, with the aid of true science, though true in itself and by itself, is nevertheless imperfect, and does not satisfy the infinite yearning within us. The idea of man, the idea of the world, the idea, in a word, of the finite and of the fact, and the Idea of the Absolute Being, are still a mystery of the spirit, and for many ages the human spirit has been occupied with the endeavor to discover the key to this mystery. In fact, this mystery would have been wholly insoluble had not Christianity enlightened the human spirit by the ideas which it revealed from heaven, and had it not elevated the human mind by its luminous teaching to the height of the mountain of the Logos, whence the human spirit can, in a sort of survey, by looking down, behold the entire mystery of knowledge of the universe, and discover the ideas and reasons of beings, and explain their nature. What is man? what is the world? What, in a word, is the fact? and, most important of all, what is the absolute Being, God? In order to pronounce an opinion about these things clearly, we must have a clear and accurate idea of them in our spirit. For an idea, as said above, is an image of a being, or, in other words, that by which we know a being. A methodical investigation of beings conducted carefully affords our spirit an accurate idea of them; and in proportion as the human spirit busies itself with the investigation of the nature of beings, it approaches closer and closer to the acquisition of an idea of them whereby it comes to know them more perfectly. By the acquisition of ideas of beings our spirit is brought closer to the beings, because an idea, if followed out, is like a road leading to the being it represents. Through comprehension of the Idea of the absolute Being, the spirit is carried to the supreme Being, because the Idea of the most perfect Being is the road which leads the spirit to it. The relation, therefore, of the spirit to beings is defined by its relation to the ideas of them. If the ego is ignorant of beings, and especially of the Being of beings, its ignorance places it at a remote distance from the beings, and especially from God. Its ignorance is like a murky, gleamless night in which a walker does not know where he is going, being assailed by and colliding with obstacles on all sides. An idea will dispel ignorance as light dispels the darkness of night. An idea draws the spirit on the one hand, towards the being which it portrays and reveals to the spirit and draws the being, on the other hand, towards the cognitive spirit. It elevates the spirit to contemplation of the being of which it was previously ignorant, and, on the other hand, it lowers the being towards the elevation of the spirit. When thus cognized, an idea may be characterized not only as an image simply of the being in the spirit not only as a bond between the cognizer and the object cognized, but also as a mediator, because it connects and conjoins the spirit yearning after the being with the object yearned after. The spirit has a strong desire to become acquainted with and to gain knowledge of a certain object. Moreover, a being was brought into existence so that it might be an object of the spirit's cognition. Its purpose is to become known through the idea of it, which reveals it in the spirit and mentalizes it, so to speak, in the spirit's cognition. For without a spirit as was said before, there can be no knowledge in our spirit. The appearance, then, of an idea in the spirit is a revelation there in of a being; consequently it is the fulfillment of the spirit's yearning to gain knowledge of the being it represents.

Let us proceed to ponder also otherwise this important phenomenon of spirit and idea. The human spirit is the room containing ideas of beings, which ideas it endeavors to garner up in itself, and thereby to know beings as they actually are; by doing so it becomes a perfect spirit of infinite capacity, capable of holding an infinite plenitude. Ideas are the food of the spirit for it is through ideas that the spirit is nourished and lives. The relation of the spirit to beings through the ideas of them spells the development, the perfection, and the immortality of the spirit. By relating our spirit with the absolute Being through the Idea of His, we relate it with the source of eternal life and of immortality, we develop and perfect it, and fulfill its infinite yearning to gain knowledge. This explains why those who neglect to acquire ideas and the knowledge of beings that can be gained by means of them, are guilty of neglecting to develop and to perfect the mind for the acquirement of immortality. Those who deprecate the acquisition of ideas, and who hold their spirit aloof from them, are obscurantists, because they try to obscure and to extinquish the light of thought; they are assassinators, because they attempt to deprive the spirit of its food, of ideas, and thus to stay it. For, if the human spirit has a tendency and yearning to gain knowledge of everything round it that is scientifically knowable; if, as a matter of fact, the Creator endowed it with this yearning to gain knowledge of everything it is ignorant of, to investigate everything divine and human, and to explain all things by means of one general, or catholic, idea, no one is able to withstand the progressive tendency of man, no one can obstruct the mind's desire to gain knowledge of everything unknown and prevent it from learning all about everything that is scientifically knowable. The deprivation of the spirit of an idea is its deprivation of its spiritual food, resulting in want of that by which the spirit is developed and perfected. One can see objects aright by looking at them in the light, since, the vivider and brighter it is, the more perspicuously and clearly the light shows the objects to the eye; but, on the contrary, the dimmer and more confused the light, the dimmer and more confused becomes the sight of anything seen by it. Thus, too, one can live well when one is nourished well with suitable food, and the more effective the food is the more effective the strength in the body becomes and propor-

tionate to the body's work ; but, on the contrary, the more inef-
fective the food is and the more unsuitable for the maintenance
of life, the more a being ineffectively nourished becomes ineffici-
ent for work, owing to its being deprived of the required stength.
The spirit cognizes and knows beings by means of the ideas of
them, these rays of spiritual light. The more perfectly it knows a
being, the more perfect an idea of it it has ; while the more it is
ignorant of a being, or the more imperfectly it knows it, the greater the ignorance or the more imperfect the knowledge it has of
the idea, and consequently the more imperfect a spirit it is. But
a spirit that is completely ignorant of what is outside of it or of
itself is naturally impossible. For a spirit is an essence and a cognizing being and a being exercising volition. Predication of utter
and absolute ignorance in regard to the spirit is a denial of its
existence; it is a contradiction. Hence it is not a question concerning absolute ignorance of the spirit which is naturally impossible and contradictory to the nature of the spirit but one concerning relative ignorance; for we know some beings and are ignorant of others, and we know nothing absolutely, nor are we ignorant of anything absolutely. The idea in our spirit like a clear
light, guides us to a comprehension of the being; and like food
adequate for the nourishment and invigoration and development
of the spiritual nature it strengthens the spirit for the execution
and achievement of every object cognized and thought about, because it becomes a d e s i g n and a w i l l and an a c t. The
influence of an idea over the spirit is nothing else than an impartation of life and of immortality, whereby the spirit lives forever
by means of the ideas of beings, by means of the idea of itself,
and by means of the life - bestowing Idea of the Absolute Being.
That age in which the human spirit shall behold in itself the entire world of ideas fitted together and combined with the Idea of
the Absolute Being will be the age of the science and of the self-
activity of the spirit the age of perfection, and of the prevalence
of the kingdom and dominion of t h e t r u t h on the earth. In
that age of the power of the kingdom of t h e t r u t h shall t h e
i d e a be actualized, and become a d e s i g n and an a c t; and
that is the kingdom of w h a t i s g o o d, of w h a t i s r i g h t
a n d j u s t, and of w h a t i s b e a u t i f u l in the world ; that
is the kingdom of God on earth, the kingdom of heaven. As long
as the spirit keeps on advancing in the acquisition of more perfect
knowledge of beings by means of more perfect ideas, and actualizes these in moral, political, and social life, and the world of art,
it progresses on the way of civilization until it arrives at perfection, which shall consist in a full and perfect contemplation of
beings by the cognitive spirit through the ideas of them. This is

what is meant by the term omniscience and by the expression fulfillment of the mind's yearning to gain knowledge. It is perfect knowledge and cognizance of the Truth.

CONCERNING PRINCIPLES

In every science there are principles whereby ideas are correlated and joined together, and the relation between the ideas and the beings of which they are images can be contemplated and considered. Moreover, in the order of beings, beings are related to one another, and their relation is regulated by ontological laws and ontological principles. This holds true also of the moral order of beings, in which moral and free beings are related to one another on the basis of admitted principles. Moreover, even in social and political life in general there are principles that regulate and define the relation of members of society to one another, and which serve to maintain the social order. These principles may be considered concretely and abstractly. Concretely they are considered as persons set to organize society and to maintain the social order; abstractly, as written laws, or as social customs, or as laws of natural right, defining social relations and maintaining them, for the sake of social good and of social order. We can distinguish the following kinds of principles: 1) ontological; 2) logical and scientific; 3) moral and social; So that there are ontological principles, scientific or logical principles, and moral or social and political principles. Out of these grow more special kinds of principles, the ones mentioned being considered more general principles as genera. We deem it needless to discuss them here, because we are mainly concerned with scientific principles.

Scientific principles are distinct from the ideas of beings, though some persons have wrongly taken them to be ideas of beings, or have confused them with ideas. The ideas of beings in our spirit are images of beings, whereas principles signify the relations and references obtaining between the beings, and explain the manner in which the spirit acquires ideas of beings, by passing from one idea to another, and thus builds a science. For this reason principles, being objects of intellection, are abstract ideas, cognized not by themselves but as references and relations between beings, as was said above. Principles serve as such in the process of thinking. In order to answer in two words or so the question, What is a scientific principle? we assert that a principle is a law of the spirit that governs thought. Thought is work of the spirit. This work may be done correctly or incorrectly. It is done correctly when in the process of thinking about beings the mind applies the law of reason. It is done incorrectly when the spirit thinks contrary to and outside the law of reason in its cognitive work. We ought, therefore, to distinguish the following three things: thought, or cognition; the law of thought, or of cognition; and the idea by means of which a being is cognized and known. The ability of the mind to conceive an idea — cognition, or thought — a law and rule of the mind for the conception and acquisition of an idea — the principle of cognition, or of thought — an idea showing a being perspicuously in the spirit — an image of the being — constitute right cognition, or correct thinking. Without principles to govern cognition and thought, the mind cannot cognize correctly and think aright. But to cognize correctly and to think aright signify nothing else than to acquire the true and actual idea of a being and to become acquainted with beings by means of the ideas of them. Thought is related to the idea of a being by means of a principle; and without the latter there is no reference, no relation between them. This fact may be succinctly represented by the scheme:

Thought (understand) — Law — Idea.

But thought is related to the being itself by means of the idea; in which case the scheme is:

Thought (understand) — Idea — Being.

Hence it is necessary that we consider separately the idea of the being from the idea of the thought (undertand) and of the law, and that we take care not to confuse them.

Our spirit is naturally in possession of the law of thought, (understand), as it is also in possession of the idea in its cognition. The Spirit cognizes itself; and in this cognition it is in possession of the idea of itself and of the law, or of the principle governing the cognition of itself. The spirit self-cognition denotes that it internally represents itself, describes its own features, and portrays itself in itself. This representation takes place in accordance with a law of the spirit. The law of the spirit is not independent of the existence of the spirit, and we cannot think cognize, of a law without a spirit, Wherever there is a spirit and thought congnition, there too is a law of thought cognition; accordingly, there is neither a spirit without a law and a principle, nor is there a law of thought cognition without a thinking cognizing spirit. As neither is there an idea without a cognizing spirit and an object cognized. The law of the spirit regulates its cognitive operation in the process of cognizing a being correctly, in conceiving the true idea of it, and in representing it clearly and perspicuously in the spirit. Hence it is logically evident that without the law of cognition, or of thought, there can be no correct and true idea in the spirit, nor any true cognition and true thought cognition but instead thereof only impressions and fancies, and simulacra in the spirit and chimerical notions. But, we may wonder, do the principles, whereby the cognitive spirit regulates its operation in thinking for the acquisition of ideas, really exist in the spirit as primary laws, or are they acquired by it and consequently adscititious? To solve this question we must first take the notion of mind, and ask, What is a mind? The essential feature of the mind is the process of gaining knowledge. Wherever there is a gain of knowledge, there it may be said that there is also a mind; and wherever there is a mind, there it may be said that there is a gain of knowledge. Whatever has not the character of mind, is not mind, but matter. Matter is s o m e t h i n g b e i n g h o o d w i t h o u t k n o w l e d g e, a kind of being that knows nothing. Mind is something having beinghood together with knowledge, a kind of being that knows something. A mind, in accordance with the conception of it as a conscious being, is immediately aware of itself through itself. In being aware of itself, the mind contemplates a relation existing between itself as subject of thought and as object at the same time. The activity of the mind in cognizing itself as an object of cognition, is applied directly to the object cognized; and the conception of the idea of itself takes place in accordance with some law existing in cognition which the mind cannot transgress in its primary cognition. Thus the cognitive mind cognizing itself cognizes in accordance with some primary law and conceives the primary idea of itself. This primary cognition may be represented as follows;

Cognizing Subject	LAW The ego—The ego OF COGNITION	Object Cognized

In the cognition of the nonego the cognitive spirit of the ego, cognizing the nonego, cognizes itself in accordance with some law subsisting in the primary cognition of the mind. It cognizes the nonego as something independent and distinct from the ego, and the idea of the nonego as distinct from the idea of the ego. This cognition, which takes place in accordance with the primary law in cognition, may be formulated as follows:

Cognizing Subject	LAW The ego - The nonego OF COGNITION THE ABSOLUTE	Object Cognized

The cognitive mind cognizes itself either as a cause or as an effect. In this cognition it outlines the law in accordance with which the mind cognizes everything it cognizes, as a cause or as an effect (causate), as a premise or as a consequence.

The principle of causality. — This law can be fittingly called the law of causality, because it shows to the intellect the relation naturally existing between the cause and its effect. This logical principle of causality shows in the mind the relation which exists between ideas of which one is a cause and the other is an effect. For instance. The mind cognizing itself and having the idea of itself within itself cognizes it in relation to the Idea of the Absolute Being, which it conceives in accordance with a logical law, either as an effect or as a cause. It is naturally impossible in the course of logical cognition of the mind for any error to creep in so as to lead the mind to think the effect to be a cause, or the cause to be an effect. Just as it is naturally impossible for the mind to think a being to be at the same time a nonbeing, an idea to be a nonidea, a principle to be a nonprinciple at the same time. A relative effect cannot at the same time be also an absolute cause; the fact cannot at the same time also be the eternal being, nor can the eternal being be a fact. Whatever has been cognized by the mind as a being cannot be cognized at the same time as a nonbeing. What has been cognized as having knowledge cannot at the same time be cognized as not having any knowledge, seeing that it has been aware of this. For everything that exists either as a cause or as an effect. For this reason we assert that:

a) Everything being and existent exists either as an absolute cause, or as a relative cause and relative effect; as an eternal being or as a fact.

b) Nothing existent, whether as an eternal being or as a fact, can at the same time not exist, as such. What is an eternal being cannot at the same time be also a fact, as neither can the fact being an eternal being.

The mind cognizing in accordance with the law of causality cognizes a being either as a cause or as an effect; it cannot cognize the contrary of this. In cognizing the being to be a being, the nonbeing to be a nonbeing, the relative to be relative, and the absolute to be absolute, the mind cannot at the same cognize the contrary of these cognita. For:

Whatever is a being is not at the same time also itself a nonbeing.

Whatever is a nonbeing is not at the same time also itself a being.

Whatever is relative is not at the same time also itself absolute.

In the fact that the cognitive mind cannot cognize at the same time two ideas of which one precludes the other, it formulates the principle and law of contradiction; and it frames this law and presents it in cognition.

The principle of contradiction: — The law of contradiction defines the relation between two mutually exclusive ideas, and by means of it the cognitive mind cognizes the nonintercommunicability of them. For we naturally cannot cognize the coexistence at the same time of two ideas contradicting each other; neither can we predicate two contradictory features or characters of one and the same idea. In contemplating a relation between the idea of beinghood and that of nonbeinghood, of which one excludes the other, we cognize the fact that one is a denial of the other, and that we ought to accept one of them as true, and deny the other as false, for there is no middle road. In cognizing itself, the cognizing ego cannot at the same time not cognize itself. In cognizing itself as a being that exists relatively it cannot cognize itself also as a being that at the same time exists absolutely. The notion of relative excludes the notion of absolute, in the same way as the notion of simple existence excludes the notion of nonexistence or inexistence. But whatever exists has a purpose of existence in the order of being. The ego, however, which cognizes a being to be a being, and not to be a being and a nonbeing at the same time in accordance with the principle of contradiction, and which cognizes a cause to be distinct from its effect, in accordance with the law of causality, cognizes the fact that in the general or catholic order of being it has some purpose, that it has regard to some end.

The principle of purposefulness. This cognition of the purpose and end of a being outlines the primary law of purposefulness or aimfulness, which is also the law of the general or catholic order of being; and upon the purposefulness of beings is founded also the method of induction. The law of contradiction presupposes the distinct existence of the beings in creation. For, if the beings were not distinct from each other, this logical principle of contradiction could not even have been in our mind. Hence it is evident that the distinct existence of beings preexisted in the totality of creation, since the ideas are cognized separately as distinct things in our minds. From this fact it follows that the logical order of ideas is a picture of the ontological order. Accordingly, just as had there been no beings there would have been no ideas in our minds, so and in like manner it may be said that had there been no principles and laws regulating the relations of being there would have been no logical laws regulating the relations of the ideas in our minds. The existence of beings preceded, of course, the existenee of ideas. The existence of ontological principles and laws preceded the existence of the logical laws and principles in us. The ideas of the mind are images of beings in it. The relations subsisting between the ideas in the mind are images of the relations subsisting between the beings in creation. Hence it appears that the logical principles and logical laws of the mind which regulate the relations between ideas are images of the ontological principles and laws which regulate the relations between beings in the universe. Just as the relations of beings cannot be the principles and laws which regulate them, without the beings and by themselves, but only in conjunction therewith, so and in like manner the relations of ideas cannot be the principles and logical laws in accordance with which they are defined by themselves and without the existence of ideas in our minds. Beings are the material of existence. The relations between them, the principles and laws in accordance with which they exist and operate in the catholic aim of creation, are their specific form and nature. They are their external image and representation. The ideas in the mind are the material of cognition, and its cognizable object. The relations between them, and the logical laws in accordance with which ideas are entertained by the mind, are their specific form and nature. They are their external form and embodiment in the mind. And just as we must not confuse in the order of beings the beinghood of beings with their relations, and with their natural and ontological laws, with their specific form, so and in like manner may it be said that we must not in the logical order of ideas confuse the beinghood with their relations, with their logical principles and laws, with their specific form. As the relations between beings, their principles and laws, coexist with the beings and immediately affect their existence, so and in like manner the relations between ideas of the mind, logical principles and logical laws, coexist together with the ideas, and immediately affect their existence in the mind. Hence it is logically evident that the specific form of beings immediately affects the beinghood of the beings and that the specific form of ideas immediately affects the beinghood of the ideas in the mind. These facts may be represented schematically as follows:

Substance (hypostasis) of a being	+	Nature of the being	= a Being
Substance (hypostasis) of an idea	+	Nature of the idea	= an Idea

The laws and the logical principles of the spirit are considered together with its ideas. Likewise the primary laws of the mind which are the source of all scientific and logical axioms are considered together with the primary ideas, without which latter the logical laws cannot even be conceived. The primary ideas are the material of the process ot cognition, the primary and first and chief object of thought cognition. The logical principles and the logical laws are the specific form of the process of cognition, the form or shape of the matter of thought. Between the matter of thought and the specific form of thought there subsists a relation and concord or consonance which the spirit contemplates in accordance with the principles of reason. It behooves us, therefore, to distinguish the beinghood of an idea as an idea in the spirit from the form and manner in which the idea presents itself therein. This distinction is a natural one, for even in the order of beings we distinguish the beinghood of every being from the specific form and the shape of the being. Accordingly, we call the beinghood of a being its hypostasis and p r i n c i p l e ; but as for its specific form, which it exhibits and by which it is separately distinguished from other beings, we call that its n a t u r e. Moreover, we even call the beinghood of every idea its hypostasis and principle; but as for its specific form we call that is form and nature, as exibiting it in the spirit and distinguishing it from other ideas. The primary ideas in our minds are also the criterion of every scientific principle and of every law of cognition. Accordingly, had there not been primary ideas and primary laws in our minds to start with, no primary knowledge would have been possible, nor any logical criterion; consequently, neither would there have been any mind, since the lack of these involves a negation of the existence of a mind, which latter is a knowing, or cognoscent, being. Hence it is logically evident that wherever there is knowledge, there also are to be found, and ideas, and a law of thought. And wherever there is a mind, there also are to be found knowledge, and ideas, and laws of thought. Whoever denies the existence of a spirit must necessarily deny also the existence of every idea and of all knowledge, the existence of every logical law. But one cannot do this, for by denying the existence of a spirit one denies also the existence of thought cognizing. But he bases his denial upon the process of cognition; and therefore upon the spirit. For whence did he learn that there is no spirit cognizing things seeing that he himself cognizes ths denial or negation? For even negation is knowledge. So if there were no spirit that knows anything, whence could come this knowledge of the negation? Hence it is logically evident that anyone denying the existence of a spirit is contradicting himself. Moreover, anyone who denies the existence of primary ideas, of primary knowledge, and of the primary laws of the spirit, is denying the basis of every idea and knowledge, of every logical law; but his denial presupposes the existence of the spirit making the denial, i. e., the existence of a being called the mind. Hence it is evident that he is contradicting himself if he disavows or abjures the principles. The acknowledgment of the existence of a spirit is an acknowledgment of the existence therein of primary ideas and of primary laws. Any denial of the existence of these is nothing more than empty words of an arbitrary will, which, however, cannot be cognized or conceived by the spirit. The spirit perspicuously shows within us primary ideas and primary laws; and we cannot conceive the inexistence of ourselves. Our will may assert in words that it denies their existence; yet it cannot actually deny their existence, and convince itself internally that these things do not exist. Hence it is logically evident that our will when perspicuously enlightened by the mind and cognizing a being as a being, a cause as a cause, and an effect as an effect, when cognizing the purposefulness and end of each and every being in accordance with the primary laws of causality, of contradiction and of purposefulness, cannot conceive the contraries of these, a being as at the same time a nonbeing, a cause as an effect and an effect as a cause; in fact, it cannot fail to cognize the purpose of beings. Those persons are lying who assert that they can cognize or conceive the contraries of these things, the opposition before the position, what is negative before what is positive; or who express themselves doubtfully as respects the cognition or conception of them. For any doubt presupposes the existence of the doubter. Accordingly, anyone doubting, for instance, his existence is contradicting himself, because on the other side he is admitting his own existence. For how can anyone doubt anything if he himself does not exist as a doubting being? Such in magnitude and habitude is the power of principles over the ego; and on this account the free will cannot resist their dominion without lying and committing an unpardonable crime.

THE DISTINCTION
OF AN IDEA FROM A PRINCIPLE

An idea is an image representative of a being in the mind. A truth is ontological; for the moment it presents itself in the mind it announces therein the existence of a being distinct from the cognizing subject, and from the idea whereby this is portrayed therein. But a principle is a law of the spirit in accordance with which an idea is conceived or cognized. and its relation to an-

other idea can be considered. In order to exhibit the distinction of
these in a concrete way too, let us take into consideration the beings themselves and the laws which regulate their relations. The
world is a totality, or aggregate, of being placed in order and
operating regularly. But the being form the matter of the world,
the substances, and cannot of themselves and by themselves establish a world operating regularly without the existence of laws
regulating their operation, and fixing or defining their relations
to one another, Beings without laws cannot have any form, or
shape, nor any relation to one another, since it is by virtue of
the principles and natural laws that they are correlated to one
another, are formed and trained, and operate regularly. Moreover,
even in the society of human beings we observe this very same
thing. Every human being is also a social being All human beings taken together constitute all society, which is operating purposefully and regularly. If we cognize all human beings as being
unrelated to themselves and to one another, and as nonintercommunicable, we are conceiving them as being without laws and
principles; and consequently as not forming and composing and
producing a society. Hence it is logically evident that it is the
principles and the laws that actually produce society and maintain and advance social life. Take away the principles and the
social laws, and you will see a society instantly dissolved and destroyed. Take away the physical laws, and you will soon see the
physical word dissolved and destroyed. Thus, even if we take
away merely in thought the existence of the logical laws, of the
primary laws of cognition and of thought, we take away the logical order itself in ideas; we take away the coherence of science
and abolish science itself. The matter, however, remains and is
not destroyed; but it is shapeless and formless matter. The removal of the laws of nature would result in the destruction of the
physical world as a consequence thereof, and not in the annihilation of the matter of it, or, in other words, of its substances and
its constituent parts. Moreover, the removal of the social laws
would involve an abrogation of the existence of society, and not
annihilation of the matter of it or, more expressly speaking, of
the i n d i v i d u a l s composing it. Thus too the removal of
the logical laws would result in the abrogation of science, and
not of the existence of the ideas in the spirit. Hence ir is logically
evident that p r i n c i p l e s ought to be distinguished from
i d e a s, as social laws are distinguished from persons, and physical laws are distinguished from physical beings. But can we conceive a world without physical principles and natural laws? Of
course not. Hence it is evident that neither can we conceive science
without logical principles and laws. We have to conceive both;

any attempt to discriminate them is made mentally, but it has no real consequence. Hence the distinction and discrimination is one made by mere abstraction, and represents no concrete reality. But just as we cannot see a being without its shape, and society without its organization, so and in like manner it may be said that we cannot cognize ot conceive ideas without the logical principles and laws of the spirit. But spirit, idea, and principle are three things which are so distinct and interconnected that the removal of one of them involves a negation of the nature of the spirit which, being naturally cognitive, cognizes the beings by means of the ideas of them by virtue of a law of cognition. By confusing ideas with principles we confuse individuals with social laws, beings with laws of nature, and we arrive at an incorrect judgment concerning them. Consequently there can be neither any negation nor any confusion in regard to the matter under discussion here ; for the operation of these is obvious. Society is under the sway of laws. The physical world likewise is under the control of physical laws. Everything in creation is under the influence of definite laws which are the subject - matter of some special science. Moreover, even the rational and moral worlds are under the control and authority of logical principles and laws. Everywhere there are principles that regulate order and guide creation to its destiny. Any revolt against the principles is an attempt to overthrow the universal order, and is an apostasy from the absolute Principle of the universe. A revolt is a work of the free will. Where there is no free will, there is to be found no revolt against any principle, under which term are included governments and authorities of all kinds. For this reason we find that the history of political states, as well as that of religions and of philosophical systems, never anywhere bears witness to any physical revolt of physical beings against the physical laws controlling creation. A free will can, it is true, revolt against social principles, i.e., against the authorities ruling society, but it can never change or alter or overthrow them, because they are deeply fixed in the social nature of man by the Creator. Hence, anyone who revolts against them is bound to be crushed to pieces before their power and irresistible might, and will return empty - handed to his own position and rank. Thinking that society was established by means of a social charter or document, by artifice and not by nature, Rousseau recommended the return of men to their primordial condition, to the wild and nonintercommunicable state in which according to him they were living originally, a state like that in which monkeys and orangutans (also spelled ourang - outangs) live. In fact, he recommended the dissolution of society. The French Revolution of 1789 attempted, on account

of the silliness and foolishness of the mobocracy, to put these re-
commendations of Rousseau and the antisocialists into practice,
after making bold to rise up against the principles of right and
of social order, and acting in the name of absolute social anarchy
and disorder! But the French radicals soon enough realized that
this attempt of theirs was far from undermining and overthrow-
ing the natural principles of right and that it merely became
the cause of enormous damages and copious bloodshed; so that,
in order to remedy the evil and halt the licentiousness it became
necessary for them te return to the legal ond natural principle of
social right, to arrange society and their own affairs in accordance with the unchangeable laws of social order, to proclaim the
Christian religion, which had officially been abolished by vote in
their National Convention, to be once more the prevailing religion in France, to recognize the principle of right respectfully as
an everlasting law of God, and to proclaim officially the existence of God, whom they had previously proscribed by vote in the
National Assembly as a result of their impetuosity and senseless-
ness. Nevertheless, a social revolution of people against the
principle of right, and against the principles of religion and of
morality, is preceded by a revolution against logical order and
against the principles of reason, and such a revolution occurs
and is usual in the scientific world in which there are a multitude of contradictory statements and much irrationality and lack
of judgment. The history of philosophy bears witness that a certain class of philosophizing enthusiasts mutinied against reason
and the principles of cognition and made and attempt to found
and erect a philosophical edifice upon imagination and illogical
reasoning. On this account at times it denied the existence of a
God as distinct from the world and man, and proclaimed a belief
in materialism. At times again it confounded God with the world
and man, and professed a belief in pantheism. At other times it
deified man and proclaimed a belief in panegoism. In consequence of adherence to vain - minded skepticism it proclaimed all
knowledge and all truth to be doubtful, and thus brought on a
confusion of spirits and provoked a commotion in the scientific
world. This revolt against the everlasting principles and laws of
reason resulted in a revolt in the moral and social order, because
it prepared men's spirit for a mutiny against everlasting principles and laws upon which the logical, moral, and social edifice
is based. A mutiny against logical principles is a mutiny against
the moral order and when the laws of the spirit, the principles of
reason, are violated, the principles of morality, the moral laws of
the will, and after these the political laws, the laws of social
right, are violated too, and the social man is thus led to perdi-

tion. From this consideration of principles it becomes plain that social life is influenced by the obedience of the will to the principles of logic and the laws of the mind. How guilty of sinning and of wronging society are those who munity against the laws and principles of logic and who build chimeras with their imagination and publish and disseminate these as scientific doctrines. They are the ones who incite society to moral and political misconduct, and undermine the bases of society, thereby threatening its desolation and ruination. But woe to those men through whom the scandals come (Matt. 18 : 7). It were better for them had they not been born.

THE NATURE OF AN IDEA

What we called an idea further above was the image of a being which we have in our spirit and by which the spirit is enabled to contemplate or consider the being. Without an idea we should be unable to contemplate beings or even ourselves. Moreover, but if we should be deprived of the spirit in consequence of our inability to contemplate beings by means of the ideas of them, nor should we be able to have ideas of them. For an idea is a fruit of mentation, a fruit of the spirit or mind; accordingly, wherever there is an idea, there too there necessarily is also a spirit and wherever there is a spirit, there too there is also an idea : but where the spirit is absent, the idea too is absent. A stone exists, a plant exists, an animal exists. But these essences, or existences, because destitute of spirit, are destitute of an idea too; and for this reason we can observe in such essences no births of ideas. Since an idea, however, is an image of a being in our spirit, it represents and explains therein the nature of the being, and it serves to express in the mind the reason of the being's essence. But a spirit which learns something through an idea desires to impart what it has learned to other spirits of a like nature, because it is by nature social. Thus it may be seen that it needs a suitable instrument for the external impartation of that which it has been taught internally through the idea. This instrument is the tongue or language and the oral speech whereby it can utter the knowledge it possesses. The spirit utters externally by means of language whatever it cognizes internally by means of ideas. If it could not cognize anything, it could not utter anything either. A stone, a plant, and an animal have no language, no articulate speech, because they have no cognition, and consequently no intestine speech: they have no spirit. But a human being, because he has a spirit has ideas and speech which can represent and explain the ideas in his spirit. But during a time when he cognizes nothing, he cannot speak anything; he is then like a senseless and irrational animal, though he possesses the power of acquiring a capacity for oral speech when endowed with a spirit and informed with ideas; and thus he will be enabled to represent and express his mind and spirit in oral speech. That is why oral speech may be said to be expression of mind, and an accurate depiction of spirit.

An idea, as an image of a being, is also an internal and external discourse of reason in regard to the being, an image exhibited in the mind and in speech and language. But every discourse of reason is either true or false. It is true when it accurately explains the nature of a being or of the idea of it. It is false when it explains it incorrectly and distortedly, If an idea depicts a being in the mind incorrectly, it is called false; if it depicts it accurately, it is called true. But in order for an idea to be imposed upon the will effectually, it must be a true image of a being and bear the stamp of truth accurately. The truthfulness of an idea depends upon the existence of the being, i. e., of the reality which it is supposed to represent. Everything that we cognize must also exist in the order of beings; for the being themselves are the measure of our ideas, and it is as a result of their existence that we form the ideas in our mind. Our mind cognizes primarily 1) itself; 2) the world; and 3) God. What is relative and what is absolute; the fact and the eternal Being. It cognizes itself because it exists: had it not existed, it could not even have cognized itself. It cognizes the world and God because both of these exist: had they not existed, it neither could have cognized them as existent. Hence it is logically evident that it can cognize anything that actually exists, and that outside of the existence of these being it can cognize no other being because there is no such being in the order of beings. Cognition of a nonbeing as a being is impossible for us. So, then, it is easy to see that all the ideas of our spirit are expressive and representative of being, or realities, including the ego, the world, and the God who is the creator of the world, Have we within us any ideas that are antiegoistic, anticosmic, and antitheistic? We have not. We cannot on any occasion observe any such ideas in our mind at all, because our spirit is unable to conceive and to cognize what does not exist. Those who contend that they can think of or conceive the inexistence of the world, or the insubstantiality of the existence of God, presuppose in themselves a cognition or conception of their existence, a cognition of position before contraposition and denial. Inasmuch as they cognize what exists, they are lying with their tongue when they contend that they can cognize what does not exist, or they are victims of their illogical reasoning, in that they confound the cause with the effect, and deify creation instead of the Creator. Inexistence cannot be cognized or conceived before existence. That is to say, the mind cannot think of inexistence without first having thought of existence.

An idea in our spirit represents an object of which it is the idea. But since there are primarily three different objects that are capable of existence, ideas too are distinguished into three different classes, namely: 1) anthropological; 2) cosmological; and 3) theological But since among these three objects, comprising the ego, the world, and God,there subsist certain relations, the spirit by means of ideas can cognize these existing among them; accordingly, it forms within itself also a fourth class or species of ideas, that of relations.

I d e a s   o f   r e l a t i o n s. According to the particular object which it represents in our spirit an idea is either simple or compound, relative or absolute, primary or acquired, perfect or imperfect, defective or complete, certain or probable, true or false. According to the manner in which an idea is cognized in our spirit it is concrete or abstract. Let us now proceed to examine these species of ideas, their features or characters, and the way in which they are cognized, commencing with the first species.

Ideas considered with reference to their primary

objects and species

ANTHROPOLOGICAL IDEAS

We distinguish and divide ideas according to their objects which they represent in our spirit into the following primary species: a) anthropological; b) cosmological; c) theological. Since beings have relations and references to one another, we can also form ideas of the relations subsisting between beings. Accordingly, we shall first discuss anthropological ideas. Anthropological ideas are images of beings in the cognizing ego which we are wont to call a human being or a man; those ideas are ones by means of which the latter acquires knowledge of: 1) the being-hood of a man, his substance (called the h y p o s t a s i s in Greek —the nearest other word in English probably being f o u n d a- t i o n) and existence; 2) the characteristics and attributes inherent in the being, which constitute its nature and structural form in which it presents itself in the order of beings; 3) the relation which subsists between its characteristics and its hypostasis 4) the extent which the being in question occupies, i. e., the space; 5) its duration in the order of being, i. e., the time. When cognizing a human being, we have an idea of him in our spirit, and by virtue thereof we have knowledge of what a man is throughout the depth and breadth of his nature and essence. Our spirit tends to knowledge and comprehension of the man and pursues the full and perfect acquisition of the idea of him. But it cannot accomplish this unless it goes about the investigation in accordance with a method, analyzing the mechanism of the man and studying this in every part and detail thereof. For, after first acguiring the idea of the existence of the man by means of consciousness of the ego through the spirit cognitive action upon the ego, and by means of perception of his body, and positing this idea as the basis and foundation of every anthropological idea, the mind afterwards proceeds in an analytical way to knowledge of each part. The ego and the body, are two distinct and co - existing things. Neither the ego is a body, nor the body is an ego. Ego and body are two essences of a distinct nature. For, the ego can think, feel, and exercise volition or will, whereas the body lacks mind, feeling, and will. While the ego is an ego, the man' s body is not an ego, but, on the contrary, something different from an ego. The idea of an ego and the idea of a body are two distinct ideas ; they are two distinct species of anthropological ideas. But what is the ego throughout its essence nnd nature ? What is a man 's body ? The idea of the ego 's existence, and the idea of the body 's existence are primary ideas, because they arise in the mind out of some first and primary cognitive action thereof upon the ego and the body, In its first activity the mind conceives the primary idea of the man 's ego and that of his body. For this reason it posits the idea of the ego as the basis of psychology, and the idea of the man 's body as the basis and foundation of somatology, and sarcology, which are two of the sciences, belonging to the circle of the psychological ane philosophical sciences. The ego, as an essence, possesses attributes and characteristics, it has a nature. It likewise has a spatial extent and a temporal duration and a relationship between its beinghood and its characteristics. Moreover, even the body, as an essence, is subject to the same law. By cognizing all these ideas of the ego and of the body we cognize the complete constitution and structure of the ego and of the body, and we then have a perfect and exact or accurate idea of them in our spirit (mind). We thus cognize the idea of a man perfectly, and obtain knowledge of what the being is which we call a man, in both his mental, or spiritual, nature and in his sentient, or sensual nature. Thus is originated the science called a n t h r o p o - l o g y. But this knowledge is not sufficient to satisfy our desire to learn about man. Othe1 perplexities are aroused within us. For instance, is the man thus cognized himself the cause of his own existence : has he in himself the reason for his existence, or is he the effect of some other cause ? But if he is the effect of a cause situated outside of him, what, we may wonder, is the final reason of his existence ? What is the aim to which he ought to pay heed and for the sake of which he was created ? Why was he brought into this world ? Again, if he is the result of a cause outside of him, what is this cause, and what is the relationship between him, as an effect, and the cause of him ? These questions of the mind are rational ones, because they are made in accordence with the eternal laws of cognition, in accordance with the principles of causality, of contradiction, and of purposefulness, and correspond to the rational order itself and to the natural order of things. By thus reflecting and considering and proceeding methodically in the acquisition of knowledge, the mind will contact the creative cause of man, the Absolute Being. It establishes, or confirms, His existence, the relations between cause and effect ; it establishes, or verifies, His infiniteness, everlastingness, and permanence, in contradistinction from the finiteness and temporality of man. This ascent of the mind to cognition of the Absolute Being 's existence is called t h e l a w o f r e d u c t i o n, in accordance with which the mind traces the existence of the effect back to the existence of the cause of it and conceives the Idea of it. (N o t e o f T r a n s l a t o r. In the philosophy af A. Makrakis, whose terminology S. Philaretos employs, the term «reduction» has not the same signification as «induction» or «deduction» because it alco involves the notion of «ascent» from lower to higher ideas.) From the existence of the effect the mind, by proceeding in accordance with the law of the catholic order of beings ascends to cognition of the existence of man 's final purpose and of his final cause ; and it seeks to comprehend this purpose and this cause. After acquiring a notion of the creative and final reason of man, and of the reason why he is on the earth, the mind possesses the idea of man, and knows not only what a man is, but also what his creative and final cause is, and what their relations are, and what the aim is to which he ought to pay heed. By means of this idea the whole mystery surrounding man can be understood, and man becomes known with respect to his past, his present, and his future, first analytically and afterwards synthetically and i n t o t o.

COSMOLOGICAL IDEAS

The ideas which we receive from the world are cosmological ideas (N o t e   o f   T r a n s l a t o r. By «cosmology» here is meant physical sciences in general, in accordance with the philosophical terminology of A. Makrakis ; likewise by «anthropology» is meant the biological and physiological science of man, including the science of psychology, etc.). It is through and by means of them that the ego cognizes the world 1) with respect to its beinghood and (hypostasis) 2) with respect to its structural form and nature, 3) with respect to the relationship between its nature and its (hypostasis) 4) with respect to its (spatial) extent, and 5) with respect to its (temporal) duration. The first and primary and fundamental idea of the world is that of its beinghood and (hypostasis) (or as might say in English its reality and substantiality), which idea is posited, or assumed, as the basis of every other cosmological idea. In cognizing the beinghood of the world we cognize in our spirit its substance by means of the idea of its existence. But the cognition of the idea of the world's existence is not cognition of the complete and perfect idea of the world: our spirit aims at a full comprehension of the essence of the world and at acquisition of a complete idea of it. The idea of the beinghood of the world leads the cognition to the idea of the nature, of the relation, of the extent, and of the duration of it. This idea accrues to the ego through some immediate cognitive action of the spirit upon the world, upon the nonego. But can we cognize the knowledge concerning the world and acquire a perfect idea of it together therewith and at the same time ? No : for this would be opposed to the progressive nature of our spirit, which proceeds from what is known to what is unknown, and ascends from imperfection in accordance with definite laws and in accordance with a logical method. By means of the analytical method, therefore, we have to study each individual part of the nonego, analyzing it into its natural elements, and thus we are enabled to acquire an idea of parts. By means of the synthetic method, on the other hand, by fitting together all the partial cosmological (physical) ideas into a single general idea, we are enabled by this to cognize the world thoughout its essence and nature. As a result of analysis of the elements of the world, and of the mind's meditation thereon, numerous sciences are established, the sum - total of which form a single cosmological, or physical, science, named cosmology, the basis of which is the idea of the existence of the world. For how can we conceive the existence of a cosmological science without conceiving the existence of the world? Likewise neither can we conceive an anthropological science without conceiving the existence of man. But the idea of the world, as actually existing, with a structural form, and a complex of relations, and a duration in time, and an extent in space, does not fulfill all our desire for knowledge of the world. Within me there is still a void which needs to be filled. I must obtain a complete and perfect idea of the world. Hence it is that. I ask questions, and these questions of mine are reasonable, corresponding to realities and actualities. Is the world, of which I have an idea, itself the cause of its existence, has it in itself a reason to serve as its efficient cause, or is it a result of another cause, which exists outside of it? But if it is indeed a result of some other cause, what, I wonder, are its relations therewith, what is the final reason of its existence, and what is the aim it seeks to attain? Why was it made? These questions of the mind are expressive of its universal laws and principles, of causality, of contradiction, and of purposefulness, the nature of which has been made known by many previous explanations. By thus reflecting and reasoning the Spirit contacts the efficient cause of the world, whereof the latter is an effect, and it conceives therefrom an idea of the efficient and final reason of the world, verifies the existence of the Absolute, and the relations of the world thereto, as of an effect to its cause; it verifies the infiniteness and the perpetualness and the everlastingness of the Absolute, in contradistinction from the finiteness and temproralness of the world, in acccordance with the law of reduction whereby our mind is led to ascend from the effect to the cause of it, from what is finite to what is infinite, from what is relative to what is absolute. In asking whether the cause of the existence of the world is contained in the latter or in something else, the Spirit is seeking to discover the boundary separating what is finite from what is infinite, what is relative from what is absolute, what is causate from what is the cause of it. But this seeking presupposes a distinction of what is relative from what is absolute in the physical and logical order. For the spirit which seeks to discover that which is absolute and to distinguish it from what is relative, cognizes the existence of the relative and of the absolute apart from each other and distinct from each other, in accordance with the primary law of cognition. Is the world, I wonder, the cause of its own existence? This question means: Is the world a relative or an absolute being? Is man, I wonder, the cause of his own existence? This question means: Is man, I wonder, something relative or something absolute? It is evident, therefore, that what is relative and the idea of the relative is something quite different from that which is absolute and the idea of the absolute. But the idea of the world, taking the latter to be studied throughout the depth of its essence and nature, is a relative idea, precisely as is also that of man. These two ideas — that of man and that of the world — depict and represent the fact; accordingly, both may be more concisely expressed in a single complex idea, that of the fact and the finite being. For the relative and finite being, as having its efficient cause in the existence of the Absolute Being, is a contingent, not a necessary, being, for it could exist or not because it exists only as depending on the volition and power of the Absolute and Necessary and Eternal Being which is the Cause of it. Hence it is logically evident that the idea of the fact is contingent and dependent upon the Idea of the Absolute as an idea that exists eternally and as one necessarily having also beinghood. It is upon this eternally existent Idea of the Absolute that the science of sciences, Philosophy, is founded, which aims at a comprehension of the perfect Idea of the Eternal Being. The other sciences, which are mere handmaids of their mistress Philosophy, the science of sciences, are founded upon the idea of the fact.

THEOLOGICAL IDEAS

Theological ideas spring out of God, who is the Absolute Being and the efficient cause of everything. Through them we are able to cognize God 1) with respect to His beinghood; 2) His nature; 3) His relationship; 4) His duration; 5) His extent. The fundamental idea of God, which our spirit acquires by means of some initial cognitive action of its own upon God, is the idea of His existence. Accordingly we take this as the basis of every other theological idea. But what is this cognition and this knowledge before the perfect Idea of God, before the mystery of our ignorance concerning God? We know that there is a God, and from this primary knowledge of His existence we are seeking further to gain a thorough grasp of all knowledge concerning God, in order to acquire a perfect idea concerning God. We are led up to cognition of God's existence, not directly and before cognizing the existence of ourselves and of the world, but after knowledge of the fact has preceded. For the existence of the fact presupposes the existence of the Eternal Being. Were the Eternal Being inexistent, neither could any fact be existent. The Eternal Being, however, could exist even without the fact, because the fact is contingent, whereas the Eternal Being is a necessary being. God as the Absolute Being exists absolutely. As a being He has characteristics and attributes, the sum — total of which is called His n a t u r e . Between His beinghood and His nature there subsists a relationship and consonance analogous to His nature and beinghood. As a being existent outside of the fact He is also situated outside of all space and exists outside of all time. For empirical space and time define the extent and duration, respectively, of the fact and of relative and finite essences. A finite being has an existence, a nature, and a relationship which are likewise finite, and therefore it occupies a finite portion of space, and comes into being (or beinghood), and lasts likewise in finite time. But above finite existences is conceived and cognized the necessary and infinite existence of the Being. Above finite natures is conceived and cognized, as necessarily existent, the infinite Nature of some infinite Essence. Above finite relationships and powers, between finite natures and finite existences, is conceived and cognized the existence of the Relationship and Power of an infinite Essence. Above the finite space and time of the finite extent and duration, respectively, is conceived and cognized the necessary existence of the eternalness, and of the everlastingness, and of the infiniteness of the Being and of the Absolute Essence. God dwells in the unlimited vastitude of infinity, and the unlimited vastitude of infinity is the house of God. God exists and lives in the domain of everlastingness. It is clear, therefore, that infinitude and eternity are the space and time, respectively, of God: they are sempiternal. In cognizing God we cognize Him as having a perfect existence, a perfect nature, a perfect power, as being forever and living forever in His infiniteness, eternalness, and everlastingness. But before we can mount up to this cognition, we have to pass through cognition and knowledge of the fact, we have to conceive in the abstract the features and characteristics of the divine nature, and above all we have to study carefully and intelligently the spiritual and rational nature of man, i.e., his mental and logical peculiarities. For we can discover the Absolute Mind in the finite nind, the Absolute Will in the finite will, and the Absolute Idea in the finite cognitive and ratiocinative nature of man. We can discover the infinite in the finite, God in man, as will be made plain in what we shall say hereinafter.

In cognizing God as an absolute being, we cognize Him as having in Himself the reason of His efficient and final existence, as being the efficient and creative Principle and end of beings, as having in Himself the efficient and final reason of the existence of beings, as the source of all cognition, knowledge, and science, as knowing Himself perfectly, as conceiving and cognizing all things before they come into being (or beinghood), and in their essence after they have come into being (or beinghood); in sum, as omnipotent, able to create and to substantify outside of Himself what is as yet inexistent, or, as we also call it, nonbeing, which He sempiternally conceives and cognizes as being existent.

In cognizing God as cognizing Himself by means of perfect cognition and having in Himself a perfect idea of Himself, we cognize Him as a perfect Mind cognizing in a perfect Spirit by means of a perfect Idea of Him; moreover, we cognize Him as a God who is essentially one in number but existing in three substances and persons who are all three equal and perfect. In cognizing Him as all — wise, we cognize Him as knowing immediately and perfectly the nature and beinghood of beings, their final purpose, and the means whereby they can accomplish the purpose of their existence. We conceive Him as cognizing being as nonbeing, and as one who is omnipotent, in His power and wisdom creating a world consistent and consonant with His Design and His Logos. We conceive God to be all — good, because He is allsufficient, being rich in everything that is good, supplying to each and every being and to all of the beings taken together whatever is good for their perfection and whatever is needed to maintain and preserve the beings. Creation, being an aggregate of all the numerous beings that have God as their cause and a purpose analogous to their nature, stands in perpetual need of means analogous to its maturation and completion, without which it cannot accomplish its destiny. Divine goodness grants these means abundantly, and every being finds whatever good thing it needs and that in which and by which it is enabled to reach its maturity. In cognizing God, therefore, as one in respect of essence, but triune in respect of persons, namely, a Mind, a Logos, and a Spirit, or, in other words, as the Being, the Cognition, and the Truth, respectively, all - wise, all - good, and all - powerful, the absolute cause of everything in the universe, we conceive Him in science and truth, and have a correct and true idea of Him, which is the basis and support or mainstay of every scientific idea in our mind.

IDEAS OF RELATIONS

The cognition of the ideas of the ego, of the world, and of God involves the idea of a relationship subsisting between these and connecting the three ideas of them together and with each other as abond, or nexus. Moreover, in conceiving the three ideas the Spirit conceives also the necessary bond or nexus connecting them with each other, Relations are: 1) physical; 2) rational; 3) moral. Physical relations connect physical beings with each other and with God's most perfect will, which is the source of the relations. Rational and moral relations connect rational and moral beings, with one another and with God's cognition and moral will, out of which spring all relations. All bodies are connected with one another and correlated in accordance with physical laws, which spring out of Gon's will as His work. The entire physical and material world, being correlated to itself and to God's creative will, depends on the will of the most perfect Being as his work and created product. Likewise all rational and moral and free beings, the entire rational and moral world, being correlated to themselves and to God's most perfect will, depend upon it as a work and created product and have their aim directed to it through the agency of a supreme and perfect relationship. The idea of the numerous and various relations, which we obtain by observing partial relations, leads us up to cognition of a single absolute and universal relationship, which is the relation of creation to God, or the relation of the fact to the Being. We can conceive this relationship by means of our reason. This relationship is the most perfect and highest of all relations, and it includes moreover every other relation. This indeed is the relationship whereby we are enabled to conceive and to gain a thorough knowledge of all other relations by simply contemplating them in it as in a picture.

The relationship by which the eternal Being is connected with the fact is a relationship by which the eternal Being is sempiternally connected with eternal nonbeing, with what is contingent and may become and be a fact (at some future time). As a sempiternal relationship sempiternally connecting and uniting the Being with whatever can become and be anything, it is analogous to the objects being related. Hence it is logically evident that is it actually and potentially a being : it is an actual being as springing out of the eternal Being ; it is a potential being and fact as a relation connecting the fact with the Being, and thereby connecting and uniting the Being and the fact. In the fact the most imperfect being is matter, and the most perfect being is man. Consequently the relationship between the eternal Being and man is the most perfect and is analogous to both. 1) It is one by which man partakes of the Being ; 2) it is one by which he partakes of the fact, and it is the explanation of the Being and of the fact, of their essence and nature, of their power, duration, and extent. The most perfect relationship, whereby the Being is connected perfectly with the fact, is revealed in the most perfect work of the Being, in man, in whom is to be seen the coincidence and association of two natures, the divine and the human, in the sempiternal substance of the most perfect relationship. Hence we are seeking to comprehend the most perfect relationship with respect to its sempiternal beinghood and the revelation of it in time in the fact. Its sempiternal beinghood, its sempiternal nature, power, extent, and duration, is revealed in the essence of the fact, in the nature, power, extent, and duration of the latter, with which essence it is associated and connected as the effect with its cause. Hence it may be said that the most perfect relationship is the object of the Being and of the fact, in which object the Being and the fact, God and man, shine forth in all their glory. So as a result of observing the numerous relations, by a law of cognition we are led up to cognition of the one most perfect and absolute relationship, which relates the Being to the fact, God to man, 1) religiously, owing to the moral downfall of the fact; 2) rationally and morally, and politically too, owing to the imperfect and naturally progressive nature of the fact; 3) and physically, owing to the perfection of the physical world. This latter form of this relationship is the most imperfect, while the most perfect form is the moral, and rational, and political form of it, in accordance with which the fact, being exempted from the influence of physical laws, is exalted and elevated to the purest sphere of rationality and of morality, and of living harmoniously and forever with the Being. The religious form of the most perfect relationship is the most imperfect, though it is also the preparation or forerunner of its moral and rational form. But in general the most perfect form of this relationship is the social form, in accordance with which an entire community or society of moral and rational beings can become connected with the most perfect and most moral Being, by means of a bond likewise most perfect and most moral, by means of a most perfect relationship, by means of the Logos. If anyone wishes to obtain knowledge of the perfect relation of the Being with the fact as revealed therein, let him look at the society of rational and moral beings which is living in harmony with the Supreme Being and which depends upon His perfect will. The most perfect relationship, moreover, involves the most perfect revelation of the Being, and the most perfect knowledge of the fact; while the idea of this relationship is identically the same as the most perfect Idea of the Being; and His most perfect work is likewise identically the same as the idea of the God - man. The highest and most perfect form of the perfect relationship between the Being and the fact is the rational, and moral, and social connection and association of logical and moral beings with the most perfect Idea and Design of the Being. This relationship is involved in the Revelation of the Idea of the Being, of the sempiternal Logos, in Christianity, which latter is the most perfect relationship of the Being with the fact. This relationship makes its appearance 1) as the rational representation and as the descriptive knowledge of the Being and of the fact, or, in a word, as t r u t h ; 2) as the common law, physical and moral, of the operation of the Being and of the fact, as a physical and moral g o o d ; 3) as a law of the external operation of both, as r i g h t ; 4) as a standard, or measure, of analogy and of harmonious unity of both, as what is b e a u t i f u l ; these four items being phases of the aforesaid highest and most perfect form of the perfect relationship between the Being and the fact. Rationality, physical and moral law, right, and beauty, in an absolute sense, are four aspects and forms of the most perfect relationship between the Being and the fact. But the idea of the most perfect relationship includes an idea of the rational, of the physical, and of the moral law, the idea of right, and that of the beautiful, truth, and whatever is good, sublime, great, grand, or beautiful. In contemplating the most perfect idea of the most perfect relationship we are contemplating the idea of what is true, of what is good, of what is right, and of what is beautiful, or we might say the idea of trueness, of goodness, of righteousness, and of beauteousness, the Idea of the Being, by which God is related to the contingent and to the fact. The social form of the most perfect relationship is the first and highest, and the purpose of its physical and of its religious, form, which are merely the means of accomplishing it. The end, on the other hand, is the relationship of the Being with the fact in the entification of what is morally good, in the association of both through what is good, in the contemplation of truth, in the practice of what is good and of what is righteous, right, and just, in most perfect love. This most perfect form in love of the rational and moral relationship between God and man abrogates the religious and the physical relationship of the accident ; it abolishes the prevailing disorder in nature, corruption, decay, and death ; it abolishes whatever is finite and whatever is extensive ; it renders the physical and the moral world imperishable and immortal, and introduces imperishability and immortality into the world ; it founds and establishes therein the kingdom of truth, of what is good, and of what is right — the kingdom of heaven, and it consolidates the everlasting order of things. Hence it will be seen that the most perfect relationship between the Being and the fact comprises a revelation of the everlasting order in creation, a most perfect union of God with man through Christ, who is none other than the relationship between the being and the fact, or, more expressly speaking, the God - man. The idea of the perfect relationship is the idea of the God - man, an idea connecting God with the world and man, and without which we cannot cognize the three objects of knowledge, because neither can these exist without a relation the sempiternal source of which is the sempiternal Being, God.

CONCERNING CONCRETE IDEAS

An idea, we have said, is an image and representation of a being in our spirit. Hence it may be seen that when I say that I have an idea of some being, I am saying nothing else than that I cognize — i. e., am thinking of — a being and know it by means of the appearance of an image of it in my spirit. For this reason it may be said that all the ideas in my spirit, as images and representations of beings, are actual concrete ideas, different from another kind of ideas called abstlact, which are formed by the spirit in accordance with logical vaws and can be conceived by themselves and without the beings from which they have been abstracted by a logical process. Concrete ideas precede in cognition, and abstract ideas follow, in the same way as the substances of beings, of their nature, precede in the order of beings. Concrete ideas represent beings, while abstract ideas represent properties, natures, acts, relations, and, in a word, attributes. For this reason it may be said that concrete ideas are images of beings, while abstract ideas are images of anything attributed thereto, or predicated thereof. Essences possess beinghood — i. e., they really exist; the attributes predicated of them, on the other hand, are not really existent — they exist merely in relation to the beings with which they are conceived to be conjoined in the spirit. Beings are conceived together in the spirit with their attributes and characteristics, because they coexist in nature, and we cannot cognize a being concretely otherwise than through its attributes and its nature, as neither can we cognize a characteristic and a nature without, or apart from, a substance of which these are predicated. Hence it may be inferred logically that in cognizing the ideas of attributes, of characteristics, and of categories of beings, the spirit cognizes them not as actually distinct from the beings proper of which they are characteristics and attributes, not as having an objective existence and substantiality distinct from the beings themselves, but only ideally and in the abstract as abstracted from the beings and their essences. For this reason, as being cognizable in themselves and independently of the beings proper of which they are the phenomenon, or that which alone is apparent, they are termed abstract ideas. But since the cognition of them is preceded by the cognition of the concrete ideas from which they have been abstracted, therefore we must first treat of the subject of concrete ideas and thereafter of that of abstract ideas.

| Ideas considered with respect to their features |

CONCERNING SIMPLE IDEAS

Concretely and actually simple ideas are images of simple beings, images of hypostasis. It is through them that we gain knowledge of the beinghood of beings, and are able to cognize the mystery of their existence. What is called a simple idea is the first representation of any being in the mind with respect to its beinghood and existence. Every object is first known to exist and afterwards its nature becomes known, as well as the relation and purpose of ite existence. Therefore it may be inferred that something first makes its appearance in the spirit as existent, as the idea of a simple existence, and afterwards this reveals in us its nature, relation, and purpose. Existence is a common predication of everything. For every being subsists and exists. For this reason it is also to be noted that the idea of beinghood, too, as being commonly predicated of every being is a general and universal idea, an indeterminate idea. Moreover, it is to be noted that every idea in our mind has its beinghood, i. e., it exists as an idea of something in our spirit. Therefore as an idea of beinghood it is simple. A simple and abstract idea has no specification of its own, no feature of its own. Hence it may be said to be indefinite; and on this account we cannot define it, except to say that b e i n g h o o d i s b e i n g h o o d . But when we specify, or qualify, the general and universal idea of existence by means of a feature of its own that distinguishes it from any other idea of beinghood, we form the individual ideas of beings; and thus in our mind we can represent a whole world of individual presentations and ideas which depict, or represent, the individual existences of beings, their substances. Consider the idea of the existence of the ego — the idea of the existence of the world — the idea of the existence of God. These are ideas of beinghood, not as conceived in the abstract, as a general idea, but as the beinghood of the ego, of the world, and of God, as ideas that are concrete and actual. When I say that I have in my spirit the idea of the beinghood of the ego, I do not mean simply and generally that I have an idea of beinghood indeterminately, but as an idea of the existence of the ego, in distinction from the idea of b e i n g h o o d of other beings. Thus even when I say that I have an idea of the beinghood of an apple tree, of a fig tree, of a dog, of a cat, of a man, of a woman, of a child, of an old or aged man or woman, what I mean is that there is an apple tree, a fig tree, a dog, a cat, a man, a woman, etc. in the order of beings. I can cognize concrete, and not abstract, ideas. This specific character or feature which I predicate of the beinghood of beings for the purpose of distinguishing and specifying them makes them a multiple idea, because it predicates of the idea of the being also an idea of its characteristic, of its featureful character, and of its nature. It has already been stated that the beinghood of any being is a simple beinghood, and that the idea of it is likewise a simple and universal idea. It is simple because it has no specification, no determinate qualification. It is universal because it can be predicated of any and every being anywhere and at any time. Every being exists. Substantiality is common to all beings; hence the idea of it is also universal.

Inasmuch as existence may be predicated of any being whatsoever, because every being subsists and exists, the idea of existence too may be predicated of every idea, and every idea accordingly has its beinghood as an idea in the mind. By abstracting from any being its own peculiar character whereby it can be distinguished from every other being, and through the process of abstraction and generalization ascending from Individuals to species, and from these to genera, we can conceive in our mind the most general idea of beinghood, which includes every particular and individual presentation of beinghood. Thus by a process of abstraction and generalization we are elevated to cognition of the simple idea of beinghood, which is a universal idea. Beings have specifications and their own features. They may be distinguished into two primary genera: 1) organic; 2) inorganic. These again may be subdivided into rational and irrational. In all of these there is commonly predicated an existence, so that both an organic being and an inorganic being are beings, and both a rational and an irrational being are likewise beings. Organicity, inorganicity, rationality, and irrationality are characteristics and specifications of the nature of the being in question for the purpose of distinguishing the many substances of the being. With these abstracted there remains a being denuded of every characteristic, and one which is consequently unspecified and indeterminate. But a being without any attribute is matter, it is the substance of every being. The simple idea of existence is merely the idea of the substantiality of a being.

CONCERNING MULTIPLE IDEAS

A simple idea has no specification (or, in philosophical terminology, no specificity), because it represents no characteristic of a being except that which is called beinghood; and on this account it is the most general and a universal idea and one which may be predicated of any being whatsoever. But when it takes on a qualifying feature, or determinate character, it becomes a multiple idea. The idea of the ego, for instance, is a multiple idea. For it not only presents in the mind the existence of the ego, but also its attributes, these being in the aggregate what constitutes its nature and form. This idea depicts the hypostasis of the ego together with the manner in which the latter makes its appearance in the order of beings. A multiple idea presupposes the existence of a hypostasis together with its nature. Accordingly, just as, were there no beings, we could not have had the simple idea of their existence, so and in like manner had there been no beings with attributes — essences — we could not have had the idea of its essence, a multiple idea. The world is an aggregate of individual hypostasis, an idea of whose simple existence we can form in our spirit. But these substances make their appearance in some manner and have various forms and various attributes and species. Our spirit therefore, forms in itself ideas of these various forms of beings, and by means of each idea it obtains knowledge of the particular being to which the idea pertains. These ideas of the nature of beings are multiple ideas the basis of which is a simple idea. A simple being becomes a multiple being when it assumes a nature. As through the process of abstraction of specific features and of generalization of common features we are elevated to a conception of the most general idea which is the indeterminate idea of beinghood, so and in like manner through the process of adding specific features, in the idea of the hypostasis of each being, we are enabled to descend to cognition of the idea of the numerous species and individuals, and are enabled to form particular and individual ideas. In our cognitive ascent we simplify ideas, whereas in our cognitive descent we compound them. We first cognize individual and particular ideas, and afterwards general and universal ideas by observing and reasoning.

A multiple idea reveals in our mind the beinghood and the form of a being. But since every being, every substance, has an existence together with a form, and is revealed in the order of beings in some specific form and in some manner or other, in our spirit too a being is depicted in accordance with the nature it possesses. Hence a multiple idea is a universal idea, because it can be predicated of any being whatsoever. We conceive characteristics and attributes to be inherent in beings, and we can conceive no attributes without a being except by mental abstraction. But we can conceive a relation and reference as subsistent between the nature of a being and its substance ; and we conceive in our spirit the idea of the relation arising from its existence : hence a multiple idea includes 1) the idea of the existence of a being ; 2) the idea of the form of a being ; 3) the idea of the relation subsisting between its hypostasis and its form. But each particular being exists in some region of space and makes its appearance during some interval of time. From the existence of the space and of the time our mind conceives the idea of space and of time ; and it contemplates these along with the idea of the beinghood, form, and relation of the being, as being related to these. It is therefore logically evident that a multiple idea is inclusive of the ideas extension and of duration, which are general and universal ideas of because they can be predicated of every being and of every occurrence. By thus cognizing a multiple idea our spirit is able to explain it by means of these propositions :

Every being subsists and exists.

Every thing that exists exists in some specific form.

Every thing that exists has an extension and a duration.

The first postulate explains the existence and hypostasis of the being. The second one explains its existence as an organic or inorganic, animate or inanimate, rational or irrational, being. The third postulate explains its existence and appearance in space and. time. We examine each being with respect to its beinghood, its nature, and its specific form in which it appears in the order of beings, with respect to the relation and reference of its substance to its nature, with respect to its extension and duration. Hypostasis nature, relation, space, time all concur in the existence of every being ; and on this account a cognitive mind cannot cognize a being without a hypostasis or a nature without a hypostasis and a relation, a being not existing in space, not having any extension, and not existing in time, not having any duration. Hence it is evident that both the idea of extension and the idea of duration are universal ideas. The conception of a nature without hypostasis or of the relation between them by itself. is effected in abstraction in the mind, and not actually. This very same remark holds good also as applied to cognition of extension and of duration for the purpose of facilitating the proncess of cognitio for the spirit. Always, however, in cognizing a being we cognize it with respect to all its elements — its hypostosis, its nature, its relation, its extent, and its duration.

CONCERNING COMPOSITE IDEAS

What is called a composite idea is one that presents in our mind the union and association of many essences in a single hupostasis This Kind of idea is to be distinguished from a multiple idea, which latter presents in our spirit a nature united with its hypostasis. When I cognize the ego, I cognize it as a simple and multiple unit. I cognize it as a simple unit in its substance as a being, but as a multiple unit in its nature, in its characteristics. But when I cognize a human being, I cognize him as a single entity so far as concerns his hypostasis, his ego, but as composite so far as concerns the whole of him which is composed of distinct parts. A human being is composed of three essences distinct from each othet, to wit, of a body, a soul, and a spirit. A body, a soul, and a spirit are what constitute a human being. Hence it is logically evident that the idea of a human body, that of a soul, and that of a spirit constitute a single idea, namely, the idea of a human being, which is a composite idea. The process of composition puts many essences together round a center, and the composite being has a single substance but many essences. The world has a single hypostasis a single center ; and round this are concentered a number of essences distinct from each other, called the earthy, the watery, and the fiery essence, of which it is composed. Hence it is evident that it is composite. Consequently the idea of the world is composite too. God is a single triune hypostasis which contains in itself three units of beings, or of persons. Hence it is logically evident that God is a unit and a trinity — a unit comprising persons and hypostasis having the same nature. God, therefore, is a simple aud multiple essence. He is a simple essence in His three hypostasis, namely, His perfect Mind, His perfect Idea, and His perfect Spirit, but multiple in His characteristics, in the attributes which constitute His nature. Such is the correct and true idea concerning God which we obtain in our spirit when we think about Him rationally, i.e,, in accordance with reason — an idea at once simple and multiple, as distinguished from the composite idea of the fact. On this account every multiple idea is one that depicts, or represents, the beinghood, the nature, the relationship, the extent, and the duration of a being. Every composite idea, on the other hand, is one that depicts, or represents, numerous essences, the totality of which has one center and one substance. In order to grasp the multiple idea of a being and essence, the mind first considers the nature of the being and then proceeds to conceive an idea of its nature. But since every nature is the nature of some being, the spirit is led to ascend from the idea nature of the being to the conception of an idea ot the being and of its hypostasis, to cognition of the being from the phenomena, and thus it possesses the idea of the substance. This ascent is one which goes from multiplicity to simplicity and unity. Since every nature is analogous to the hypostasis of which it is predicated, and since between hypostasis and nature there are references and relations, therefore when thinking of this relationship the spirit acquires the additional idea of the relationship, and the latter is a third element of the idea of every being. But inasmuch as every being occupies space and lasts for some time, the mind conceives the idea of the extension and that of the duration of the being ; and thus it cognizes in itself the whole idea of the being in its unity, simplicity, and multiplicity. The idea of the being is simple and multiple. It is simle with respect to its beinghood, but multiple with respect to the elements composing it, namely, the nature, the relationship, the extension, and the duration. The idea, on the other hand, which depicts the synthesis, or combin- ation, of many essences in the order of beings round a single hypostasis, is a composite idea, the basis of which is simplicity and multiplicity. The synthesis presupposes the existence of the simple and multiple essences. On this account by analyzing things that are compound we can discover their simplicity and multi- plicity, by simply ascending to the simplest, indivisible, and undecomposable particles, whose existence we presuppose, as they aie things which do not come under the perseption of our senses. The analysis of a human being into the parts of which he is composed enables us to ascend to the idea of the undecomposable, indivisible, and simple substance of the ego, which idea we acquire through consciousness. All composite ideas of what is finite lead us to ascend to the cognition of a simple, undecomp- osable, and indivisible essence which is infinite and absolute and the idea of which is an image of its infiniteness, of its multipl- eness, of its undecomposableness, and of its indivisibleness — an Idea which is equal to and exactly like the perfect essence which has perfect beinghood combined with infiniteness, simpleness, undecomposableness, and indivisibleness. For if there exist es- sences that are finite and composite, or compound, there neces- sarily exists above them some essence too that is simple and multiple as the source from which they have acquired and possess beinghood. But the world and man are composite essences. Hence it may be inferred that they have of necessity a simple and multiple cause to which they owe their creation. For how other- wise could they have aquired their composition ? Hence it follows that just as the simple and multiple existence of the fact reveals to us the absolute existence of some simple and multiple essence, so and in like manner the composite essences of what is finite reveal to us the existence of some absolute simple and multiple essence which we call God.

CONCERNING RELATIVE IDEAS

An idea is called a relative idea when it depicts a being that exists in the order of beings not as something self - existent but as something depending upon another being which is higher and more perfect than it. A relative being owes its existence to some other being. It exists because its cause exists: if the latter did not exist, neither could it exist. I have in my mind the idea of a sheep, say. This idea is a relative idea, because the existence of the sheep is due to something else which caused it to exist or produced it by the process of generation und which originated in the initial pair of sheep created by God and not begotten in accordance with the law of coition. All these ideas of a sheep, together with the further idea of its original pair, or primary couple, are relative ideas. The idea of a male or female human being is a relative idea, because any human being owes his existence in the world to his parents, while they in turn owe theirs to their parents, and so on back to the first - formed pair of human beings who received their beinghood directly from God and were not begotten of genitors, or generators and generatrices, by a law of natural procreation. The idea of the ego and that of the world are relative ideas, for both of them owe their existence to God, who is the absolute cause of beings. A relative idea is that of the fact, because the fact is not anything that is self - existent, but, on the contrary, owes its existence to God, who is the Eternal Being.

A relative idea is the idea of the fact, of what is finite, of what is temporal, of what is extensive. In it is included the idea of the beinghood of the ego, the idea of the beinghood of the world, and that of their relations; the idea of the form and of the nature of the ego and of the world; the idea of finite space and time. In the relative idea is comprised collectively everything that may be predicated of the fact. From individual and partial ideas of the fact our mind ascends to the general idea of the relative being and represents in itself the idea of the fact. By thinking about the fruit it is led to conceive by a law of cognition the idea of the tree which produced it. From cognition of the tree the spirit ascends to cognition of the productive cause of it, until at last it stops and stands before the Idea of the absolute Cause. In thus thinking about the relative effects in succession and ascending to the conception of the relative causes, our mind does not relax, but, on the contrary, continues to seek to discover the uncaused cause of every fact and of every relative cause. Hence it is led to conceive the idea of the existence of the absolute Cause, which contains in Itself the cause of Itself, and which is both self—existent and self—caused.

CONCERNING AN ABSOLUTE IDEA

We call the image formed in our spirit of the self—existent and self—caused Being an absolute idea. Such an absolute idea is one, because the absolute Being too is one. Our mind cognizes this Idea after having previously cognized that of the fact and that of the relative effects and causes. After first looking for the cause of every being and trying to find out whether the cause is in it or in any other relative being; after first cognizing that all beings are not causes of their own existence, but, on the contrary, that they are due to a cause which resides outside of them, the mind proceeds to think as follows. I cognize myself; I cognize my own existence. But in cognizing myself, I cognize at the same time also the fact that I myself am not the cause of my own existence. I cognize the fact that I am the effect of another cause, which latter exists, or has its beinghood, outside of me. I cognize at the same time also the world and its existence. But I cognize at the same time also the fact that the world is not the cause of itself, but that it is an effect of some cause having its beinghood outside of the world. This cognition is a cognition of the effect, of the fact, of that which exists relatively. In thus cognizing the existence of what is relative the spirit conceives the idea of the existence of the Absolute cause outside of the ego and outside of the world. Without cognition of what is relatively existent there can be no cognition of the Absolute Being and no representation of the Idea of it in the spirit. We must therefore first cognize the existence of what is relative, in order to be able with the help of this cognition to cognize the existence of the Absolute. But just as it is impossible for what is relative to exist without the Absolute, so neither can the idea of the relative exist in our spirit without the Idea of the Absolute Being. Accordingly, if our mind has a yearning to seek the cause of all being, it has also the Power to discover it by thinking in accordance with right reason and proceeding methodically in the endeavor to discover it. It has the ability to lift itself up to the idea of the existence of it and to discover therein what it cannot find in relative beings, in what is finite and in the fact. By ascending to the Idea of the Absolute through the fact, it ascends to the Idea of the Eternal Being, of that which is infinite, sempiternal, and everlasting, to the Idea of eternal beinghood, of perfect specific form, and of perfect rational relation, and thus it succeeds in cognizing the sempiternal essence of the Absolute, His everlastingness and infiniteness.

CONCERNING PRIMARY IDEAS

A primary idea is one that has been in our spirit initially (i. e., from the beginning) as an image representing the Being. It is called primary because it exists in the mind without any work or operation being required to acquire it. It coexists together with the spirit, and is revealed immediately and directly before (i. e., in front of) the ego with all perspicuity. so that any denial of it is in the very nature of the case impossible. Primary ideas are: 1) the idea of the ego; 2) the idea of the nonego; 3) the idea of the Absolute Being and of the relations between them ; that there is an ego ; that there is a world ; that there is a God; and that there are relations between them. These ideas are primary ideas because they are imposed upon the spirit's cognition as principles, but these ideas are rather opinions than ideas. For by means of them we declare that there is an ego, a God. But primary ideas are mainly the idea of the hypostasis of every being; the idea of its form and that of its relationship; the idea of its extent an that of its duration, or that of space and that of time, respectively. From these primary ideas we can proceed to form primary judgments, which are the criterion of every judgment, just as primary ideas are the criterion of every other idea. Primary ideas are what make up a primary or initial cognition, and are the mainstay of every idea. From the fact these ideas exist in every human being conscious of his own existence, some persons speculating in philosophy inferred that they are innate in the mind, that they are selfplanted and spontanteous ideas of the spirit. Consequently they doubted whether these ideas which grow up in the spirit spontaneously are ideas corresponding to beings existing outside of them, and consequently whether they represent (real) beings. Hence they sought to find a good and sufficient reason in proof that innate ideas are images of (real) beings, and not mere simulacra and fancies of the spirit. The belief about innate ideas has had as a consequence the terrible delusion of speculators in philosophy, of whom some split the unity between beinghood and knowinghood in twain and sought reasonable arguments to prove and verify the agreement between knowinghood and beinghood, or, as it is more usual to say in English, between knowing and being. Those, on the other hand, who took the ideas to be fancies of the ego, and to be mere simulacra of the spirit, denied the existence of any being independent of the ego, and proclaimed the ego to be a God! Kant, however, without denying the existence of the world and of God, declared knowledge of beings outside of us to be impossiple, and particularly knowledge of the Absolute; accordingly he turned all his attention to classification of the ideas in the spirit. Thus the matter of the innateness of ideas wound up in subjective Idealism, which declared that the ego is the source of ideas, and that outside of it and its ideas there exists nothing else. The end, therefore, of Idealism was a denial of all objectivity.

The primary ideas of the Being, of structural form, of relationship, of space, and of time, are not innate, nor are they spontaneous creatures of the finite ego. For, if the ego had the ability to produce the ideas out of itself, as the earth produces plants, would not all our ideas be innate and be produced spontaneously? For, why should it be correct for us to believe that some of our ideas are innate, and that others of them are produced by our mind, but not all of them? Why should we agree with those who believe that some of our ideas are innate, are primitive ideas, and disagree with the uncompromising idealists, who maintain that all our ideas are fancies and mere simulacra of the ego, and spontaneous products thereof? Why should we be of like mind with the eclectic philosophers and not with the subjective idealists? We can nowise see any sufficient reason to be convinced that only universal, necessary, and general ideas arise from the finite ego, and not all ideas. For, if some of these are not a product of the ego, whence does it become plain that the others are? The eclectic school has no convincing reason in proof of what it asserts, and on this account Idealism triumphs over it. Eclecticism, without solving this problem, was founded upon the false supposition that necessary, and universal, and general ideas are produced by the ego, and it ensconced itself upon a tottering and rotten support. Being unable logically to untie the Gordian knot respecting the question as to whence ideas arise within us, Eclecticism cut it asunder by means of the false supposition, and not by means of right reason and logical proof. When its support was taken away, it had to go along with it; accordingly, it may be said, those who are speculating eclectically are speculating upon a basis which has already been vitiated. On this account Idealism and Materialism now rear themselves haughtily against Eclecticism, which is unable to kill them logically and scientifically, and to vanquish them triumphantly. Eclectics either ought to admit that all our idea have their source in experience, as the materialists hold, or to admit that all their ideas stem from the ego, as

the idealists hold. Otherwise, let then prove why some of them
ought to be taken to be innate, and others not.

Our primary ideas are primary images in the spirit which
are impressed upon it, when the ego comes into contact with beings. They are produced from the contact of the cognizing ego
with the objects cognized. For, after coming in contact with
itself, after cognizing itself, the ego immediately gains an idea
of itself, and by means of that idea, as by means of some image,
it considers the ego to be itself. It thus acquires an idea of beinghood. In cognizing the world, on the other hand, it gains an
idea thereof, and by means of that idea it contemplates it. It
thus acquires a more general idea of beinghood. By means of
the idea of the ego and that of the world, it cognizes also the
Absolute Cause of beings, God, and gains an idea of Him, and
thereby contemplates Him. It thus acquires a general idea of beinghood, and ascends to a conception of the most general idea of
the being. In this manner the ego acquires also the primary ideas
of the structural form, of the relationship, of the extension, and
of the duration, of the being, relatively in so far as respects cognition of the ego and of the world, but absolutely in so far as
respects the cognition of God. Primary ideas, therefore, are so
called, not because they are innate, or because they are produced
out of the nature of the ego — i.e., not because they are out-
growths of the ego, but because they are acquired from the bri-
mary cognition of the soul, and result from the immediate contact
of the spirit with the objects. This is verified also by a consideration of the manner in which all our conscient and percipient
and ratiocinant ideas, or, in other words, by a consideration of
the contact of the ego with the objects of knowledge through
the spirit, or mind.

CONCERNING ACQUIRED IDEAS

Primary ideas, to wit, that of the being, that of its nature,
that of its relationship, that of its duration, and that of its extension, are immediate products of the cognitive spirit, when the
latter cognizes the ego, the world, God, and the relations between
them, the finite and the infinite, the temporal and the sempiternal. These ideas are the first impressions of the spirit which
are formed therein as a result of its immediate contact with the
objects of the ego, of the world, and of God, and of its initial
and first cognition in regard to them. For the mind, or spirit, is
evident at the same time as cognition of the existence of a being,
and of its nature, and of its relationship, and of its duration, and
of its extension. But the being is cognized as an ego, as a nonego,

as a relative being, as a fact, as an absolute being, as a temporal being, as a sempiternal being, as a finite being, as an infinite being. An acquired idea, on the contrary, is so called because, being acquired by means of logical processes and laws, it has to be consistent and concordant with the primary ideas, which are the criterion of every acquired idea, in order that it may thus be also true. By means of the primary ideas the ego cognizes itself, the world, God, and the relations subsisting between them. It cognizes the fact, and the Eternal Being, the finite and the infinite, the temporal and the sempiternal. But it cognizes only their existence and beinghood. It cognizes the fact that each being really exists, that it possesses some nature and some mode of existence, that its nature is related to its hypostasis that it is situated in a region of space, and that it is subject to the lapse of time. But in the very beginning it is ignorant as to what the beinghood of beings is in itself — what the thing really is — their substance, what their nature, their relationship, their extension, their duration are; accordingly, it persists in seeking to acquire in addition an idea and notion of these unknown entities. This endeavor of the cognizing ego, and the existence of the objects in regard to which its cognition exercises cognition, are the occasions for acquisition of ideas which on this account bear the appellation of a c q u i r e d   i d e a s,   o r   d e r i v e d i d e a s . If we deprive the ego of its primary ideas, we deprive it also of its primary knowledge, we deprive it of that very thing which is the cognitive spirit of the ego, and in that case we cannot form and gain acquired ideas. Along therewith we then remove also the primary judgments, and are left unable to think and to judge about any object. An acquired idea is true if it is consistent and consonant with the criterion of the primary ideas. Otherwise, if it contradicts them, it is false. Yet, although a falsehood usually creeps into them, it can never creep into primary ideas. Primary ideas are always true; they are certain: accordingly, they rule in cognition and hold sway therein, regulating its operation and activity for the acquisition of ideas in regard to objects of knowledge. On this account even the primary judgments resulting therefrom have a universality as universal laws of the spirit, which latter always and at all times cognizes the truth of the being, of its nature and relation, and of its duration and extension. Everything that exists is either something divine, or something human, or something mundane, or something relative to those three objects. In other words, whatever exists is relative or absolute, or subsists as some relationship between the relative and the Absolute. Whatever is cognized, therefore, is cognized either as something divine or as something human or as some-

thing mundane, or as some relation between these. It is cognized
as a fact or as an Eternal Being, or as a relation between them,
or, more expressly speaking, as a ratio of the Being and of the
fact. These notions are represented by the following scheme:

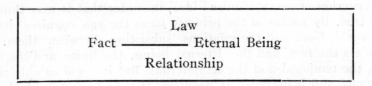

```
                              Law
            Fact ——————— Eternal Being
                        Relationship
```

Cognition cannot cognize anything that does not exist ·in
the order of beings: instead it can cognize only that which really
is and that which is actual. Hence it is evident that it cannot
even conceive an idea of what is not and of what does not exist.
Inasmuch as beings exist, we therefore can cognize them; and
they are not because we cognize them, as idealists speculating
contrary to nature and reason absurdly think. The existence of
the idea within us, whether primary or acquired, depends upon
the existence of the beings which affect our spirit. Those persons
are in error who think that the existence of beings depends on
the existence of the ideas in us. Such a delusion had as a consequence the attempt to verify the existence of beings by means of
the existence of idea in our spirit, which had been taken to be
innate, and the precipitation of idealists into the chaos of a complete denial of the existence of a God and of a world — a really
illogical and fantastic denial, and not a logical or rational denial,
because right reason and the testimony of the spirit (or mind)
verify the existence of the fact and of the Eternal Being, of the
relative and of the Absolute. Nevertheless, what is cognized by
us respecting the ego, the world, and God, and their relations,
even as an acquired idea introduced into the mind from without,
may be true if it consists and does not conflict with the criterion
of the primary ideas, but false if it is contradictory thereto. But
this falsity of an acquired idea is not considered such by itself,
for there is no idea that is false by itself, since every idea has
its beinghood in thought; but, on the contrary, that aspect is
observed in the relation and reference of the idea to the primary
ideas which constitute the criterion of ideas. If, while I have in
my spirit the three primary ideas distinctly, viz., of the ego, the
world, of God, and of their relations, I predicate some cosmological idea of God, or predicate some divine idea of the world,
thus contemplating an absurd relation and reference between
them, it is plain that I am judging incorrectly; accordingly, this

idea is false, not by itself, as was said hereinabove, but in its relation and reference, which the ego absurdly attempts to cognize, to another idea which is at variance and in conflict with it. Thus are gained all acquired ideas consistent and consonant with the primary criterion of ideas, which is infallible and unerring.

CONCERNING ASCERTAINED AND PERFECT IDEAS

An idea is called perfect and complete when, upon being compared with its legitimate standart (or measure), it is found to be equal thereto ; when it has all the features of its depth and breadth within itself. The standard of every idea is the being depicted by it in the spirit. If we wish to obtain knowledge of the perfectness of an idea, as we entertain it in our mind, we ought to compare it with the being whereof it is an idea. When we are thinking the idea of a perfet human being, and wish to see the complete picture of it, we compare it with the perfect man of the prophets and of history, that is to say, with Jesus Christ, and we thereby are enabled to contemplate the totality of it, its clear and complete character. Its complete agreement with Christ establishes in us the truth of the idea of a perfect human being which we have in our spirit, ahd by means of it we truly cognize a perfect human being, by contemplating his perfect image. The perfectness of the idea is the truth of the being, its faithful and exact image and representation. For a perfect idea represents in the mind the beinghood, the structural form, the relationship. and whatever else may be predicated of a being to a degree of perfection such complete equality and agreement is observed between the idea of the being and the being itself. The perfect aspect of the being presupposes also an analogous mind for its cognition ; while cognition of the Absolute Being pressupposes the acquisition of a perfect Mind (or Spirit) analogous to the cognition of an equal Idea. As an absolute Mind cognizing in an absolute Spirit, God cognizes His own absolute Idea, which is equal to Him in perfectness. But we, having imperfect cognition, cognize imperfectly ; and on this account every cognition of ours and every idea of ours are imperfect, though not also false, being capable of perfection in proportion as we enter into communication with the objects of knowledge, and particularly with the absolute creative cause of beings. For by entering into communication with God mentally, we obtain from Him additional spirit, or mind, and broaden our knowledge, and know beings perfectly, by acquiring within us the complete ideas of them. Perfectness of an idea is also its completeness, because what is perfect has in itself everything that it ought to have in order to be considered perfet. What is perfect excludes from the idea want and surplus; and any idea that is perfect is also complete and ascertained.

CONCERNING DEFICIENT AND IMPERFECT IDEAS

An imperfect idea is an imperfect cognition of a being. But an imperfect cognition is also deficient. Moreover, an imperfect idea is likewise deficient, because nothing that is imperfect is complete. Hence it is logically evident that it is deficient, being in need of perfection and completion. Cognition is perfected through perfectness of the spirit, or mind, and is completed through a supply of spirit, or of mind, analogous and proportionate to the perfect cognition of the being. Since, however, the ego yearns to cognize the perfect and absolute Being, but is now spiritually— i.e., mentally—imperfect and deficient, therefore it needs must receive a spirit analogous and proportionate to the perfect cognition of the absolute Being. It must commune with the source of the absolute Spirit. Because otherwise for what purpose is all its yearning after cognition of the Absolute? For what, we may wonder, is the primary cognition of the Absolute in our mind, or spirit, ant its yearning and straining to acquire a complete idea of Him? Why should we then desire that which we can never be able to cognize and which we shall never be able to enjoy? Our mind can nowise understand this contradiction. Never shall we be able to accept this illogical tenet of the Kantian school as a scientific fact by thinking logically. This is truly a contradiction and a terrible delusion. This is really a monstrous falsehood! If we have in ourselves some very imperfect idea of the absolute Being, a primary idea, and a yearning to comprehend the absolute Being, and to acquire a perfect idea of Him, we necessarily have also the ability to proceed to comprehend Him, by making use of the right method, and taking the straight course, which the spirit (i.e., the mind) and right reason prescribe, these two witnesses to the truth. It is wholly contradictory to suppose the contrary. In cognizing the Absolute we get near Him, we commune with His nature, we gain from Him an additional supply of cognitive spirit; and after becoming partakers of His perfect Spirit, we shall be able to cognize and understand the latter perfectly and to acquire a perfect idea of It.

CONCERNING CERTAIN AND PROBABLE IDEAS

An idea is certain when it represents to the soul the Being, the fact, or the future, on account of which it is also believed to be true. An idea is called probable when in representing in the soul what is likely to occur it holds the soul in doubt as concerning what has occurred whether it has actually occurred, as concerning a being whether it actually exists or is, and concerning what is to occur in the future whether it actually will occur. But certainty and probability are not features of ideas, but states of the ego in regard to the ideas and knowledge it possesses. In so far as ideas depict beings in our spirit and exhibit their existence perspicuously, they are true and certain. In the first instance certainty attends primary ideas and ideas consonant therewith which we acquire by observing soundly and reasoning aright, acquired ideas. But in so far as these are taken to be impressions rather than ideas, lacking clearness ant perspicuity, they are probable, their probability increasing or diminishing in proportion to the clearness or vagueness with which the idea presents itself in our spirit. What is probable becomes more probable, whereas what is certain cannot become more certain, just as what is true cannot become more true. The ego meets the perspicuity of an idea by demanding certainty. It meets the obscurity of what is vague and confused by demanding probability. Primary ideas produce in the soul unhesitating certitude owing to their perspicuity, and because they are products of the immediate operation of the spirit upon the three objects of knowledge. Who can entertain any doubt in the face of the perspicuity of these ideas? Who can misunderstand these ideas? Moreover, all acquired ideas gained and introduced into the soul in accordance with the laws of thought are certain, as representing perspicuously and clearly the beings of which they are ideas, or their relations and states.

CONCERNING TRUE OND FALSE IDEAS

An idea is characterized as true when it depicts in the spirit a being or relations of a being. It is false when it conflicts with the being of which it is an idea, and represents it incorrectly. For there is no idea that is absolutely false. An idea which represents in the spirit the existence of a being is true. In representing the nature of a being or its relations to another being it may represent these either as they really are or as they really are not. Hence it may be seen that the falsity of an idea does not reside in the beinghood of the being which it represents, but in the representation of the form and nature of the being, and in the things predicated of it. False ideas are also called chimerical, because their falsity may be observed in their composition, or combination, and not in their simple elements. The idea of a tragelaph, for instance, is true as to its simple elements of which it is composed, but false as to its composition. The notion of a goat and the notion of a stag combined together constitute the idea of a tragelaph, which has no objective existence, because there is no tragelaph in the order of beings. But a goat and a stag do exist, and on this account the ideas of them are true. But the idea of a zoophyte is not chimerical and false, because the existence of a zoophyte is attested by perception and experience. The falsity of every idea may be proved from the inexistence of its object in the order of beings. And for verification of an idea we must have recourse to the nature and order of things, of beings, and of their relations, comparing it with the being of which it is an idea. The falsity of an idea may creep into the cognition of acquired ideas, but, never into the cognition of primary ideas, which are always possessed of the character of being true, correct, and infallible. The character of being infallible is further possessed by the general idea of the being, that of it nature, that of its relationship, that of its extension, and that of its duration. All acquired ideas that are introduced into the cognitive faculty of the soul in accordance with the laws of thought are true. Those, on the other hand, are false and chimerical which are introduced thereinto contrary to the laws of thought, both through impression and through unreasoning imagination. An idea is true in so far as it agrees with the being it represents, but is false in so far as it disagrees therewith and explains its nature diversely. A false idea is wholly different from one which is imperfect and deficient and which, though representing the being deficiently, does not actually stand in contradiction and contrariety thereto. Christianity, for instance, cognizes God and thinks of Him as one existing in three persons, namely, the Father, the Son, and the Holy Spirit. It cognizes Him as He is—a unit as respecting His essence, but a trinity as respecting His three persons. Hence it is logically evident that it entertains a correct and true idea about God. For God actually is such. That is to say, the idea about a God who is one and triune is true. Every idea opposed thereto is false. Mohammedanism conceives God to be one both in respect of essence and in respect of persons; consequently, to be a God in a single person. It is thus opposed to the true idea of Christianity about God. Consequently it has a false idea about God. Yet its falsity is not absolute; for it serves to represent the beinghood of God, though it is to be rejected because this God who exists is indeed a unit in point of essence, but a trinity in point of persons.

Herein lies the falsity of the idea of Mohammedanism about God in one respect. This idea of Mohammedanism which it cherishes about God is a chimerical and false idea. Materialism maintains that it cognizes the absolute in matter—God in the material organization of the physical world. Hence it is evident that it entertains a false and chimerical idea about God, which is opposed to the Being who really and actually is God. It entertains an impression rather than an idea about God. Nevertheless, this belief or impression is not absolutely false, because it shows in the mind of the materialist the existence of the Absolute, God. It is, therefore, a true idea in so far as it represents the beinghood of the Absolute. But it is false because it represents His nature incorrectly; because it confusedly and tragelaphically depicts in cognition what does not really exist in nature. The idea of the Absolute held by Materialism is a tragelaphic combination of the idea of the relative with that of the Absolute: it is an illogical and fantastic mixture and hodgepodge of things presented in the mind, in distinction from the idea of the relative and from the idea of the Absolute. On this account we say that false and chimerical ideas, being the fruit of irrational imagination, are not images of (real) beings, relations, and categories in the nature of existing things, but, on the contrary, are subjective impressions, and illogical mixtures and combinations of true ideas, and, in a word, fancies of the impressionistic cognition.

CONCERNING ABSTRACT IDEAS

An abstract idea is a presentation in the mind of anything that does not exist in the order of beings as a (real) being, but as an attribute, or as a predicate of a being, conceived by itself. Abstract ideas are formed in our mind in accordance with logical laws, and by means of them we can cognize what is general and what is universal—what we should otherwise be unable to cognize by means of individual and particular ideas. The logical operations required for the acquisition of abstract ideas are the processes of abstraction and generalization. Abstraction is a mental process whereby in the cognition of many individual essences the spirit abstracts their peculiar features and the attributes unlike them. Generalization is a mental process whereby the spirit combines all the individual essences into one, out of their common character, and thus forms a general idea. Out of the individual essences we can form an abstract idea of the species; out of the species, the idea of the genus; and out of the latter we are led to ascend up to the most general idea, which is predicated of every genus, species, and individual. I have in my mind, for instance, the idea of an egg which is white, and I cognize its whiteness in relation to milk, snow, cotton, all of which things are white. As long as I cognize what is white along with its whiteness, that is, an egg, milk, or snow, and the like, I am cognizing the being discretely, and this cognition of mine is concrete. When, however, by the process of abstraction I reject all the differences of more or less whiteness subsisting between these beings, and by the process of generalization conceive what is common to all of them, I form the abstract idea of whiteness, and cognize it by itself in my spirit. Thus I judge that whiteness is predicable of every egg milk, snow, cotton. Relying upon the principle of contradiction, according to which whatever is is, and cannot at the same time both be and not be, by the process of induction I judge that every white being is everywhere and always white—for instance, snow is everywhere and always white. But if I compare many abstract ideas, such, for example, as whiteness, blackness, redness, all of which may be predicated of essences, and I abstract from these what is peculiar in all of them, by the process of generalization of the common feature or character in all, I form the general idea of color, which idea is predicable of all essences. The whiteness of an egg, the idea of the whiteness of every essence that is white, and the idea of the color of every essence are three abstract ideas, of which one — the egg is white — is an idea of a particular whiteness; the second idea — everything white is white—is an idea of general whiteness; the other idea — every essence has a color—is a judgment of a universal abstract idea of color inclusive of every color, white, black, red, and the like. The idea of color is the most general idea, species of which are the ideas of blackness, of redness, and of the other colors.

By the processes of abstraction and generalization the cognitive spirit assends from observation of many existences and hypostasis to the most general idea of the Being, which idea is inclusive of every particular and individual existence. For everything that is a being really exists. Under this most general idea of beinghood the spirit cognizes as included therein the idea of every rational and of every irrational being, of every animate and inanimate, organic and inorganic being : it thinks of that idea of the being as one which comprises all things. The most general idea of beinghood, as being a product of the most perfect abstraction and generalization, is also the most imperfect, because it is denuded of every attribute and element, as the idea of simple existence. Hence it is evidently an indeterminate idea. While in the order of beings the highest and most perfect Being is that which has the most attributes and most characteristics, a complete and perfect nature, in the logical order of ideas the most imperfect idea is that of the being, without any attribute or characteristic.

```
                    B E I N G
        Inorganic                      Organic
        Inanimate                      Animate
        Irrational                     Rational
```

What simply is, without any attribute, is the basis of the inorganic and of the organic being. That which is inorganic and organic is the basis of what is inanimate and animate. This, in turn, is the basis of what is irrational and rational. The idea of the being is predicable of every being, and has breadth in inverse ratio to its depth. Being the most general idea in respect of breadth, it is the most imperfect in respect of depth. In the order of beings inorganic beings have more features than the very imperfect particle of matter. Organic plants have more features than the inorganic things. Irrational animals have a more perfect nature than plants. Of animals rational man has more features than the animals below him. The Being, on the other hand, who is supremely higher than man, namely, God, has a complete and perfect nature and is the most perfect of beings.

Abstract ideas cannot be conceived before the idea of the concrete, which precedes in cognition. For we first cognize the being concretely, and afterwards by the process of abstraction we conceive the abstract idea of existence. Our primary and first knowledge not only distinguishes the Being from the fact through essential differences of their respective natures, but also combines them by means of the necessary bond between effect and cause in accordance with the principle of causality. And though the idea of the Being excludes the idea of the fact, because the Being is not a fact, yet the idea of the fact does n o t exclude that of the Being, because the fact partakes of beinghood and is a being, but a finite and dependent being, unable of itself to become and to be—i. e., to come into existence and to remain in existence on its own initiative. Thus too the simple and abstract idea of the being may be predicated both of the Being and of the fact, whereas the idea of a necessary and perfect and sempiternal b e i n g h o o d may be predicated only of the Eternal Being, though the idea of a temporal and finite and contingent b e i n g h o o d may be predicated of the fact, of the world, and of man. On this account the simple idea of b e i n g h o o d when predicated of the sempi-ternal Being is called specific, whereas when it is predicated of the contingent and of the fact it is called a general idea. Moreo-ver, the abstract ideas of living, of knowing, of being able (i. e., of having some ability or other), when predicated of the Eternal Being are called specific. But in reference to the fact they are called general ideas, because they may be predicated of animals and of men. All beings partake of beinghood, temporally so far as respects all of them except God, who partakes of beinghood sempiternally, i. e., independently of time. All living beings par-take of livinghood (or, as we usually say in English, of life) contingently and temporally, except God, who partakes of living-hood necessarily and sempiternally. Likewise all thinking and able beings partake of cognitivity and of ability : those in the fact, temporally; but eternally existent God, sempiternally. We possess beinghood in common with God, but not also eternal beinghood. Likewise we possess vitality (or livinghood), cognitivity (or thin-kinghood), volitivity (or willinghood), ability (or powerfulness) in common with God, but not also e t e r n a l vitality, awareness (or knowinghood), volitivity (or willinghood), and powerfulness (or inherent ability). The adjective e t e r n a l presents the nature of these concepts with special reference to God. But the term being-hood, vitality, ability, etc., without the qualification e t e r n a l merely generalizes it with reference to the fact. In the proper sense it renders the simple idea of existence most general. The simple, abstract idea of beinghood is destitute of determinateness and, being the most imperfect in the logical order of beings, it is conceived in contrast to the most perfect Idea of the Eternal Being, which Idea has a perfect nature, and perfect characteristics and attributes. To the same extent that the abstact idea of being-hood is the most imperfect, the Idea of the Eternal Being is the most perfect and is inclusive of every idea. The most imper-fect idea of beinghood, without any character or determinateness, is the idea of matter, of undifferentiated, amorphous, crude mat-ter in the condition in which God put it after He created and brought it into beinghood through the process of entification. The most perfect Idea of beinghood, on the other hand, is the hypostasis Idea of the Eternal Being, by means of which God cognizes Himself, and depicts Himself in the prosess of thinking, and through His most perfect cognition contemplates the har-mony and consonance and concord of His Idea with Himself, the Absolute Truth.

Ideas are ideas either of the Eternal Being, or of the fact, or of what is to be (in the future) and of what has to be done (in the near or distant future). The ideas of the Eternal Being have the quality of necessariness and of absoluteness. Those of the fact, on the other hand, have the quality of being contingent, relative, and finit. Those of what is to be (in the future) have the quality of being possible and contingent, because the things cognized by means of them as things that can be done may be done or not, the actualization of them depending on the Eternal Being. For this reason whatever we cognize we cognize it either as an eternal Being or as an occurrence, and consequently as something past, or as something present, or as something that is to be in the future. But just as we cognize the Eternal Being logically through the exercise of the power of reason, as an eternal Being, and the fact as something past which we cognize by means of our memory, or as something presend which we cognize though the process of perception, so and in like manner we cognize what is future as a result of the cognition of the Eternal Being and of the fact. In the process of cognizing the existence of any fact and any being, both in the past and in the present, as the effect of the sempiternal existence of the Being, but the fact as something imperfect and progressive and related to the Eternal Being by the law of causality and that of purposefulness, we can find out their relations, and we discover the final purpose of the fact in the existence of the Eternal Being. The fact has been formed and made naturally progressive, because after receiving simple existence as a result of the sempiternal volition of the Being it received the start of its beinghood. From this start of simply being a being it is gradually led on, by virtue of a law of progress, to its end. But just as the start of the fact, its simply being a being, before receiving existence was an idea in the intellect of the Eternal Being, possible and contingenty susceptible of actualization, so and in like manner the end of the fact, its perfect being hood, before being actualized in the future, was a complete and perfect idea in the spirit (or mind) of the Eternal Being. This, moreover, is the ideal of creation which we conjecture from the cognition of the Eternal Being and of the fact, from the perfect essence and nature of the necessary Being, and from the imperfect and progressive nature of the fact. So we may assert that abstract ideas are ideas either of the necessary Being, or of the contingent and possible, with respect to what has occurred or been done in the past, and what is in the present, or what is to be in the future. The ideas of all - wiseness, of all powerfulness, of all - goodness, af absoluteness, of sempiternalness, of eternity, of eternal entity, of eternal immortality and bliss, of everlastingness, of all - holiness, of perfectness, in which are comprised all of God's properties and peculiarities, are logical ideas, formed in the mind (or spirit) as a result of the necessary existence of the perfect Being and pred-

6

icated of God. For whence could we have received these abstract ideas and have had them in our mind (or spirit) if the concrete Being God had not existed? Whence could have come these ideas in us if right reason had not revealed in our spirit the perfect existence of the Eternal Being. Hence it is evindent that because the perfect Being exist, therefore and on this account we can also cognize His perfect properties, qualities, and peculiarities. On the contrary side of the picture we find that the abstract ideas of mortality, of corruption, of decay, of imperfection, of temporality, of spatiality, are empirical ideas, formed in the mind (or spirit) as a result of the contingent existence of the world, and predicated of the fact. We could not have had them though if there had not existed the concrete Being from whom they are abstracted, the world, and the fact, and if the cognitive spirit had not revealed in us the existence of them. But yet, as a matter of fact, there is to be observed not only mortality, but also life, not only decay but also imperishability, in the fact. Not only vice, but also virtue. Life, imperishability, and virtue exist sempiternally in God, and they constitute the ever-living, imperishable, and perfect nature of the Being. Their existence, on the other hand, in the fact is an imperfect revelation of God's life, imperishability, and virtue. For this reason life is opposed to mortality, imperishability to decay, and virtue to vice. Mortality is predicated of sentient life; decay, of compound bodies. Life and immortality are predicated of the spiritual (or mental) and logical (or rational) life of the Being, while imperishability is predicated of every simple unit and of every simple essence. But what is imperfect can be perfected; what is perishable can be made imperishable; what is mortal can be made or can become immortal. This possibility is also proper and right, because it is congruous with the progressive nature of the fact. What is imperfect naturally has regard to what is perfect; what is mortal, to immortality; what is perishable, to imperishability. And, in a word, all creation has regard to what is perfect, to its · final purpose. So if I think creation immortal, imperishable, everlasting, and perfect, able to acquire everything that it has need of, I am thinking of it with respect to its future condition, a condition which is possible, needed, and contingent. I am thinking of the possibility and need of the revelation in creation of the Logos of its purposefulness, and am thinking of the possibility and need of its perfection, i.e., of its being perfected. In thinking of the possibility and need of the perfection of creation, I cognize as possible and proper and right the incarnation of its efficient and final Logos (or Reason), the revelation of the absolute Principle of causality, of contradiction, and of purposefulness in God, the manifestation and exhibition in creation of God's most perfect Design. Hence it is evident that I am thinking of the everlastingness, immortality, and imperishability of all creation in the everlastingness, immortality, and imperishability of all creation in the future, and the kingdom of God which is destined to prevail therein in the future, the kingdom of truth, of virtue, of beauty, and of justice. This thought and cognition of the future is logical; but the actualization of it lies in the future. Hence it is evident that it is a thought and cognition of an Ideal, of what is ideally perfect. But when this Ideal becomes actualized and realized, the logical truth will become a reality and will become an ontological and actual truth.

THE SOURCE OF IDEAS

Ideas, as images of beings in our spirit, originate in us from the relation of the subject (or thinker) to the object (or cognitum), a relation created by the spirit (or mind). For in every thought or cognition there are three things that we can distinguish: 1) the cognizing subject; 2) the object cognized; 3) the cognitive spirit. From this relation of cognizing subject and cognized object there is originated in the thinking subject the idea of the object of his cognition by the cognitive spirit, which idea exists in the latter as an image of the being that is being cognized. Every being is cognizable, or thinkable. For this reason the cognizing being not only can cognize other beings, but can even cognize himself, thus becoming at the same time both a subject and an object of cognition. The cognizing subject is the model whereby cognition springs forth. For just as a photographer makes a picture by means of the art of photography, while having regard to the person being photographed, so and in like manner the cognizing subject conceives an idea by means of the spirit and the art of ideography, while having regard to the object being cognized. Could the photographer have made a picture of any person without the help of the art of photography and the instruments thereof? Impossible. Could he have photographed an imaginary person who did not exist? Impossible. But neither could any photograph be made without there being anyone to take the photograph. Now, thought and cognition is in effect a process of photographing and ideographing various beings, analogous on the whole to the process of photographing persons. Hence it is evident that there are three conditions that constitute the law governing the acquisition of ideas: 1) the existence of an object of cognition; 2) the existence of a subject of cognition; 3) the existence of a cognitive spirit (commonly called «a mind» in English). That which cognizes or thinks is the void which admits and receives the idea proceeding out of the object cognized. The object cognized is that which fills the void in the cognizer. The spirit is the means or agency by which communication is established between both, and the filling of the cognizer is effected. This filling is what produces the truth, because the cognizing subject cognizes the being by means of the idea of it. The first truth to result from this communication is the idea of the simple existence of the being, an imperfect idea merely representing the beinghood of the being. The equality, however, between the cognizing subject and the object cognized begets the truth, which is a complete and perfect cognition and idea of the object cognized. But just as the picture of a person is a product of photography, so and in like manner is the idea of anything a product of pneumatography. (N o t e o f T r a n s l a t o r.—The reader is supposed to know that «pneumatography» as employed here is a Greek word meaning the art of taking pictures and of writing by means of spirit, in contrast with «photography», which is the art of taking pictures and of writing by means of light.) The light is the source and cause of the picture of a person made by photography ; the spirit is in the cognizer the cause and source of the idea of the being. The spirit is analogous to the light which shows the objects to the eye, and photographs therein the images of visible objects. For it is thus too that the spirit shows to the cognizing ego the objects, and «pneumatographs» in cognition the ideas of cognizable beings. For this reason during the time that the ego is destitute of cognitive spirit, even though it exists and coexists together with other beings, it has no knowledge and no idea, being destitute of every idea and knowledge. Hence it is logically evident that the spirit is the source of knowledge and of ideas.

The spirit is the region of ideas. In the initial state of its cognitivity the ego acquires three ideas from the three objects of knowledge, which objects it contacts through the spirit immediately and perspicuously. For this reason all three of these ideas — that of the ego, that of the nonego, and that of the Absolute Cause— are primary ideas, and the first thing to become known to the ego, the origin of all knowledge and science. To begin with, the cognitive spirit possesses these three ideas in itself, by means of which ideas the ego cognizes the existence of itself, of the world, and of God — ideas distinct from each other, yet combined together in accordance with the principle of causality. So the source of primary ideas and of primary knowledge is the spirit ; accordingly, if the ego had not had a cognitive spirit, it would have been nowise able to cognize the nonego, nor indeed even itself. But the cognitive spirit as cognizing primarily the beinghood of the ego, of the world, and of God, and transmitting the primary idea and knowledge of these to the ego, is rudimentary and imperfect, because it imparts to the ego a very imperfect idea and knowledge about God, about the ego, and about the world. The first thing to become known is proportionate and analogous to the primary allotment of the spirit by means of which we exercise cognition and think. As the primary spirit is very imperfect, it cannot help producing an imperfect cognition and showing beings imperfectly as respects their beinghood. But in view of the fact that the cognitive spirit is imperfect to begin with, any knowledge obtained through it is also imperfect ; and the ego 's thought, or, more expressly speaking, its cognitive power and ability, is imperfect, being perfected in the course of time through exercise and training and continual consideration and cognition of beings. For the exercise of the cognitive power of the ego in regard to the contemplation of beings makes it able to think in a more perfect spirit, which is imparted to it out of the source of the absolute Spirit in proportion to the exercise of it and meditation on the beings. The eye may not see visible objects exactly in accordance with their nature, not for want of proportionate light, nor on account of any ailment, but because of its not having been properly exercised and trained in the process of seeing. But even when it has been properly trained to see, can it do so when there is no light? Or can an eye that is diseased or injured see in broad daylight? It can do neither the first nor the second. Hence it is logically evident that together with soundness of the eye and together with light for vision, there needs to exist also the ability to see which is acquired by exercise and training. Thus in connection with the ego mention ought to be made of its spiritual and moral soundness, its cognitive spirit, and the ability of its cognitive faculty which is acquired by exercise and training. In primary cognition the cognizing ego possesses a primary ability to think and to cognise, a primary spirit, primary ideas: it has primary knowledge. The beinghood of the ego, the beinghood of the nonego, and the beinghood of God — this is what is immediately given by the spirit, and it is that which is known to start with. But this first item of knowledge is very imperfect knowledge : it is the first food of the ego and is its very imperfect life. In brief : An imperfect spirit, — imperfect knowledge, — its fruit. Hence it is evident that the ego is imperfect, because it thinks and knows imperfectly, notwithstanding that it yearns for the most perfect knowledge, which is what is unknown and mysterious. But in view of the fact that it has become known that the source of ideas is the spirit, and consequently also the source of primary knowledge, it may be inferred that the spirit itself is the source of the ideas of what is now unknown to the ego and recondite. For ignorance presupposes a want of spirit, just as knowledge presupposes a possession and existence of spirit. To know signifies to have a spirit of knowledge. To be ignorant, on the other hand, signifies to be in want of spirit. Throughout the time during which, being infants, we are altogether ignorant of even our very existence, notwithstanding that we exist, we have no cognitive spirit. Hence it is evident that the cognitive spirit is something other than the ego, and not the same.

THE SOURCE OF THE COGNITIVE SPIRIT OF THE EGO

We have shown that the source of the ideas in us is the spirit, which is the source of primary as much as it is of acquired ideas, and that the spirit is something else than what is called the ego. Accordingly, those persons err exceedingly who identify the spirit with the ego and confuse it with the cognitive abilities and powers. For if the ego were the same as the spirit the source of the latter would have to be the ego : therefore the spirit would have to be emitted by the ego or would have to emanate from the ego. But if the spirit did spring out of the ego as its source, it is evident that ideas and knowledge would have to spring out of the ego too. The ego, therefore, would be cognizing itself through itself, and the cause of its cognition would have to be something which it had innate in itself, and not something given to it out of anything else. But any being that cognizes through itself also cognizes of itself, or, more explicitly speaking, produces ideas out of itself and of itself, as being a source of knowledge. But whatever produces ideas out of itself may be supposed to have them in itself innate. Thus was begotten the hypothesis of innateness of ideas, on which hypothesis are based the modern philosophical systems from Descartes down to our own times, not excepting even Eclecticism, which modified the hypothesis of innateness by substituting another hypothesis no less fantastic. Out of this false hypothesis of innateness of ideas there was fated to be educed all the ideal world derived from the ego, and the irrational imagination was to be developed out of it, and finally ideas and knowledge were to be taken to be subjective phantoms of cognition having no subsistence outside of the cognizing ego ; in addition the illogical question w h e t h e r b e i n g s e x i s t, which is contrary to the primary knowledge, was to be put, and scholastic proofe were to be adduced respecting the agreement of thought and beinghood, and respecting the external existence of beings. This strange conclusion was arrived at by modern philosophy, which has loomed in all its bulk latterly in order to contribute to the regeneration [of the spiritual world, by dispelling the darkness of ignorance and taking pains to eradicate prejudices besetting the spirit of man. But instead of dispelling the darkness of ignorance it darkened still more the philosophical horizon ; and instead of eradicating prejudices it diffused doubt over the ocean of knowledge and ignorance, and imagined that it had learned everything through innate ideas from the very beginning, or else that it knew nothing, but even entertained doubts about the thinking subject and wondered whether he really existed. But if the hypothesis of innate ideas were true, sould such conclusions ever result therefrom, we wonder, seeing that they are confutative of all true knowledge ? Could it have led to the conclusion either through Idealism that man is God, or through Skepticism that man is a stone, ignorant of everything ? For the tenet that man knows everything signifies nothing else than that man is a God, being himself the cause of his knowledge as having obtained it through himself ; likewise the tenet that man is ignorant of everything or that he ought to entertain doubts about everything, signifies nothing else than that he is a being without a spirit, such as a stone or a silly, irrational animal, for instance. There is, however, a time when a man is ignorant of everything and of himself, having consequently no spirit of cognition, though existing as an imperfect being that has merely beinghood. This time is that of infancy, when the sentient ego, living sentiently and in an organic body, is destitute of all knowledge. Hence it is evident that he is destitute of spirit. During this interval of time the ego, living a sentient life, and in association with the body, exists and lives without thought and knowledge, without awareness. Hence it is evident that awareness is something acquired and imparted after beinghood, and living sentiently is something which follows the birth of the ego through flesh and its manifestation in the world. But there will be a time when the ego shall become the possessor of all knowledge, God-equal, not through itself, but through the spirit being imparted to him, out of the source of the absolute Spirit. The present time is a time of learning, of exploration and search, and of intellectual and moral development of the ego, a time of mental (or spiritual) progress accomplished by the exercise of the cognitive ability of the ego upon cognita, or objects of thought, and by the impartation and acquirement of a cognitive spirit. Progress takes place from what is known to pursuit of what is unknown, and from what is imperfect to pursuit of what is perfect. Whoever starts by departing from a state of absolute ignorance is giving rein to his fancy and not reasoning. On this account he winds up in dubiety and skepticism, or in an utter denial of knowledge. Whoever sets out from a state of absolute ignorance is not reasoning, but merely playing with his imagination ; and on this account after many contradictions and delusions he winds up in a denial of all objective knowledge, and he takes his ideas to be mere simulacra of the cognitive process, and effusions of the spirit. This is equivalent to the state of absolute ignorance into which the vain idealists of the West fell. But we, who philosophize soundly, and distinguish what is known to cognition at the very start, from what is unknown in the beginning, who admit primary knowledge and ignorance, what we know originally and what we are ignorent of, who do not identify the ego with the spirit, are free from such absurd conceptions, and on this account we arrive at conclusions that are true and consonant with our present imperfect and progressive nature, which yearns for perfect knowledge. So the spirit is not the same thing as the ego, but, on the contrary, is something different, associated with the ego, true enough, precisely as light is associated with the eye, but distinguished from the ego by peculiar attributes. The association of the spirit with the ego ought to be conceived in analogy to its nature. It ought to be conceived, not in chemical combination, such as occurs in material bodies that are compound, but in an association of one guiding and one being guided, wherein the one being guided is enlightened and illuminated by the one guiding him, and can walk with his guidance freely and without constraint, being attracted by the operation of the enlightenment. The ego was naturally endowed with a receptivity of cognition, or capacity for thought. But it is the spirit that imparts to it in the beginning the primary cognition, the primary awareness, when it accrues, or becomes present. This transition of the ego from sheer beinghood and living the life of sentience to the order of awareness is evidence of the progress and progressive nature of the ego. This awareness is a property of the ego, which acquires it from association with the spirit. Anyone can be guided by another when he is inherently or naturally capable of this, when he is susceptible of guidance by someone else. The guide imparts to him the knowledge he has need of. This is the process of learning ; for a man ignorant of the way and what is being sought can learn this through the guide, and when he knows it he acquires something that he did not previously possess, he acquires knowledge ; and, if he has learned it well enough, he himself can become the guide of another man. Thus too the ego, starting with mere beinghood and sentient living, through the help of the spirit gradually becomes an ego that is aware and conscious, consequently a spirit through the Spirit. Beinghood is the most imperfect essence, matter, in its primary atoms and indivisible particles. The ego, before receiving sensation and cognition, is possessed of mere existence. Hence it is evident that it is matter : a mere hypostasis undecomposable, indivisible, imperishable, receptive of life and of cognition. The initial association of the spirit with the ego gives the latter primary awareness, which is something that is common to all and inalienable ; because God, who gives awareness to the ego and promotes the latter from a state of mere beinghood to that of awareness, is the cause of the perfection of the ego. Hence it is evident that He does not take away what He has given of His own free will, without reducing the ego to the state of mere beinghood, or that of matter. The primary spirit, as the cause of the ego 's awareness, is formative of the ego, because it molds and forms its nature, and from its unconscious and formless condition it exalts it to the order of conscious beings, rational and free. For this reason the spirit, as being formative and depictive of the ego, after the image and likeness of the perfect Being, imparts to the ego a spiritual nature, which consists in thinking, willing voluntarily, and being affected. It imparts to it the attributes of the divine nature. The ego and the spirit are distinguishable, like beinghood and awareness : beinghood without awareness is the unconscious ego, the hypostasis of a human being ; beinghood with awareness is the spirit, from the association of which the hypostasis of the ego acquires in addition awareness by virtue of a law of nature. Hence it may be seen that we ourselves are not the causes of beinghood and of awareness, but He who has created us, not in accordance with our mind, but as He willed. If we had existed of ourselves, being the causes of our beinghood, we would have existed as perfect Gods. Likewise it may be said that if we could cognize and think on our own initiative and by our own efforts, ourselves being the causes of cognition and of thought originally, we would have cognized like Gods perfectly, having knowledge of everything and being versed in all sciences from the beginning. If we had the power and ability of ourselves, being the causes of our power, we should have been able to wield power perfectly like God, having ourselves omnipotence. But being imperfect as respects beinghood, cognition, and ability to exercise power, we exist, cognize, and wield power not of ourselves and through ourselves, but as having beinghood, cognition, and ability to exercise power derived from God. We cognize and wield power primarily only so much as is given to us ; any further cognition and power have to be gained by us through the processes of work and training. Hence it is evident that the primary impartation of cognition and power is a very different thing from that which is acquired. The spirit which imparts cognition and which is the source of the ideas in us is a ray of the absolute and universal Spirit, the Spirit «which lighteth every man that cometh into the world» (John 1 : 9). This spirit is imperishable, infinite, and immortal, and sempiternal, being distinct from the ego, which latter is temporal, and finite, imperishable, to be sure, as a simple unit, but mortal as respects its sentient life in the body. Through association, however, of the spirit, after the ego additionally acquires awareness, and the power to exercise volition, and feelings, and the ability to exercise power, it becomes immortal, because it cognizes itself, and the Absolute Cause of it, the source of immortality. To think and to be conscious eternally is immortality. In becoming self-concious through the spirit the ego becomes also immortal : possessing consciousness everlastingly, it possesses life everlastingly ; accordingly, it is at the same time everliving and immortal. Hence it is evident that life and immortality are imparted to the ego in the spirit and through the spirit; and for this reason the spirit, being the source of the knowledge in us, is the source also of life and of immortality. But the perfect Spirit in God, whereof we have in ourselves an illuminative ray, is the source of the ideas and of the knowledge, the source of sempiternal immortality.

THE MODES OF COGNIZING

The ego cognizes through the spirit. In the process of cognition it cognizes either itself or something else; the nonego, or the first and highest cause of the ego and of the nonego. In the cognition of itself the ego cognizes itself as a subject and as an object at the same time : i t i t s e l f c o g n i z e s i t s e l f. But in the process of cognizing itself it cognizes its identity, it cognizes itself distinct from other beings, distinct from the nonego, and from the Absolute Cause of it.

ego — ego

In the cognition of the ego, as subject and object at the same time, the spirit is called consciousness ; and this mode of cognition is called the conscient mode. By the conscient mode of cognition the ego cognizes itself as a being : 1) that is the same as itself ; 2) that is relative ; therefore causate ; 3) that is purposeful, in accordance with the primary laws of the spirit, i. e., of contradiction, of causality, and of purposefulness. All knowledge and all ideas that the ego gains through direct consciousness of itself, through the spirit's internal introspection of it, are knowledge and ideas which are consient and psychological and by means of which the ego acquires and possesses self — consciousness and self knowledge. Hence it is evident that the first mode of cognizing is the conscient and self — knowing, wherein the ego itself is at the same time the subject and the object of cognition, or of thought.

But the ego cognizes also the nonego through the spirit. In cognizing its identity it cognizes also the alterity outside of it which it both discerns and expresses through the nonego.

ego — nonego

This explains why cognition of the ego is simultaneous with cognition of the nonego, or, in other words, why it is that when we cognize the ego we at the same time cognize also the nonego, what is something other than ourselves, our body, and the world about us. In the process of cognizing the nonego the ego is the subject of cognition, while the nonego is the object thereof. Now, the process of cognizing the nonego is called p e r-c e p t i o n, which is another and different mode of the cognitive spirit whereby the latter cognizes our body and beings outside of the ego, in a word, the world. The concient mode of cognizing the ego in its essence is an internal process. The perceptive mode of cognizing the nonego, on the other hand, is an external process, because it is that through which the ego cognizes, not itself, but what is outside of, i.e., external to, itself — what is something other than the ego. In this cognition the ego cognizes the nonego as a being 1) that is the same as itself ; 2) that is relative ; therefore causate ; 3) that is purposeful, in accordance with the principles of cognition. All knowledge and all ideas that the ego gains through the perceptive mode of the spirit, a mode carried on through the senses, are knowledge and ideas which are perceptual and cosmological and by means of which the ego acquires and possesses knowledge of other things and knowledge of the world. Hence it is evident that the perceptive mode of cognizing is a second mode wherein the ego is the subject of cognition while the nonego is the object thereof. In cognition of the ego as ego there is combined also cognition of the nonego. For, in cognizing the ego as ego, I simultaneously differentiate and distinguish it from the nonego. So that cognition of the ego and cognition of the nonego are simultaneous and combined. At the same time as cognition of the ego takes place there takes places also cognition of the nonego, and there intervenes no interval of time between cognition of the ego and cognition of the nonego. The nonego, in the cognition of the finite ego, is finite : it is the being which is called the world. For in its finite cognition, perceptive as well as conscient, the ego cognizes itself and what is other than itself as finite beings. But in the absolute cognition of the Absolute Being and of the absolute Essence, the nonego, that which is something other, or different, than the cognizer, a nonbeing, conceived as a being in the intellect of God, may receive existence and hypostasis. So that, although in a human being's finite cognition the ego and the nonego are cognized as finite beings, in God's infinite cognition both are cognized as infinite. Thus it may be said that inasmuch as God is an infinite Being, that which is a nonbeing, conisting in privation and the state of a being in p o s s e, is likewise infinite.

| Eternal   Being   —   eternal   nonbeing |

Thus, in cognizing Himself and begetting the perfect Idea of Himself in the process of cognizing Himself, God cognizes Himself absolutely, as an absolute i d e n t i t y, whereas He cognizes the nonbeing as an absolute p r i v a t i o n.

The ego cognizes the Eternal Being, who is the Absolute Being, through the spirit. In this cognition the ego is the subject of cognition, while the Absolute Being is the object thereof. The ego cognizes the nonego, not as a finite being and in a finite sense, as in cognition of itself and of the world, but in an absolute sense. It cognizes it by a cognitive mode unlike the conscient and the perceptive mode. In cognizing itself and what is other than itself as finite beings, it cognizes them as causate beings. Hence it is evident that by some sort of anagoge, otherwise termed reduction (as distinguished from deduction and induction) in accordance with the primary law of causality, which is inherent in our spirit, the ego ascends to cognition of the Absolute Being. The conception of the notion of something causate immediately leads the ego up (or «reduces» it) to cognition of the Cause. This cognition takes place simultaneously : in other words, cognition of what is causate occurs at the same time as cognition of its cause. Through the conscient mode the ego cognizes itself as causate, while, on the other hand, through the perceptive mode it cognizes likewise the nonego, the world, as causate too. But through the upward thrust of the spirit it cognizes the Absolute Cause. I am a c a u s a t u m. The world is a c a u s a t u m. Hence it is evident that the cause of both of them is the Absolute Being. This cognitive mode of cognizing the c a u s e is called the logical mode of cognition, that means whereby this cognition is effected is termed r i g h t   r e a s o n (as distinguished from motive reason, etc.). Thus we are enabled to ascend to cognition of the Being by cognizing It 1) as something which is the same as itself in alterity and in distinction from the ego and the world;

2) as the Absolute Being ; as the efficient, or creative, cause ;
3) as the final cause. In other words, as an absolute i d e n t i t y,
and as an absolute c a u s a l i t y, and as an absolute a i m f u l-
n e s s   or   p u r p o s e f u l n e s s. In every cognition there is
cognition of the cognizer, cognition of the cognized, and cognition of that means whereby the cognizing being cognizes—cognition of the spirit. But in this cognition the ego cognizes itself and
the world as relative and finite beings with the testimony of consciousness and of perception. And as a result of this finite cognition of the ego and of the world, the ego is reduced, or led back
up, to the infinite cognition of the infinite Being, and through
the logical mode of cognizing it cognizes the absolute and the
infinite. Cognition of the absolute and of the infinite can be effected neither through the conscient nor through the perception
mode of cognition, because this cognition, as being a cognition
of what is finite, takes on a finite character and is thus finite.
Cognition of the absolute and infinite Being, on the other hand,
can be effected through the logical mode of cognition, because
this cognition, as being a cognition of the infinite and absolute
Being, is characterized as infinite and absolute cognition. We
therefore distinguish cognition of what is finite from cognition
of what is infinite. Accordingly we call conscient and perception
finite cognition, while, on the other hand, we call logical cognition, as being cognition of what is infinite, infinite cognition.
Through these three modes of cognition the ego cognizes itself,
cognizes the nonego, or, more expressly speaking, the world,
and cognizes the Eternal Being named God. Cognition of what is
finite is cognition of what is contingent and of what is possible,
whereas cognition of what is infinite is cognition of the necessary
and sempiternal Being. Through cognition of what is finite we
cognize it as a being having a substance, and a nature, and a
power, and an extension, and a duration likewise finite. But
through cognition of what is infinite we cognize what is infinite
as a Being having a beinghood, and a nature, and a power, and
an extension, and a duration likewise infinite, sempiternal, and
everlasting.

conscient	perceptive	logical
Ego — ego	Ego — world	Ego—Eternal Being
mode	mode	mode

These are the three modes of cognizing with respect to the three objects of knowledge of which we have a primary idea and knowledge in our spirit, simultaneously, and not at different times, in accordance with the primary laws of the spirit — an idea and knowledge which is perspicuous and certain, perspicuously showing in us the existence of the ego and of the world as finite beings, and the existence of the Eternal Being as both absolute, sempiternal, and infinite. But we ought to examine these three modes of cognition more accurately and explain all their nature and power.

The Conscient Mode of Cognition

CONSCIOUSNESS

The ego is the subject of cognition: 1) of itself, 2) of the world; 3) of God, and of the relations subsisting between them. In cognition of itself it is at the same time a subject. The cognitive spirit in this cognition is called c o n s c i o u s n e s s, and is an internal introspection of the ego. It amounts to c o n t e m p l a t i o n   o f   t h e   e g o   i n   i t s e l f   t h r o u g h   t h e   c o n s c i e n t   s p i r i t   w h i c h   s h o w s   t h e   e g o   i n   r e l a t i o n   t o   i t s   i d e a s,   t h e   e g o   w i t h   i t s   i d e a s,   w h i c h   h a v e   r e f e r e n c e   t o   t h e   b e i n g h o o d,   t h e   n a t u r e,   t h e   r e l a t i o n s h i p,   t h e   p o w e r,   t h e   e x t e n s i o n,   a n d   t h e   d u r a t i o n   o f   t h e   b e i n g   w h i c h   i s   c a l l e d   t h e   e g o.   T h i s mode of cognizing is called the conscient mode of cognition. The cognitive spirit is called c o n s c i o u s n e s s, because it conjoins or connects in this cognition the cognizing ego with the ego cognized, and internally ideographs the ego by means of this immediate introspection, while the ego contemplates itself by means of the idea in consciousness. The ego, the spirit, and its idea — these three are known together and in conjunction by the ego, and it is on this account that the spirit takes the name c o n s c i o u s n e s s. The word consciousness, being derived from the Latin verb c o n s c i r e (the corresponding Greek substantive s y n e d e s i s being derived from the Greek verb s y n e d a), signifies association of knowledge of which the ego is the subject. And such is really the case. In the ego all our knowledge is connected together and associated, and its basis and subject is the ego. For in every cognition the cognizer is the ego, and every knowledge and idea is revealed before the ego by the spirit. The spirit conceives the ideas and reveals them before the intellectual eyes of the ego, and through these the ego obtains knowledge of objects. Never and nowise does the ego cognize anything without also cognizing its own existence. On this account all our knowledge and every idea of ours has the idea of the ego as its basis and subject. Without being aware of myself I cannot cognize anything at all. But in cognizing myself I can cognize any other idea. Since therefore in every cognition, whether of a finite being or of the infinite Being, there is presupposed a cognition of the ego as a cognitive, volitive, and sentient (or sensitive) being, all other knowledge and ideas are revealed before the intellectual eyes of the ego through the spirit ; and since between these and the idea of the ego there is a relationship, the spirit, in which the ideas are, therefore this internal cognition is called c o n s c i o u s n e s s. The term consciousness is to be understood 1) generally, and 2) specially. Generally, when the ego in itself observes through the spirit its relationship to all the ideas that it has in itself, and it acts upon the ideas internally. So, then, contemplation of the relationship of the ego to the ideas and knowledge in it is what constitutes the general consciousness of the ego, through which it contemplates all the ideas and knowledge in it by turning its attention to itself, without reasoning or paying attention to the world and to God. This contemplation is an internal observation of the ego, an internal introspection and intuition, whereby all ideas and knowledge are contemplated together and in conjunction with the ego. In a word, what we called g e n e r a l c o n s c i o u s n e s s is contemplation of the ego together with its ideas which is effected in it through the spirit. The ego turning its attention to itself and looking at itself and the ideas in it through immediate introspection of the spirit, is conscious of itself, and has consciousness of itself, as the center of its knowledge. Hence the expression I a m c o n s c i o u s o f m y s e l f signifies generaly : I know myself as the subject, and as the center of the knowledge and ideas in me ; I have the idea of myself as the basis of the ideas and knowledge within me. Specially, on the other hand, the term consciousness signifies knowledge of the ideas of the ego, independently of every other idea that is in the spirit. When the ego cognizes itself at the same time as both subject and object of cognition, in this cognition it cognizes also every other idea having reference immediately and directly to it as cognizing and at the same time being cognized. This direct internal introspection of the ego, cognizing itself together, with its ideas, is called psychological cognition, and that is what c o n s c i o u s n e s s is. Our discussion here is mainly concerned with psychological consciousness.

Consciousness, as a bond and relationship of the cognizing

ego with the ego cognized and its ideas, conjoins the cognizer and the cognized thus:

```
Consciousness

Ego —— Ego
```

As a result of this association the ego knows itself as a being, and forms an idea of itself which is true in so far as it represents it faithfully, or with fidelity, but is false in so far as it represents it incorrectly. On this account psychological consciousness is distinguishable as false and as true. When the ego cognizes and thinks that it is perfect, and that it has been aware of everything about it ever since the beginning, it has a false consciousness concerning itself. But when it cognizes and thinks that it is a being having imperfect cognitivity and ability, and by nature adapted to progress, and when it cognizes and thinks that it exists in time and space, it has a true consciousness concerning itself. Nevertheless, when the cognitive power of the ego cognizes in accordance with the testimony of the conscient spirit, which testimony is infallible, it always cognizes correctly and truly, and acquires true and correct ideas within itself, and stores these in the memory. When, on the other hand, it cognizes contrary to the testimony of consciousness, it errs, and stores false ideas concerning itself in the memory, termed consciousnesses, comprising psychological and conscient knowledge. Cognizing a single being by itself is to be distinguished according to the mode of cognizing the objects. Through each mode of cognition the ego acquires knowledge of each particular object, because it cannot at the same time and together cognize a scibile by a single general and immediate intuition, as can the perfect Mind. In cognizing itself by consciousness, the ego cognizes itself as a cognitive, volitive, and passive being. It cognizes itself as an essence existing in time and space. It cognizes itself as a being that is imperfect in respect of life, thought, cognizing power, feeling, as progressive, and as having a yearning to be perfected. It cognizes itself as a being having volition and yearning that are perfect, but cognition and power that are imperfect. This is the subjective knowledge of consciousness, knowledge that is true, perspicuous, and certain, because it is knowledge attested by the spirit of truth, whose validity as a witness is absolute. Upon this primary knowledge is founded the science of psychology, which professes perfect knowledge of the ego, self-knowledge and self-consciousness. When knowing itself through consciousness the ego knows itself imperfectly. Hence it is evident that its knowledge concerning itself is imperfect. Though ignorant of itself in the abstract of the primary knowledge concerning it, is ignorant of itself not absolutely, but relatively. Therefore, just as it knows itself relatively, it is also relatively ignorant of itself. But first it knows itself with respect to what it is, and afterwards with respect to what it is not — I know some things and am ignorant of other things — I am a being who know and do not know. But what do I know and what am I ignorant of as concerning myself? For knowing and not knowing one and the same thing and in regard to one and the same aspect or particular at one and the same time, is a contradiction of terms. I know and am ignorant does not mean, of course, that I am ignorant of what I know, just as to exist and not to exist mean : it means that I know this and am ignorant of that. I am a being who know and am ignorant of myself, means that the ego primarily knows itself as respects this, but is primarily ignorant of itself as respects that. 'It knows that it is, but is ignorant in that it does not know what it is. It knows that it possesses beinghood, but it is ignorant in that it 'does not know what this beinghood is. It knows that it cognizes, i.e., that it thinks ; that it wills, i.e., that it exercises volition ; that it has power, i. e., that it can do things ; that it feels, i. e., that it has sensations ; and it knows that it possesses a nature, but it is ignorant in that it does not know what its nature is in its depth. It knows that it is in time and space, but it is ignorant in that it does not know what time and space are. It yearns to acquire all knowledge ; starting with the primary knowledge with which coexists the primary ignorance, and to supersede the primary ignorance concerning it with full and perfect knowledge of it. In this psychological journey consciousness is a traveling companion of the ego, or one might better say, the unerring and accurate witness to the truth, whom the ego ought to follow, and to whose utterances of testimony it ought to listen attentively for the purpose of acquiring sure knowledge of the truth.

> The Perceptive Mode of Cognition

PERCEPTION

In the process of cognizing itself the ego cognizes itself apart from every other essence as distinct therefrom. The idea of the ego is an image of the ego in distinction from the idea of every other being. The limit of its cognition is the consciousness which it has of itself, or, more expressly speaking, psychological cognition. But this ego is together with another essence in this world, which essence is called an organic body, suitable for the habitation of the ego and for its operation upon the physical and material world. This body, being united with the ego, is latter's instrument or tool, for by means thereof the ego has communication with the material world, and is developed by being exercised upon and trained in regard to its objects, cognizing them with respect to their nature and essence and various relations, and being perfected in knowledge of the monego, while acquiring full knowledge of things other than itself. While cognizing itself through the spirit of consciousness, the ego cognizes through the spirit of perception the nonego, the body with which it coexists and along with which it is developed, and the physical and material world. Where conscient cognition of the ego ends is where perceptual cognition of what is other than the ego begins, as a being that is distinct from the ego. But if the ego were the same thing as matter and as our material body, it could not have the ability to distinguish itself from the essence of the body through inner consciousness as a being having attributes of which matter is wholly destitute. For cognition, volition, and voluntary activity are attributes of the ego imparted to it through the sempiternally cognitive and volitive Spirit of God. The fact that the ego cognizes and thinks by means of the brain is no proof whatsoever that ego is identical with the brain. For neither is the fact that the eye sees in light and by means of light only proof that the eye is the same thing as the light ; neither is the fact that the hand writes with a pen any sign that the hand and the pen are one and the same thing. Just as neither is an artisan identical with the tool with which he produces the works or products of his art. The brain is the tool of the ego by means of which the latter cognizes and thinks as long as it is in this organic body. Hence it is evident that one must distinguish the ego, in and by itself, as a cognizing and thinking being, from the brain, by means of which it evinces as by means of an instrument its thoughts in the world and its spiritual activities. The ego and the body are two things distinct from each other yet so connected together and conjoined as to permit the one to act through the other in this world. The will resisting the impulses of the body, and acting independently of of the body, is proof of the ego's self - action and self - mastery, of the fact that the existence of the ego is distinct from the existence of the body. For if volition were a property of the body, and not a power or faculty of the ego, how could it resist the body ? How could it conceive a plan and actualize it many times in spite of the inclinations and impulses of the material body ? Can the body itself oppose itself, and sometimes even destroy itself ? And yet volition can conceive a plan that is opposed to the impulses and impetuosities of the body, and can actualize it even at the sacrifice of the life of the body, glad that it is fulfilling a duty of self - abnegation, though pained as a result of the pangs of the body, which, however, are not able to overcome and defeat it and to turn it aside and dissuade it from doing as it wishes. We ask, if the will were identical with the body, how could it oppose the latter and sacrifice it voluntarily, experiencing a joy over fulfillment of a duty through sacrifice of the life of the body, but anguish on account of the pangs of the body ? Hence it is evident that one must distinguish the attributes of both. In identifying the ego with the body materialists have identified also the spitit with matter, and have denied the existence of an immortal soul distinct from the mortal body. They have denied even the existence of an immaterial, ever - living, and immortal Being, and in their lunacy they have taken matter to be sempiternal and absolute. But consciousness proves them to be deluding themselves, like lunatics, and leaves them speechless in that they cannot refute it. Perception, too, as joining consciousness in apprehension for the completion of the ego' s knowledge, bears witness to the existence of the body and of the material world, to its nature and properties, and as a result of experience it affords evidence that materialists are self - deluded in regard to their contention that the cognitive, and volitive, and passive ego is the same thing as unintelligent and will - less and senseless matter. Perception bears witness that in a certain interval of time our whole body is renewed. But if the thinking and willing being within us were the same thing as the body, it too would be renewed, and this renewal would be known to our consciousness, which bears witness to the identity of the ego and to its unity and simplicity and self - action. But consciousness bears witness to no such thing at all, but, on the contrary, it even frownes upon it as a foolish assertion. Hence it is evident that the fact that the ego is distinct from the body is clearly attested by consciousness. Likewise both the reality and the actuality of matter, and the fact that it is mindless and will - less, are attested clearly and impressively by perception.

Perception begins where consciousness leaves off. For, wishing to get beyond the cognition of itself, it immediately meets with the nonego, with the material world. As long as the ego is cognizing itself, consciousness performs its own function, while perception remains in abeyance. But when it goes beyond cognition of itself, perception takes a hand, and consciousness remains in abeyance, retaining possession of the idea of the ego. As long as consciousness is active the ego cognizes itself in relation to

its body and its efficient cause. For this reason we can neither separate the cognitions of the o n e spirit and of the o n e cognizing
ego, nor take them to be acting at different times. For we can never
remember any time when we were cognizing ourserves alone,
without cognizing our body, the world about us, and the efficient, or creative, cause of us. At the same time that cognition of the
ego takes place, there always occurs also cognition of the nonego
and cognition of the efficient cause of us at the same time. In
point of logical order, however, cognition of the ego precedes in
cognizing, and is followed by cognition of the world, and as a
result of these two cognitions the ego is enabled to ascend, or is
led back up, to cognition of the Absolute Cause. For this reason
we say that perception of the nonego begins where the limit of
the ego, or of consciousness, ends.

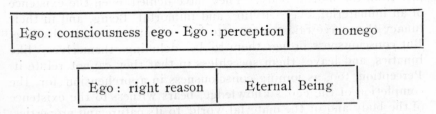

| Ego : consciousness | ego - Ego : perception | nonego |

| Ego : right reason | Eternal Being |

In acting through the senses perception employs them as
instruments or tools, without in any way kecoming identified
therewith. The senses are the doors by which knowledge of the
sensible world is introduced into the soul, and this knowledge is
absorbed by the ego through perception. The ego perceives the
external world through the senses. Perception is distinguished
from the senses in the same way as the mind is distinguished
from the brain. Perception is the workman ; the senses are the
tools by which the workman performs his function. But in the
same way that Materialism identified the mind with the brain
and incorrectly dogmatized that the mind is a property of the
body and of matter, so did it identify perception with the sense
organs, the essence of the spirit with the essence of the material
body, the workman with the tools of his art or trade. But in the
same way that it was exposed above, it is now exposed again as
dogmatizing incorrectly and identifying things distinct from each
other. A tool can nowise act by itself, but only in relation to the
workman does it perform its function through him. Thus too the
senses cannot act at all by themselves, but only in relation to the
ego, which through them perceives the sensible world. But if the
ego through consciousness turns its attention upon itself and
looks at itself, the senses remain idle, and perception nowise acts
through them upon the external world. Or, if the ego perceives

through one of the senses carefully, the other senses remain idle ; and for this reason many times when objects pass before our eyes we fail to behold them, because our attention is fixed upon some other object. For this reason, too, the ancients used to say that it is the mind that sees and the mind that hears. If the ego were the same thing as the body, and the spirit were a property of matter, as materialists believe, how could the property be superior to its essence, and stand in contrast thereto ? How could the senses wrestle with the ego and be brought into subjection to it, unless this ego had authority over the senses — unless it were itself an essence distinct from the essence of the body, ruling and governing the latter essence ? This contrast and opposition between the senses and the ego indisputably bears witness to nothing else than the fact that the senses are distinct from the cognizing ego which perceives things through the senses, like a tool in the hands of a workman.

But Skepticism entertains doubts concerning the validity of knowledge of the sensible world acquired through the senses, and concerning the certainty of it, taking a cue from the illusion which often results from our superficial perception in respect to sensible objects. But the illusion due to a superficial perception is an accident, and not a law of the spirit. The law of the spirit consists in careful observation in respect to objects which serves to verify and confirm their beinghood and nature in the spirit. Perception, in fact, is the criterion of every sensible idea and knowledge. When perception acts carefully through the senses, the ego acquires ideas that are true and accurate. Hence it may be seen that the senses never deceive us when acting in accordance with the law and in accordance with the spirit's percipience. The illusion is due to an action of the sense contrary to the law of perception : it is the result of an automatic sensation. The ego, therefore, is deceived because it does not observe correctly, and not because the senses of the body fail us, as the skeptics believe who foolishly doubt even their own doubt.

Perception is like consciousness : the one is the source of the perceptions in us, and the other is the source of the consciousnesses within us. Hence both are the law of the spirit acting upon sensible objects, on the one hand, and upon the ego, on the other hand. Perception is the criterion of all ideas derived from the sensible world. Consciousness is the criterion of all ideas accruing from the ego. Deliberate and careful perception in respect to perceptible objects, and consciousness in respect to what is cognoscible through consciousness, are what produce the correct and true perceptions and consciousnesses within us. In perceiving the nonego, we come into contact with its existence through the spirit immediately and directly from the very beginning, and are perspicuously assured that what is being perceived is a (real) being having an identity, a nature, a power, an extension, and a duration of its own — that it is a being with its attributes and categories. Thus through perception we learn of the existence of our body, and of the existence of the external and sensible world. While through consciousness we learn with certitude and perspicuity of the existence of ourselves, through perception we learn with the same certitude and perspicuity of the existence of the nonego. This cognition takes place within us at the same time, and not at some subsequent time. Thus, therefore, we may be as sure that the nonego, i. e. , the sensible world, exists, as we are sure that we ourselves who cognize it exist.

The Logical Mode of Cognition

RIGHT REASON

In the process of cognizing itself ego cognizes through consciousness. But in the process of cognizing what is outside of itself, that with which it is coexisting, the sensible world, the ego cognizes through perception. But in cognizing itself and the world, it cognizes these objects as effects, as c a u s a t a . And from this cognition it is led back up to cognition of some absolute cause whence these objects received their beinghood, nature, power, extension, and duration. In the process of cognizing the Absolute, therefore, the ego cognizes It as a Being that is outside of it and outside of the world, outside of every causate and finite fact. This cognition of the spirit, proceeding as it does from c a u- s a t a to their causes, is cognition in accordance with right reason, nowise deviating from the right line running between the c a u s a t u m and its cause, between the fact and the Eternal Being. The cognoscitive and cognitive power, or faculty, of the ego is one, though it cognizes the scibile in three different ways, namely : 1) consciously ; 2) sentiently ; 3) logically. In the process of cognizing consciously, the source of knowledge is consciousness. In the process of cognizing sentiently, the source of ideas is perception. In the process of cognizing logically, the source of ideas is right reason. Consciousness, perception, and reason are the essence of the spirit, the primary and true witnesses of our knowledge, the criterion of the truth. Consequently we ought to avoid identifying the cognitive and cognoscitive power of the ego with the spirit of consciousness, of perception, and of reason whereby the ego comes to know the truth and is assured with respect thereto.

The cognitive power, or faculty, of the ego, though cognizing the ego through consciousness, and the world through perception, cognizes God through right reason.

$$\text{Ego} \xrightarrow{\text{right}} \text{Eternal Being}$$
$$\phantom{\text{Ego} \xrightarrow{}}\text{reason}$$

Cognition in accordance with right reason relies upon the c a u s a t u m and the fact, and starting thence it soars aloft in quest of the cause. Every relative c a u s a t u m is due to some relative cause: for there can be no c a u s a t u m without a cause according to the law of causality in our spirit. But relative causes, like absolute c a u s a t a, are necessarily due to an absolute cause. The acts of the ego are its causata, its effects, whereof it is the relative cause. The wishes (i. e., desires), the decisions, and the outer acts of the ego are relative effects of it, by which we are led back up to cognition of the ego, as of the relative cause of them. The phenomena in the world are relative and causate, effects of some relative cause, which latter is the world, or the beinghood of the world. The beinghood of the ego, and the beinghood of the world, as relative causes, presuppose the necessary existence of some absolute cause, from which they have received their beinghood and on which they depend, because they cannot exist by themselves and of themselves.

(relative effects : relative causes)
(: : relative causes : Absolute Cause)

Logical cognition begins where cognition of the finite — cognition through consciousness and perception — ends. Conscious cognition ends in knowledge of the ego. Perceptive cognition ends in cognition of the world. These two kinds of knowledge are the limits of the conscient and of the sentient cognitive faculty, beyond which the logical cognitive faculty begins acting. The ego, failing to cognize the creative, or efficient, cause of it either in itself or in the world, goes beyond cognition of itself and of the world, and ascends to a circle of higher cognition, called logical cognition, by means whereof it conceives outside of itself and of the world the efficient reason of its existence, the Absolute Cause of beings. Logical cognition, starting from the data of experience, from the phenomena, soars aloft to the cause of beings, to the

Real Being, to the Eternal Being; and it seeks this outside of the ego and of the matter of the world, as something independent thereof. This law of ascent to the cause through observation of effects is called r e d u c t i o n (the corresponding Greek term being a n a g o g e, which, however, is used in a different sense in English) ; and this logical mode of cognition is called accordingly the r e d u c t i v e mode, and the law of causality. (N o t e of Translator. — It is called r e d u c t i o n on the ground that it leads back up to the original cause). In cognizing the Eternal Being outside of the ego and outside of Creation, we cognize It as something distinct from these and not the same ; consequently we cognize It as the efficient and creative cause of them. We cognize It as the cause of the beinghood of all beings ; as the cause of the livinghood (or life) of all living things ; and furthermore as the cause of the cognitivity (or cognitive capacity) of all cognitive things, i.e., of all thinking beings ; in fact, as the source of all existence, life, and thought.

In the process ef cognizing the Absolute Cause of beings through right reason, the ego comes into immediate and direct contact with Its very existence. The reason, or rational relation, between the cognizing ego and the Absolute Being who is being cognized, makes itself felt as a nexus, or bond, and as a law of cognition, leading cognition directly back up to a conception of the idea of the Absolute. Consciousness and perception find their equilibrium in right reason ; and all experimental ideas and knowledge become unified in the idea and knowledge of the Eternal Being. For the existence of the ego and of the world depends upon the necessary existence of the Being. In the process of contacting the Being through reason, the ego becomes connected with the Being, and the Being then reveals Itself in the ego as an absolute idea that is necessary and universal. Consequently the ego cognizes the Eternal Being as having a perfect existence, a perfect beinghood, a perfect nature, a perfect power, infinity, and eternity. Finite existences, natures, powers, extension, and duration, lead cognition back up to the conception of the idea of a single perfect existence having a perfect nature, a perfect power, eternal duration, and infinite extension, or, in other words, eternity and infinity.

Right reason is the source of the ideas of the Being which are in us. Through it we cognize the Being as an absolute Mind cognizing in the absolute Spirit the absolute Truth, which latter is the Idea of His perfect essence, and nature, and power, and infinity, and eternity. Through right reason we cognize the Being as a perfect Will which engenders a perfect wish (i. e., desire) depictive and representatiye of a perfect volition. Through right reason we cognize the Being as a Power which is infinite and absolute, able to create things out of nonbeing, and to preserve and maintain what has been created forever. We cognize, or conceive, the Being as the absolute source of joy and gladness, as One enjoying Himself and cheering Himself in contemplating His own perfectness and His sempiternal life : in a word, as the source of bliss. But as for what the Absolute, the Infinite, the Eternal, the Sempiternal is in respect of His nature, that is something which we do not know directly from the beginning, though we yearn to learn it by thinking in accordance with reason and law, and by advancing from knowledge to knowledge. The perfectness of the existence, of the nature, of the power, of the infinity, and of the eternity of the Being persist as problems to us whose solution we can accomplish by means of right reason. The idea, however, of the existence of the Absolute Being which we have in our spirit is so perspicuous and certain that we cannot deny it. Right reason in the law of cognizing the absolute, the necessary, the universal; and were it not for this law we should be perfectly ignorant of the existence of the absolute and necessary Being. By means of right reason we cognize the perfect beinghood of the Being, and all His perfectness ; accordingly, we are led back up to the idea of the absolute Cause of beings. When conceiving the beinghood of the Being by means of reason, we thereby cognize also what the Being of beings is what His nature, and essence, and power are. By commencing with reason and proceeding through reason, we end in reason, and thus build and found the science concerning the Being upon right reason. Conscious and perceptive and logical cognition may be represented to the eye by means of the following diagram: *

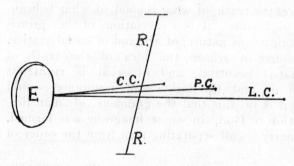

The ego in cognizing itself delineates in itself the idea of itself through consciousness. In cognizing what is something other than itself, the world, through perception, it delineates in itself the idea of the world. In cognizing God through right reason it delineates in itself the idea of God.

---

* The E denotes the cognizing ego. The straight line marked C. C. stands for the power of the cognitive spirit which is called conscious cognition (C. C.) and which cognizes the ego. The straight line marked P. C. stands for another power of the spirit which is callep

Thus by means of the three laws of cognition the ego cognizes what is finite and what is infinite and everything that is
understandable (i. e., every scibile), and it builds the sciences of
the fact and of the Eternal Being. To the same extent that the
Eternal Being is higher than the fact, knowledge of the Being is
higher than knowledge of the fact; accordingly the law of cognition of the Eternal Being is higher than the laws of cognition of
the fact. In the same way that the Eternal Being takes precedence
over the fact as the absolute cause of it, right reason too, as the
law of cognition of the Eternal Being, takes precedence over the
laws of cognition of the fact, the knowledge of which it completes and perfects, because it reveals the efficient and final cause of
beings. Accordingly, in the same way that we can assert that
were it not for the Eternal Being nothing could exist, we may
also assert that were it not for right reasson neither could consciousness and perception exist within us. In reason and through
reason God is revealed within us 1) as the absolute efficient cause;
2) as the final cause of beings; and 3) as an absolute contradiction. He is revealed as an e f f i c i e n t c a u s e, as the Creator of the universe, and as the conservator of the world and its
provider and governor. As a f i n a l c a u s e He is revealed as
a lawgiver, and ruler, and judge of rational and moral beings.
As a c o n t r a d i c t i o n He is revealed as an unchangeable entity, and as ever the same, immutable in His nature and essence,
and as the real Being, or, in other words, as the B e i n g H i m-
s e l f, the T r u t h H i m s e l f, the G o o d O n e H i m s e l f,
the B e a u t i f u l O n e H i m s e l f, and the R i g h t e o u s O n e
H i m s e l f. He is revealed in general as an ontological and logical, moral, physical, and social law: as a perfect Being. This
internal revelation of God through right reason before the eyes of
the ego is a revelation of the truth, of what is good, of what is beautiful, and of what is righteous; it is a revelation of the principles of science, of morality, of nature, of art, and of social justice.
Were it not for the source of reason, the idea of the truth, of
what is good, of what is beautiful, and of what is righteous
would be unknown to us, and the darkness of ignorance would
beset our souls. And it is in this that the grandeur of man lies,
and also his assimilation to God, in whose image he was formed.
Right reason is the party—wall separating man from the order of

---

perceptive cognition (P. C.) and by which we cognize the world. The
straight line marked L. C. stands for logical cognition (L. C.) of the
spirit whereby we cognize the Eternal Being. The straight line trans-
versal thereto and radiating from the common center of the ego, marked
R. R., is to be taken as representing right reason, in which they meet
together.

(the lower) animals, and the nexus connecting him with God, i.e., the bond tying him to God. For through right reason man is enabled to ascend to cognition of God, while God is revealed in man as descending in the fact. Man, being a fact, is led back through reason up to cognition of the infinite, while the infinite is brought down in the fact and is revealed therein. In right reason God contacts the creature, while the creature contacts God. What is infinite contacts what is finite, while what is finite contacts what is infinite. Through right reason God speaks in man, and explains His perfect essence and nature, and reveals to him the efficient and final cause of the universe. Man, on the other hand, is enabled through right reason to ascend high enough to hear and listen to what God speaks within him. Thus right reason is the necessary intermediary between God and men serving to enable both of them to come to an understanding with each other, and forming a necessary logical and moral bond between them. The recognition and admission of the existence of the absolute and necessary Being is a recognition and admission of the existence of right reason, as of a law leading the ego back up to cognition of the Absolute. The quest of the Absolute in the relative and in the fact presupposes ignorance of the primary law of cognition, and consequently a failure to apply it in cognition. Every quest of the Absolute, asking W h a t i s t h i s? and pursued outside of right reason, leads the ego into error. Indeed, since those who have in the past speculated illogically respecting the Absolute Being were led astray and they identified the Absolute with the fact and what is relative, or else in the Absolute they denied the existence of the fact in opposition to the testimony of consciousness and perception, therefore and on this account skeptics inferred absurdly from this abuse an argument against the use and legitimate validity of right reason, proclaiming that right reason may be led astray and deceived, and that no reason can convince us of its truthfulness. But the law is unerring and never makes a mistake, unerringly guiding us to the truth. Anyone who follows the law never makes a mistake. But when he disregards or violates the law, he is led astray and commits a mistake. Hence it is evident that right reason, as the primary law of cognition, is unerring and inerrable, and those who think and cognize in accordance with it are likewise inerrable and infallible. These, on the other hand, who think and cognize contrary to it are the ones who go astray and commit mistakes. On this account reason is an implacable enemy of error. The skeptics who predicate ego's errors of reason are exposed and shown to be ignorant of the nature of reason, and to be identifying it with the ego, which is subject to error and delusion.

THE NATURE OF CONSCIOUSNESS

Consciousness is the law of cognizing the ego as a finite essence having its r a i s o n d' ê t r e and end outside of itself. In this respect it is distinguishable from the cognizing ego as a law of the spirit. The spirit naturally knows itself as at the same time subject and object of cognition. Well, this law of cognizing is called c o n s c i o u s n e s s. Consciousness, as a law of the spirit, being distinguished from the ego, has the nature of showing unerringly to the ego: 1) the latter's substance and beinghood; 2) its nature and properties; 3) its power and relations; 4) its duration; and 5) its extension. This showing is immediate; and the one which does the showing is the unerring and true and immediate witness to the truth. The ego is connected with it through the spirit of consciousness. In so far as it knows itself through consciousness it (sc. the ego) is true, but it errs in so far as it declares anything thoughtlessly (i. e., unreflectingly) and contrary to the testimony of consciousness. Thus it may be said that consciousness is a metaphysical and spiritual light showing what is in us plainly and clearly and unmistakenly. In this inner light of the soul may be seen the essence and nature of the ego, the simplicity of its substance, and the manifoldness of its nature, its power, extension, and duration; and in it is plainly apparent the entire psychological world within us. Were this light not in us, the ego, being unconscious, would remain in deepest night, wholly ignorant of itself, and would be like stones and other unconscious things in which this bright light of consciousness does not exist. But just as the eye was made receptive of light, by means of which it can see visible objects, so and in like manner the ego was made receptive of spirit, by means of which it can cognize and know itself, beings outside of it, and the Absolute Being. In the process of cognizing itself through the spirit, by the law of consciousness, the ego is aware of itself in the metaphysical light as a being that is the same as itself, causate, and the subject of cognition. It is aware of itself in truth, because consciousness is the veracious witness to the truth, the law of the spirit operating in the process whereby the ego becomes aware of itself. Consciousness, as a law of the spirit, has the nature of directing the cognizing ego immediately and directly towards the object of its cognition, of connecting it therewith, and of attesting unerringly and infallibly the truth it is aware of. For this reason we have no other more certain testimony than that of consciousness to assure us that we are existing. For consciousness alone shows us that we are existing. Our existence, in fact, is shown so perspicuously that we cannot deny it if we are sane. For this reason in regard to every psychological idea and item of knowledge consciousness ought to be proclaimed and recognized as the infallible and unerring witness.

THE NATURE OF PERCEPTION

The ego, in the process of cognizing the nonego, with which it is coexisting, cognizes it through the spirit of perception ; and this law of cognition is called p e r c e p t i o n, or, more exactly, p e r c i p i e n c e. Percipience, as a law of the spirit, involved in cognition of the world, is distinguishable from the ego, and has the nature of perspicuously and clearly showing the world : 1) as respects its beinghood; 2) its nature; 3) its power; 4) its duration; and 5) its extension. The showing of the nonego, of the world, through perception is immediate; and percipience is unerring and true in so far as it shows the ego through the sense organe the idea it gets of the outer, or external, world. The cognizing ego is connected with the nonego, or what is commonly, called the world, through perception. It is true in what it knows about the world through perception, but errs in what it declares contrary to the latter's testimony, or in what it observes carelessly and superficially. In acting upon the external world through the sense organs, percipience is the metaphysical light in which the ego cognizes the objective existence of the nonego, and assures itself respecting the external world. Percipience and consciousness, in fact, are two laws of one and the same spirit, through which spirit the ego cognizes itself and what exists outside of itself. If the law of consciousness is correct and true and certain, it follows as a logical inference that the law of percipience too is correct, true, and certain. It is impossible for consciousness to be true in what it attests and for percipience not to be true in what it affirms. Those who deny the validity of consciousness, and its legitimacy, ought to deny also the validity of percipience, and the legitimacy of knowledge acquired through it. For the very spirit of truth, being naturally true, cannot be true and false at the same time, nor be true in some things and false in others. Error and falsehood come from the ego when the latter cognizes contrary to the testimony of the witnesses to the truth, and contrary to the laws of the spirit; they do not come from the spirit and its laws. By connecting the cognizing ego with the object being cognized, perception shows it the truth about the nonego, and directs the ego's cognition to it directly and immediately. It bears witness with all certitude to the existence of the external world. For this reason we have no other more certain testimony than that of perception to assure us that beings outside of us are actually existing. For perception alone shows us the existence of the world outside of us. This showing is so perspicuous that we cannot deny it if we are sane. It is in the nature of percipience that the element assuring us of the world's existence and showing us the truth of it resides. For this reason percipience ought to be proclaimed and recognized as the infallible, and indefectible, and unerring witness in regard to every cosmological idea and item of knowledge.

THE NATURE OF RIGHT REASON

In cognizing the Eternal Being, the ego cognizes Him in the spirit through reason. On this account right reason is the law proper of the spirit, and one which is primary too. In the process of cognizing the Eternal Being right reason is distinguishable from the cognitive power, or cognitive faculty, of the ego, as a law of the spirit, perspicuously and unerringly showing the ego: 1) the existence of the Eternal Being; 2) His nature; 3) His power; 4) His eternity; and 5) His infinity. Cognition through right reason is direct, and immediate, and true. For the ego is related, and is connected, and communicates with the Eternal Being through right reason; moreover, it is through this relationship that the Eternal Being reveals Himself to man, and emits to him His unapproachable light. Thus the ego is assured as respects the existence of the Being. Right reason, by connecting the ego with the Eternal Being, shows the ego the truth so perspicuously that it is impossible for there to be any denial of it, so long as the ego is sane. Reason not only bears witness to the truth of the Eternal Being, to His existence, but also shows His creative and final reason. Were there no right reason in us, we should be ignorant of the Eternal Being, owing to our inability to lift ourselves up to the cognition of general and universal ideas, to the cognition of the eternal and necessary existence of the Being. As light out of the light of the sempiternal Logos (or Reason) in God, as a ray of the unapproachable metaphysical Sun, reason enlightens the ego in connection with cognition of the truth, and perspicuously shows it the Being of beings, and the source of all truth. This showing is perspicuous, immediate, and certain. For reason, being, unerring, and infallible, leads the cognizing ego unerringly to cognition of the sempiternal Truth. Hence it may be inferred that it is in the nature of right reason that what assures us of the Eternal Being's existence and shows us His truth in the spirit resides. On this account right reason ought to be proclaimed and recognized as the unerring and infallible witness in regard to every scientific, and logical, and theological idea and item of knowledge. Hence it may be inferred that the unerring character of consciousnsss, of percipience, and of right reason — of these three laws of the spirit through which the ego cognizes — has been scientifically proved, and that there can be no error or delusion in the face of this proof. The laws of the spirit are true, as laws of the truth of the spirit. On this account whatever is attested and shown by them before the eyes of the ego is perspicuous ; and consequently it is also self - evident and insusceptible of any doubt. Consciousness and percipience constitute the law of cognizing the fact. Right reason, on the other hand, constitutes the law of cognizing the Eternal Being. The existence of the fact is perspicuous and certain ; the existence of the Eternal Being is likewise perspicuous and certain. The laws of the spirit by which the fact is cognized are particular and relative and confingent because of the object being cognized through them; whereas the law of cognizing the Eternal Being, right reason, is an absolute and necessary law which possesses the characteristics of being eternal, sempiternal, and ever the same in habitude. Hence it is evident that right reason is a primary and absolute and universal law operating in the process of cognition. If, indeed, it is through consciousness and percipience that we know the existence of ourselves and of the world outside of us, it is through right reason that we know the efficient cause of ourselves, and the creative reason of our own existence, and can utilize the knowledge obtained through consciousness and percipience. Hence it is evident that reason is also the highest light within us, affording more and higher enlightenment than the light of consciousness and that of percipience, and revealing to us more and better knowledge, which is as superior as the Eternal Being is superior to the fact.

FIRST AND PRIMARY IDEAS

What we call first and primary ideas are those which we conceive in our spirit first and in the beginning of cognition, when we cognize in accordance with the laws of cognition which we considered in the foregoing pages. The first and primary ideas are the foundation and basis of all our ideas which we acquire from objects of knowledge in accordance with the primary laws of the spirit. As first they are the criterion of secondary ideas. As primary they are the criterion of derived and acquired ideas. When the ego receives awareness and knowledge of its own existence, it receives at the same time also knowledge of the existence of the world, and of the efficient cause of it. Consequently it possesses and contains within itself three first and primary ideas, concrete, and distinct from each other, which it contemplates in its spirit. But where were these ideas previous thereto? Were they in the ego, we wonder? But if the ideas were in the ego, the latter would have cognized them directly in the beginning; in addition, it would also have remembered these ideas in time subsequent thereto. But experience denies the truth of this assumption. Experience shows us that the ego exists before receiving consciousness of its existence, in an infantile body, feeling but not cognizing. Hence it is evident that there was a time when the ego, though really existing, did not cognize anything. Consequently, it had no idea of knowledge of anything, but, on the contrary, remained under the dominance of absolute ignorance. But if it were utterly ignorant, how could it have had any ideas? This is an obvious self - contradiction. The source of ideas is the spirit. If the ego had been a spirit directly in the beginning of its formation and at the time of its entification, it would have had ideas, not only first and primary ones, but also secondary and derived ones. It would have remembered them and its former condition before being born with a body and appearing in the world as a person. But experience nowise proves or bears witness to any such thing as true. Hence it is evident furthermore that the ego was not a conscious spirit from the beginning. Through the spirit it becomes a spirit, or, more explicitly, a being which cognizes itself and beings outside of itself, and the Eternal Being called God. The first spiritization of the ego is its initial consciousness, its initial perception of the nonego, and its initial cognition of the Eternal Being. Hence it is evident that it was through the spirit that the ego received the first and primary ideas; for it is the spirit that is the source of ideas: and through the spirit it was connected with the three objects of knowledge; for the spirit is the region of ideas, the relationship and nexus of beings.

THE FIRST AND PRIMARY IDEA OF THE EGO

In cognizing itself through the spirit the ego initially forms an idea of its own existence. It cognizes itself as a being, as an essence with its attributes, of power, of extension, and of duration. This first idea accrues to the ego directly, when the latter comes into contact with the cognitive spirit and receives self - consciousness, or consciousness of itself. The idea of the ego, as of an essence, which the ego receives directly in the beginning as a result of its contact with the spirit, is imperfect, imperfectly depicting the ego as respects its substance, nature, power, extension, and duration. The ego exists the ego feels, thinks, wills ; the ego has power to do things ; the ego exists in space and in time. The existence and beinghood of the ego is the principle of it, of which the attributes constituting its nature are predicated. Time and space are categories of the finite essence and nature of the ego. The ego, as a being, is in space and exists in time. The nature cannot exist by itself. It grows upon the substance of the being ; the substance can exist even in the absence of the nature, as a simple substance. Hence it is evident that the substance is preexistent to the nature. Feeling, thinking, willing (i. e., sensation, cognition, and volition) constitute the nature of the ego, a nature conceived in the abstract apart from its substance, yet not existing by itself. For this reason cognition of the ego is cognition of its hypostasis, and not of its nature in the abstract apart from its hypostasis, which is the appearance of the being, its specific form, and its structural form. Some persons have contended that it is impossible for us to cognize the substance of the being, and that our cognition can cognize only its nature. Consequently, there is no reason convincing us of the existence of the principle and substance of the ego. But this contention is not true. For, if it is impossible for the nature to exist by itself, in the absence of the hypostasis and if it can exist only together with the hypostasis, the latter serving as the basis of it, and only as a specific form, as a stuctural form, and as an attribute, we infer logically that the substance is preexistent to the nature of the being, and that it underlies the nature, though it cannot be seen by the ego directly, but can only be cognized logically. The nature is the specific form and image of the being. Hence it is the appearance of the being, or what is called the p h e n o m e n o n of the being, i.e., that part or aspect of the being which is apparent or manifest. Cognition cognizes the phenomenon of the ego, its nature. But through rational cognition (i.e., cognition attained through reason), by which we can cognize underneath the phenomenon the being itself and what is real — beneath the nature the hypostasis — we discover the existence of the hypostasis, and see the relation between it and its nature. Hence it is evident that we cognize the idea of the hypostasis logically and rationally, and by means of reason can assure ourselves of its existence In thus cognizing the beinghood of the being, we distinguish it from its attributes, by which it is revealed in the world; and by means of the relation subsisting between both we join them together, and get an idea of the being together with all its elements, its substance, its nature, its relationship, its time, and its place (or space). Hence it may be seen that the first and primary idea of the ego, though an imperfect idea, embraces all the elements of the being.

From the idea of the existence of the ego as a being, I induce the further fact that all beings that cognize as I do can cognize themselves, and have an idea of their own existence as I have of mine. In other words, they cognize the fact that they have a hypostasis, a nature, an extension, and a duration. I am convinced of this fact because I conceive the same law to hold between the same things and like things in accordance with the principle of identity. For I cognize the fact that inasmuch as there are beings that cognize as I do, these beings cannot cognize themselves otherwise than as I cognize myself, nor have any other idea of themselves than such as I have of myself in my spirit (or mind). So I say that both those men who have lived before me, and those now living contemporaneously with me, and those who will be after me, all have cognized, or cognize, or will cognize themselves as beings with a substance, a nature, and a relationship, in a time as well as in a place (i.e., in time and space). The first, therefore, and primary idea of the ego is the first and primary knowledge concerning it, viz., that it is a substance with a nature, a relationship, a duration, and an extension. This means that it is a creature (i.e., something created) and a fact (i.e., something originated in time) : that the ego is a being that exists in space and time — in a place, and during an interval of time. Consciousness unites and combines this phenomenon with the hypostasis of the ego — the specific form with the being; the image with the reality it depicts. Hence when I say «I», with reference to the ego, I am announcing thereby nothing else than my own b e i n g h o o d and my own e x i s t e n c e , though with sensation, cognition, and volition, and power to do things, coupled with the fact that I am at a time and at a place, an imperfect being susceptible of being perfected, and the fact that I have a tendency to progress, to grow, and to attain to maturity.

HYPOSTASIS — relationship — nature

= Ego.

— time — space :

The b e i n g h o o d of the ego, or what is called its hypostasis, denuded of every characteristic quality, is matter, a simple, and undecomposable, and indivisible particle of matter. It is a simple and indiscreptible unit. Its nature is its specific form, which is formed through the spirit.

The discussion here having turned to the hypostasis and and nature of beings, we must explain in a few words the principle of the hypostasis and that of the nature of the fact. The hypostasis is the principle of the being, the matter of the being. The nature is the specific form and structural form of it. The hypostasis of the being without the nature is amorphous matter, shapeless, formless and featureless; but with its nature it is a being, an essence. The hypostasis has a beinghood and existence outside of the Eternal Being, God; it is a fact: the nature has no beinghood and existence, but, on the contrary, is a substanceless, or unsubstantial, idea in the cognition of the Eternal Being, a sempiternal idea in the Spirit of God, on the model of which matter is formed structurally, and the hypostasis of beings are formed specifically, and beings receive a structural form and a specific form, and the substances become distinguishable from each other. The substance, or, in other words, the matter of beings, combined and correlated with the sempiternal ideas of beings, manifests the world of real beings and the variety of essences therein. Hence the world of real beings is the product of the association and combination of substances with their natures — of matter with its specific form and structural form.

Matter — relationship — idea, form, structure

But matter, or the world of hypostasis — the world which is imperceptible to the senses, but apprehensible by the cognitive faculty and spirit, is the fact, which before becoming such was a nonbeing, and a potential being, contingently capable of becoming such or not, depending on the free will of the Eternal Being. It became such because of the goodness and benevolence of the Being, amorphous and formless in the beginning, having mere beinghood and destitute of every other attribute. But this formless and featureless b e i n g h o o d , matter, is the most imperfect beinghood, and the lowest grade of being. From the simple substance of the being up to its state of perfection, how many degrees are there, we well may wonder? From simple beinghood to perfect beinghood, what is the distance, we wonder? And it is to be inferred that the ego in its substantial existence is very imperfect beinghood without life and consciousness, devoid and destitute of every attribute. But God impresses upon this matter the image and specific form He wills and desires, and makes beings by His form — creating and world — creating action. The image and the specific form of beings come from the sempiternal Idea of God, while looking at which God creates and endows with a specific form and imparts a structure to the world in accordance with His sempiternal Idea, which is the center of the ideal world and of the real world. Plato, thinkning inversely, considered the sempiternal ideas, in accordance with which primordial matter was structurally formed, to be sempiternal beings in God, to be sempiternal substances, while as for matter, or what we call hypostasis, he considered it to be a sempiternal principle coexistent with the Eternal Being called God. As for God, on the other hand, he took Him to be, not one who had produced the first matter out of a nonbeing, but as one endowing sempiternal matter with a specific form and imparting a structure to it — as one who fits matter with its specific form and as the creator of the present world. But the idea of sempiternal matter and of sempiternal ideas as beings in God, is a chimera, because it conflicts with and is opposed to the idea of a God who is an Eternal Being, all — powerful, all — wise, and all — good, and it is incompatible therewith. Plato and all who profess this idea were unable to see this discordance, because they failed to lift themselves up to cognition of the omnipotence of the Being, and failed to cognize the infiniteness of His omnipotence, and to see that the idea of the existence of sempiternal matter and of sempiternal ideas, as beings, contradicts the idea that His omnipotence is infinite. God's power, being infinite, cannot be limited by anything, nor can it be obstructed by anything. The idea of existence of sempiternal matter in accordance with the belief of Plato and of dualists limits the infinite power of God and obstructs His unlimited action. Hence it is evidently a false idea. But even the idea of the existence of sempiternal beings in God, which Plato calls ideas, is likewise at variance with the existence of a most perfect and all-powerful Being having a perfect Idea of Himself which is at once ontological and substantive; moreover, it is at variance with the creation of beings, or, more precisely, with the creative order, and predicates want of design and reflection on the part of God as having subjected the ontological world, which according to Plato is sempiternal and consequently perfect, to this fluent world of appearance and seeming which is on the way to destruction, on account of incoherence and inconsistency, otherwise excluded from the perfect world. Finally, these ideas, as being contradictory, are devoid of truth, which is to be found in the idea that the Eternal Being, with His infinite power, His good will, of His own accord freely created the present world out of nothing, out of a nonbeing, while looking at the one in His perfect Idea, and that upon the primordial matter previously created He formed the structure of the primary mold, and endowed the beings with a specific form, and produced out of the amorphous and formless and featureless state a world of beings, a world formed structurally in accordance with the sempiternal ideas in Him and in accordance with the substanceless ideal world in His Spirit, wherein the substantive and absolute Idea of the Eternal Being, God, who is ever the same in habitude, is ruler and sovereign.

THE FIRST AND PRIMARY IDEA OF THE NONEGO

Together with the primary idea of the ego there exists in my spirit also the idea of another thing, the nonego, distinct therefrom. The spirit shows the existence of the ego and the existence of the nonego together. The idea of the nonego — i. e., of the world — embraces all the elements considered to depend on its existence. The elements of a being are the hypostasis, the nature, the relationship, the extension, and the duration of it. Hence the primary and first idea of the existence of the world is the idea of it conceived as an essence. In perceiving the world, we perceive its essence, i. e., its beinghood together with its nature. We cannot conceive the existence of the nature apart from the substance and beinghood of the world. Every characteristic feature is a characteristic feature of some being, and without a being there can exist no characteristic feature. Consequently even the nature of the world is the nature of a being, and not of any nonbeing. In perceiving the nature of the world, we perceive its very substance; therefore it is evident that we have an idea of the world's existence. The nature, as we said further above, is a specific form and image of the being. For we comprehend beings in their substance through their nature. The idea of the nature enables us to ascend (or reduces us) directly to cognition of the hypostasis because there is a relationship and nexus (or bond) between the hypostasis and the nature. In cognizing the nature, we simultaneously cognize also the hypostasis of which it is predicated. But the hypostasis of the world is matter. In regard to the question we are discussing the same law holds true as we considered and applied for the purpose of cognizing the substance of the ego. Phenomena are images of beings, which, however, we know, not directly, but through the phenomena. The nature of every being is its phenomenon, beneath which its beinghood and principle are consealed from observation. Thus we are logically led up and back from the phenomenon to the being, from the nature to the hypostasis; accordingly we conceive the substance of every being to be preexistent to the being itself. Hence we cognize the idea of the substance through reason, and predicate it of every being. Every being has a hypostasis and beinghood. Every hypostasis makes its appearance in conjunction with some nature. Every nature is analogous to the hypostasis of which it is predicated. Every being resides in a place in space, and exists in an interval of time. From the idea of the existence of my body, as a being distinct from the ego, I logically induce the inference that all bodies exist, that they have a nature, a relationship, an extension, and a duration. On this account I inductively judge that every body exists, that it has a nature, a relationship, an extension, and a duration. From the principle of identity I judge that all the same bodies, all the same beings, have the same nature, and relationship. Thus, in the same way that the idea of the ego's existence may be logically extended to every ego in the past, present, and future, so too may the idea of the existence of the nonego, of the other thing, of that which is something else, or, in a word, of the world, be logically extended to every being distinct from the ego, in the past, present, and future. Every ego has a hypostasis, a nature, a relationship, a duration, an extension. Logical perception unites and joins the nature of the nonego with its hypostasis the phenomenon with the being, the image with the thing imaged. Consequently the first and primary idea of the existence of the nonego is complete as respecting its elements — substance, nature, relationship, extension, and duration, but imperfect as respecting its development, and for this reason is subject to repletion.

$$\text{Substance — relationship — nature — time — space.} = \text{Nonego}$$

The beinghood of the ego is matter. Its nature is its specific form and its image. The primary idea of the ego is the first and primary knowledge about it — namely, the fact that it is a being, in time and space. Hence it is evidently a creature and fact subsisting in time and space.

THE FIRST AND PRIMAPY IDEA OF THE ETERNAL BEING

The first and primary idea of the existence of the ego, and of the nonego, is not independent in our spirit, of the idea of the existence of the Eternal Being. In cognizing itself and what is outside itself the ego is cognizing not absolutely, but relatively. In this relative cognition there is immediately revealed also the existence of the Eternal Being through the idea of Him in the

spirit. I am. But I am not as I want to be. Therefore it is evident
that I am not the cause of my own existence. The nonego is,
and it coexists together with me. But it is far inferior to me who
can cognize and be conscious of my own existence. But if I, who
can cognize things, am not the cause of my own existence, when
it is considered that I have a more perfect constitution than the
nonego, how could the world, which is more imperfect than I, be
the cause of my existence? But if I am not the cause of my own
existence, how could I be the cause of the world's existence?
Hence it is logically evident that neither I nor the world have
within us the efficient (i.e., creative) raison d' être. Hence it is
to be inferred that we are creatures of some efficient cause which
is outside us and distinct from the essence of the ego and that
of the world. Thus we come to cognize the idea of the existence
of the Eternal Being. Hence the idea of the Eternal Being God
is in our spirit along with the idea of the ego, and with that
of the nonego; accordingly, the ego cognizes the idea of the existence of the Eternal Being by means of reason, perspicuously
and with certitude. It cognizes it as respects its substance (hypostasis), nature, relationship, eternalness, and infiniteness, which
are the time and space of God. It cognizes it as a perfect idea.
From the idea of the existence of the fact the ego is directly reduced to cognition of a necessary, sempiternal, and perfect existence. From the existence of the nature of the fact it is reduced
to cognition of the inevitable existence of a sempiternal, and necessary, and perfect nature. From the existence of the relationship of the fact it is reduced to cognition of a sempiternal relationship. From the existence of finite time and space it is
reduced to cognition of a sempiternal eternity and infinity. Hence
by this process of reduction it comes to conceive the idea of the
perfect and sempiternal and necessary existence of the Being, together with the latter's perfect nature, relationship, duration, and
extension. The ego, in cognizing the Eternal Being, cognizes
Him as a perfect Mind cognizing Himself perfectly, in a perfect
Spirit, and sempiternally generating, or begetting, the perfect
Idea of Himself. It cognizes that that which is cognized perfectly,
the Eternal Being, is cognized also with respect to His beinghood.
Consequently the Idea of God, as a perfect image of the Being,
represents Him as a Being perfect with respect to His beinghood,
nature, relationship, extension, and duration. But what images
anything does not image it faithfully and accurately and perfectly
as the being it is unless the latter possesses an existence and a
reality and an existence of perfectness. Hence it may be concluded
that the Idea of God is itself a perfect Being, having a beinghood
of its own, a beinghood distinct from that of the B e i n g whom

It represents, or images. Moreover, the Spirit through which this cognition is effected must be nothing less than an existence distinct from the existence of the cognizer and that of the one cognized, but is indeed a cognitive Being Itself able to cognize the Eternal Being perfectly. Hence it may be concluded also that the Spirit is another Being than the cognizer and the one cognized, a Being together with a nature, a relationship, an extension, and a duration. The Being, and therefore the Idea of Him, and the Spirit are the three principles and substances (hypostasis) in the Eternal Being, all three of which have a common nature, relationship, infinity, and eternity. Thus we know that God is one in point of essence, but triune in respect of hypostasis and persons. Consequently the first and primary idea of the Eternal Being is the idea of His perfect existence, nature, relationship, eternity, and infinity — an idea which is absolute, necessary, and sempiternal.

Beinghood — — relationship — — nature

— — eternity — — infinity.   = Eternal Being.

The b e i n g h o o d of the Eternal Being, as something that is ever together with His nature and relationship, in His infinity and eternity, as sempiternal essence, is the Spirit. The beinghood of the Eternal Being is not preexistent to His nature, but, on the contrary, coexists together with the latter sempiternally. The Being, and at the same time His nature, and relationship, and infinity, and eternity, all coexist simultaneously. But the b e i n g h o o d of the fact is preexistent to its nature. For first the fact receives its existence through the entifying power of the Eternal Being, and thereafter receives its nature through His mundifying (or world—creating) power — or, in other words, it receives its specific form and its structural form in accordance with the sempiternal ideas in God, and in accordance with His most perfect Idea, which latter is the criterion, or standard, of every idea and of every being.

Concerning the elements of the Idea of the Bein

THE HYPOSTASIS

The Hypostasis of the Being is His principle and the foundation of which His nature is predicated ; on this account the idea of the hypostasis which we receive through cognition of the idea of the nature of any being, in our spirit, is the first idea. The hypostasis of the ego and that of the nonego, when denuded of every attribute and characteristic property, is matter, a formless and featureless and shapeless, and undifferentiated, and invisible, and undecomposable and imperishable, and indivisible unit. Everything that is and exists and possesses reality is called in general a hypostasis in distinction from an attribute, which latter cannot exist by itself, without a hypostasis. Every hypostasis of a being, being without a structural form and without a shape and without a specific form, is matter. Matter is anything that exists without being aware of its own existence. The hypostasis of the ego and nonego, before receiving a structural form and a specific form, and a nature, are matter. They possess beinghood without awareness. A psychological analysis of the phenomena of the ego reduces us to cognition of the substance of the ego, which hypostasis is a simple, undecomposable, and indivisible unit. In like manner a cosmological analysis of the phenomena of the body and of the world at large reduces our cognition to the conception of the idea of the hypostasis of bodies and of the world, which hypostasis we cannot behold with our eyes in any wise whatsoever. The hypostasis of the ego, and the hypostasis of the nonego, of the material world, are one and the same, because they both have a common beinghood, when denuded of every characteristic property and every attribute. By analyzing the phenomena of the ego's cognition, sensation, and volition, we can discover underneath them the hypostasis of the ego, or, more explicitly speaking, the ego which cognizes, feels, and wills. By mentally abstracting from the ego the powers of willing, of feeling, and of cognizing, we can cognize the ego denuded of its attributes, by which it reveals itself and appears to us, and becomes known, and is distinguished from other beings. We cognize it as the simple principle, or starting—point, of a being, as something which is potentially a being, as a simple particle of matter and one that is incomposite and indivisible. Thus even by analyzing the nonego chemically, that is to say, by analyzing the phenomena of the world, the bodies of which it is composed, by the processes of chemical analysis, we can ascend to the point of dividing matter a d i n f i n i t u m, where we can cognize the existence of numerous units and indivisible particles of matter, as a result of the combination of which bodies are shaped and the material

world is formed. Though we cannot see these simple units and
hypostasis with our eyes, we can cognize their existence logically
from the phenomena, and with the aid of reason we conceive the
idea of their existence, which we postulate logically, because
every phenomenon has an analogous cause, and there is no phenomenon without a cause. Thus we are led by reason back up
to cognition of the hypostasis of matter as a result of observing
the phenomena, and are thereby enabled to cognize the beinghood
of the ego and of the world. Analysis of phenomena, and their
decomposition, reduce our cognition to the conception and notion
of the world of hypostasis and of simple units. But the world of
hypostasis, which reveals itself in the face of reason as a logical
postulate, has not the cause of its existence within itself, because
of its being potential, of its being imperfect, and of its being
subject to being perfected in process of time. What is potential
may be or may not be : it is therefore contingen. The world
of simple units, of hypostasis, because of its being potential, is
contingent : it is therefore a fact. For whatever is contingently
capable of being or of not being, does not depend upon itself,
but upon some other being necessarily existent, whence it received
and has existence. What contingently may become something
does not actually exist until it receives a beginning of existence:
but that which necessarily is — that which is a necessary being
— ever is even in the absence of the fact. Anything that may
contingently become something, but has not yet become anything,
is an idea in the Spirit of the necessary Being and of the Eternal
Being : in other words, it is an unsubstantiated (i.e., substanceless) idea, contingently capable of becoming or of not becoming
something, and being sempiternally cognized in the Spirit of the
Erernal Being. Now, let us ask, where was the fact, the world
of hypostasis, before it received its existence and hypostasis? In
the entifying power of the Being, we answer, and in His infinite
Spirit, as mere ideas, cognized without any hypostasis. For the
infinite cognitivity of the Being, and His infinite power, concur
in providing the hypostasis of the fact, of matter, of the world
of hypostasis. As one who can cognize what is not as though it
were something, God can also entify it; for cognizing what is not
as though it were is much more difficult than entifying and creating it. But if God could not cognize what is not as though it
were, then neither could He entify what is not. For how can
anyone create anything that he is not previously aware of?
According to a natural law we first have to cognize anything,
and afterwards actualize what was previously cognized or conceived. For we are actualizing an idea. But before declaring
that God can create beings out of nonbeing, and make them such

as He wants them to be, we must first show whether God cognizes what is not, as though it were. For, if He does cognize this, He can, if He wishes, also actualize it. For anything that it actualized is first cognized as such in the intellect of the one actualizing it.

If God can cognize Himself, who is a perfect Being, much more can He cognize what is not, nonbeing, a being that is most imperfect. God is the perfect Being. In cognizing Himself, therefore, He is cognizing the perfect Being. Cognition of a nonbeing is the contrary of cognition of a being. God, as a perfect Being, possesses perfect cognition, volition, action, and freedom. A nonbeing, as something very imperfect, is something that does not cognize anything, does not exercise volition, does not act, and is not free. It is therefore a negation of a being or, more expressly speaking, something that is not a being. God, therefore, in cognizing Himself cognizes in contrast to Himself that which is a nonbeing; if He could not cognize this, neither could He cognize Himself perfectly, nor would He possess perfect cognition, nor would He be a perfect Being — which is absurd. For God cognizes Himself perfectly; consequently He also cognizes whatever is a nonbeing; accordingly He possesses perfect knowledge of the Being and of the nonbeing. How can it be said that one who knows what is more difficult and what is the greatest cannot know what is easier and the least? Being able to cognize easily enough what is not as though it were something, God can, if He so wiches, also substantiate and actualize it. For perfect cognition is necessarily attended by perfect power; since otherwise God would not be perfect, which is absurd. Therefore it is evident that God, as cognizing what is not actually existent, can also actualize it and substantiate it outside Himself, distinct from His essence. The principle of the actualization of the idea of a nonbeing is the principle of entification and of creation — a principle according to which what is sempiternally cognized as a being in the Spirit of God, though not actually existent, is endowed with reality and hypostasis and the idea of it is entified. Hence it may be said that creation is entification of the idea of something that is not actually existent. That which has been entified is matter and the world of substances. This matter is something very imperfect, the imperfectness of which is, in fact, as great in measure as the perfectness of God. It was predestined to become a being out of nonbeing, and from a most imperfect existence to ascend to a degree of perfectness, and to be equalized to the Eternal Being. It is thus that we cognize, by reflecting in accordance with reason, the world of hypostasis and primordial matter, out of which God made the beings, and the being of beings in creation, namely, man. This matter is the fact; the Creator and Maker of it is God, the Eternal Being who maintains the same habitude forever.

> Eternal Being — entification — Matter

The world of hypostasis is the sum-total of the simple, undecomposable and indivisible units of which creation consists. The making of these was God's first work. After making the hypostases, God determined which of them was to receive this and that nature in its time. He determined furthermore the time that each hypostasis must remain incarnate in the world of phenomena, and according to what laws it was to be embodied and to receive its specific form and its structural form in accordance with the eternal types, or models, and the eternal ideas in Cod's cognition, and to be revealed in the world. The beinghood of primordial matter is a most imperfect image of the Being's most perfect existence. In the actualization of the idea of nonbeing God gives a most imperfect image of His most perfect existence in the creature. It is because God possesses beinghood that He gives matter, beinghood; matter, indeed, is an imperfect being, yet it is susceptible of perfection. Thus the idea of the hypostasis of the ego, and of the nonego, of the fact, is the idea of matter.

THE NATURE

The nature is the image and form of a being in which the latter makes its appearance in the order of beings. It is the sum-total of all the attributes and characteristic properties that are predicated of a being. The attributes and characteristic properties may indeed be conceived by themselves and so cognized, though they do not exist by themselves, but only as predicaments predicated of the beings. Hypostasis and matter has beinghood; and, after acquiring the nature which belongs to it, it becomes distinguished and separated in the order of beings, and is differentiated by a character of its own. The nature of the ego and that of the nonego differ, and on this account these two beings are distinguished and separated. The ego feels, wills, cognizes. The nonego either feels, or grows, or exists simply in some condition or state of being. The powers of feeling, of willing, and of cognizing are the nature of the ego. But the power of feeling without cognizing, and willing, the power of growing, and that of simply existing are the nature of the nonego, of material bodies. Matter, or, more explicitly speaking, the world of hypostasis in the process of being

made, was without specific form and structural form and undifferentiated, but receptive of a specific form and a structural form
and a figure or shape. In cognizing nonbeing as though it were
a being, God cognizes it as a perfect being. He created it imperfect in order that He might gradually advance and perfect it,
with reference to His own perfect Idea, in accordance with which
He planned and willed to create beings. Cognition of nonbeing
as of a perfect being, and creation of nonbeing as of an imperfect
being, demands complete agreement between what is being cognized as a perfect being, but is being created as an imperfect
being. For upon this agreement and equalization of God's perfect
thought and the perfect creature or product depends the fulfillment and accomplishment of the divine design, and the realization of the purpose of the creation of the beings. Between cognition of nonbeing as of a perfect being, and the creation of it in a
state of perfection, there is to be cognized the law of progress
and of God's progressive action, in accordance with which God
first actualizes nonbeing not as He cognizes it, as a perfect being,
but as an imperfect being, and afterwards gives it a type analogous to its hypostasis and by imparting a nature to it He advances and perfects it. For the nature is nothing else than the being's capacity to be perfected. The world of hypostasis is the entification of the idea of the nonbeing, or of that which is not actually existent, but which nevertheless is cognized as a perfect being in God's cognition. But this world is not on an equal footing and in agreement with the world of ideas which subsists in
God's cognition ; that is to say, it is not equal to the ideal world.
It was predestined, however, to become equal to it. Accordingly,
the ideal world which subsists in God's cognition is to be impressed completely and perfectly upon the substances of beings, upon
matter, and in the same way as a specific form and a structural
form are stamped upon matter and hypostasis. For this reason
and on this account God proceeded to engage in a second operation, mundification (i. e., the creation of a world), wherein He
clothes the entified matter and invests it with its apparel, stamp-
ing and applying upon it a specific form and a structural form,
and furnishing it with a nature analogous to its needs for the accomplishment of its destiny, or purpose. Mundification is the specification of matter, and the formation of beings, the totality of
which form the world.

Eternal Being — mundification — beings.

Just as the substances of °beings are a product of God's

entificative power and action, so are the natures of beings a product of God's mundificative power and action. Whoever can do the first, which is the most difficult thing can much more succeed in doing the second thing, which is the easier. How can it be said that He who entifies nonbeing is unable to specify and form a being and a fact? How can it be said that He is unable to perfect it? Nevertheless, it is to be noted that the specification of the fact supposes knowledge of its specific form. For how can anyone who has no direct knowledge of the type be able to specify anything? Hence it may be inferred that the specific form, the type or model, is in God's Spirit, and so is the idea of the formation of the being. This type or model which we have just been speaking of is what is called the nature of the being. A perfect type or model makes the beinghood of the being perfect. The natures are analogous to the hypostasis. The hypostasis which has a more perfect nature is also a more perfect hypostasis and has a more perfect destiny. The ego and the nonego, these two hypostasis possess a nature characterized by the fact that the hypostasis of the ego possesses a more perfect nature than the nature of the nonego. Hence it is evident that the former of the two is also the more perfect and possesses a more perfect destiny or purpose in the order of beings. But inasmuch as the substance and nature of the ego is more perfect than all substances and natures of the nonego, we conclude that it also has a more perfect destiny. Since the ego has a cognitive and volitive nature, while cognition and volition are attributes of God, we infer that the ego partakes or receives a share of God's cognition and volition. Hence it is evident that it partakes of God's nature. But since the nature is the specific form of a being, the idea thereof, we infer that the ego, being a partaker of the divine nature, possesses God's specific form and structural form and His image, upon the model or type of whom it was formed. Nevertheless, the impartation of the nature is not effected forthwith, but only in the process of time. The ego has an imperfect nature, and very slight cognition and power. God, on the other hand, has a perfect nature, as well as cognition and power that are equally perfect. Hence it may be expected that in the course of time the ego will receive all of God's nature. Reception of the nature may be equated to its standard, to the Idea of the Being residing in God, and His ultimate destiny. But the perfect nature possesses also a perfect standard, the perfect Being. It is admitted on all hands that the ego is an image of God, having reference to His perfection and to reception of God's perfect nature. Hence the ego tends to become altogether like God. For God is the standard of perfect nature. The perfect Idea of God is the true and real entity of the ego, just as it is also the true image of the perfect Being.

The nature is the perfection of the being. If the nature be taken away, or abstracted, the being is left behind as a simple hypostasis. If the latter is also taken away, there is left behind a nonbeing which is cognized as though it were a being, as a potential being, in God' s cognition. Hence this would be tantamount to taking away creation. But can we make any such absurd supposition? Impossible! For having willed to create beings, God created them purposefully; and, as having infinite power He can bring them to the purposed end. Thanks to His wisdom God is well aware of the end, the purpose, and the means for the accomplishment of His work; and thanks to His power He can do that which He has conceived and willed. For it is supreme Wisdom, perfect Volition, and infinite Power that created and governs the world. So, being cognizant of God's progressive and irremissible action upon beings, we are cognizant of the indefeasibility of their natures, and consequently we recognize also the inalienability of whatever they have received and hold of God. The ego has received and holds a b e i n g h o o d, a n a t u r e, a n d a r e l a t i o n s h i p. It is therefore evident that it will hold perpetually whatever it has received inalienably. It holds the power of cognition, of volition, and of sensibility (or feeling). Therefore it will hold these powers perpetually. Therefore it may be inferred that the ego will perpetually be cognizing, wishing (or exercising volition), acting, living. It will therefore be immortal forever. For exercising cognition and volition is really living. Thus we are perspicuously assured that the ego really is immortal, and that it cognizes, wills, and acts forever. But when this ego becomes equalized to God's perfect Idea, it will receive perfect cognition, and power, i.e., omniscience and omnipotence, and consequently perfect life, i.a., perfect and complete immortality. The nonego, on the other hand, as being incapable of receiving God's nature, will serve as the means of perfecting and deifying the ego, which ends are the purpose of creation. Thus the idea of the nature of the ego and of the nonego, or what we call the fact, are the eternal ideas in God, and the eternal types or models in accordance with which God specifies matter and constructs the world of hypostasis, and advances beings through His mundificative action, according to their genera and species, to perfection and equalization of the real world to the eternal ideal world in Him.

THE RELATIONSHIP

The relationship is the law in accordance with which the nature is connected and associated with its hypostasis. In regard to every being and every occurence we can distinguish the length of time involved in the existence of the fact and of the occurrence, from the length of time involved in the specification and formation of it. During the time that the hypostasis acquires a nature it is being specified, and the relation of the nature to the hypostasis is being determined, as well as of this to the nature, so that the nature bears an analogy to the substance, and the substance bears an analogy to the nature. From the nature we know the value of the hypostasis of the being. Whence could we have known the value of the human hypostasis if we had not known the value of the human nature? The relation is the analogy of the nature to the hypostasis. For the nature grows upon the hypostasis in due proportion and analogy to the value of the hypostasis. This proportion and analogy is the bond and law subsisting between the hypostasis and the nature and evidenced to us by right reason. This law as well as the existence of the hypostasis are revealed to us by reason from the phenomenon of consciousness and perception, from the nature of the being. On this account we admit the existence of a law according to which every nature belongs to some hypostasis and the statement that the nature is proportionate and analogous to the hypostasis. We are thus led back up to the idea of the existence of sempiternal laws and relationships in accordance with which natures are connected with substances in such a manner that each hypostasis is capable of receiving a nature that is proportionate and analogous to it, and so that it is incapable of receiving a nature that belongs to any other hypostasis. Admitting the inalienability of hypostasis, and their unchangeability, we logically infer also the immutability and unchangeability of relationships, and the immutability and unchangeability of the genera and species of the natures, in that the hypostasis of a horse cannot assume the nature of a man, nor can that of a man assume the nature of a horse or of any other animal. But the hypostasis of the God Logos can assume the nature of a man, because there is a likeness between the God Logos and man, man, on the one hand, being an image of God, while God, on the other hand, is the original of man. Wherever, therefore, there is a likeness, a communication of natures is possible ; but wherever there is unlikeness, such communication is precluded : accordingly, every hypostasis assumes the nature that belongs to it in accordance with the law of likeness and of analogy, in accordance with the law of relationship. The notion of relationships enables us to cognize the stability of the law in accordance with which every substance is analogous to its nature, and every nature to its substance; and the fact that, in view of the existence of this law, it is not possible for it to be otherwise. In the process of specifying the hypostasis and forming the beings stracturally, God instituted relationships between the nature and the hypostasis, and gave to every hypostasis the nature belonging to it, and constructed every substance in a manner analogous to its worthiness and to the purpose for which it was made. In cognizing a nonbeing, God cognizes it as though it were an actual being throughout its hypostasis. He cognizes it with respect to its substance, nature, relationship, duration, extension. He cognizes it complete and perfect. Nevertheless, in the process of entification He makes it exceedingly imperfect in the beginning and perfects it gradually and little by little in the course of time in accordance with the requirements of some law of progress and development. Though God might have made the being perfect directly in the beginning out of a nonbeing, this possibility is opposed to His wisdom, which is the source of order and of analogy, precisely as it is also to His design to make rational and free beings progressing and being perfected through their own free action. God does not make everything that He can, but only whatever is consistent with His design and is known by Him to be superior. In other words, He makes only what needs to be made. His power follows His wisdom; accordingly, it does whatever God's wisdom cognizes to be superior. Hence it is evident that graduative creation is a product of God's wisdom. In cognizing the nonbeing as a perfect being, God cognizes the relationship which exists between the nature and the hypostasis, as a bond of both; He sempiternally cognizes in His idea of it the association and relationship of the natures to the hypostasis of the beings; He cognizes the genera and species of the beings; He cognizes in Himself the ontological scale of creation. But it is to be kept in mind that the word c o g n i z e as applied to God signifies that God possesses in Himself sempiternally all the ideas of beings even before they become beings — that is to say, all the ideas of the fact (meaning what has become such), of what is becoming (a fact), and of what is going to become a fact (in the future), and also of what ought to become a fact even before it becomes a fact. In sempiternally cognizing the constant and unchangeable relationships of beings subsisting between their hypostases and natures, God cognizes the sempiternal ontological laws, and their constancy; He cognizes that a horse is perpetually a horse, and that a man is perpetually a man. He cognizes the constancy and unchangeability of relationships, and the incommunicability and unimpartability of unlike natures in reference to unlike hypostases. If the constant law of relationship did not exist, and instead thereof arbitrariness and fortuity ruled, we should continually be observing an inconstancy in beings, the impartation and communication of unlike or even of contrary natures. As a result of the sexual copulation of a man with an irrational animal we should observe the birth of a human being, or of some other animal; as a result of the copulation of a sheep with a dog we should observe the birth of a sheep or of a dog; and as a result of the hatching of the eggs of a hen by a duck or other bird, we should observe the birth of ducklings or of other fledgelings. But no such thing has been attested by past experience, or what is called history; nor does present experience attest it now; nor will future experience be able to attest it, seeing that the law of impartation of natures is constant and unchangeable in the onto-logical scale of genera and species. What has been observed in the past and is observed at present as an exceptional example in nature of the birth of a mule as the result of the copulation of a horse and an ass is attended with the consequence that the mule cannot bring forth young, because of the fact that it does not belong constantly either to the genus of horses or to the genus of asses, and that it forms an order, so to speak, which is peculiar and hermaphroditic. The barrenness of the mule is proof of the constancy of the law of natures, according to which unlike natures cannot be shared, but, on the contrary, are excluded. Hence, just as we admit in accordance with the principle of identity the iden-tity of the substances of contingent beings, so and in like manner we admit, in accordance with the same principle, also the identity of natures, and the identity of relationships, according to which like natures can be communicated to like hypostases. Hence the universally valid law of contradiction is controverted by any theory that teaches the impartability of unlike natures, as does also the inconstancy of their communication, and the vitiation of the constancy of the relationships which subsist in the commu-nication of natures and in the impartation of a nature to the substance analogous thereto. According to these the theory of the evolution of beings from some primordial protoplasm, and of the mutation of genera and species, is quite hostile and repugnant to the nature and order of things, and is discountenanced as false, fantastic, and chimerical by past and present experience, and by right reason, which affords proof of and testifies to the constancy of natural laws and confirmes the identity of beings. The constant relationships between the natures and substances of beings pre-suppose that the substances are constant, and imply that the natures are constant. Hence it is evident that the relationships, the natures, the hypostases, have always been the same ever since the creation of them in the beginning, and that they will be the same until God's disign is actualized. For this reason it may be said that the occurrences of the present bear witness to the facts of the past, as they afford evidence of the necessariness of the Eternal Being, from whom they have received whatever they have. Occurrences are either beings without life, or beings with life but without cognition, or living and thinking beings. In other words, everything that occurs is either a lifeless and mindless being, or an animal, or a human being. Beings are minerals and plants. Animals are beings with life. Man is a being who lives, thinks, and exercises volition (i. e., has desires and wishes). But whence have these facts and occurrences originated? Can it be that the animal has received its life from a plant, or that man has received his cognition from an animal? A plant has no life, but is a means of maintaining life. An animal has no cognition, but is an object of cognition, just as are all other beings. For this reason it is that the plant is born of the seed of a plant, and the animal from the seed of an animal, and a human being from another human being like him. This is attested by the experience of the past and of the present, whence we infer a constant relationship of the genera and species of beings. But what are the causes of occurrences and of facts? It cannot be gainsaid that they are the primordial genera and species of the beings. For, in view of the fact that experience testifies through the history of the past and the eyes of the present that everything that occurs may be said to occur as the result of a like being, and that nothing comes to be out of nonbeing, reason reduces us to cognition of the existence of primordial genera and species of beings, to cognition of the existence of a first genus of minerals, of plants, of animals, and of men, from, which have arisen all the beings that grow, live, and think. But whence have come these primeval orders of genera and species of the beings? It is evident that they have come out of the Eternal Being, who created them according to His ideas of them and according to His design. It is from Him that beings have received their beinghood. It is from Him that living things have received their life. It is from Him that thinking beings have received their cognition and power to think. Hence it is evident that creation is an image of the Eternal Being. Between it and the Eternal Being there obtains a law in accordance with the fact is connected with the Eternal Being, and in accordance with which the fact is perfected so as to become equalized to the Eternal Being. This law and bond is God's design, or, more explicitly speaking, it is the efficient and final Reason of creation.

— Eternal Being — Logos (Reason) — Fact —

Every hypostasis is capable of receiving some nature. But according to the law of relationship between nature and hypostasis, the nature must be analogous to the hypostasis. For, if God sempiternally cognizes man even before creating him, He cognizes him, of course, as having a hypostasis, and a nature analogous thereto. He cognizes him continuously and sempiternally as being the same throughout his essence, in accordance with the principle of identity; and it is impossible for God to cognize rationally a hypostasis of a human being with a nature of an ass, or a hypostasis of an ass with a nature of human being. A human being is equal to a human being, and an ass to an ass. This is the necessary law of the spirit, according to which law that which is cognized as a human being cannot at the same time be cognized also as an ass, and vice verca. This law is the law of contradiction and the principle of identity. As God cognizes, so too does He do. Hence there is identity in point of thinking (cognizing), and identity in point of doing. If God cannot cognize rationally a hypostasis, of a human being with a nature of an ass, it follows that He cannot create or make any tragelaphic being either. It is for this reason, too, that we do not observe any tragelaphs in creation. It is for this reason that a man has never conceived with a bitch and begotten a dog, nor has a dog conceived with a woman and begotten a human being. What is logically possible is also actually possible. But what is logically impossible is also actually impossible. What is logically possible is also naturally possible. But what is logically impossible is also naturally impossible, or, in a word, unnatural. God cognizes what is logically possible, and creates what is naturally possible, what ought to be made. Whatever God cognizes is logically possible, and for this reason it is also actually possible. He creates what is best and finest and most consonant with His design. All of God's cognitions, or thoughts, are consistent with His final design, which is the criterion of every thought and of every act of His. But God's thought is an external judgment or decision of His which becomes also an external fact. So thus it may be said that God sempiternally judges or decides that man must remain forever man, the sheep forever a sheep, the plant forever a plant; accordingly He mades it a rule that their identity must exist everlastingly. But as He judges and decides, so He does and creates; and it is for this reason that if anything that has been created or made in time be compared with God's sempiternal judgment and decision regarding it, it will be found to be consistent and consonant therewith. But a being is to be compared with God's sempiternal judgment and decision only after it matures and assumes all its nature and becomes perfect in its species and order. For then will a harmony and conconance and wonderful equalization become evident as between the idea and the being. In becoming thus perfected and exalted, the real world of beings becomes equalized to the sempiternal ideal world in God; and the latter is the ideal towards which the temporal real world is directed by God's action.

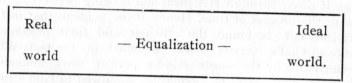

Real		Ideal
world	— Equalization —	world.

The ideal world is an image of the real, its model and idea. The real world is the ontological world. The ideal world is the standard of the ontological. The ideal world is the sempiternal; the real world is the temporal and eternal (i.e., agelong or world - long), because, having received a beginning it shall have also an end, which will be its perfection, and its equalization to the ideal world. In the ideal (or ideological) world God's idea rules all the ideas that exist in God, because it possesses hypostatical beinghood, as the idea of a perfect Being, and not as the idea of a nonbeing, like the hypostatical ideas of what are only possibly or contingently beings. The Idea of God is identical with His Design, because God judges and wishes and decisively determines things not in accordance with the ideas of contingent and finite beings, but in accordance with His infinite and absolute Idea, which is the product of His perfect Essence, a product which is begotten of Him through His perfect cognition, or, more expressly speaking, through His Spirit. In the real world, on the other hand, that which rules all beings that have been made in time is God's most perfect being, His most perfect work, that which has been made in accordance with God's design, and has been wrought out after His image and likeness. Between this being and the onhypostatic (or substantiated) Idea of the Eternal Being there exists a likeness and analogy; and for this reason communication is possible on the score of the mutuality of their natures (N o t e o f T r a n s l a t o r. — The meaning of the word «mutuality» here is not perfectly clear to me; it probably was meant to signify much the same as «interchangeableness»). God's perfect Idea, which He has within Him, and God's most perfect being, which is embodied in the fact, bear a resemblance to each other, or have a likeness. For God's perfect Idea is an image of the essence of the Eternal Being, whereas, on the other

hand, the Eternal Being's most perfect work, which is embodied
in the fact, is an image of His perfect Design, which, in turn, is
the same thing as His perfect Idea. Hense it is evident that both
of these are images of one and the same original; the one of them
is sempiternally perfect, whereas the other is imperfect in the
beginning, being subject to perfection with the passage of time.
But since God's perfect Idea is the type, or model, of God perfect
work embodied in the fact, we conclude that the latter was created
through it (i. e., through His Idea) and is being perfected through
it now in the process of time. Hence it is evident that in God's
perfect Idea is to be found the efficient and final reason of the
existence of God's perfect work embodied in the fact. What is
here referred to by the words «God's perfect work embodied in
the fact» is man, who is becoming equalized to God's infinite
Idea and ultimate Design. The nature of the perfect man, and the
nature of the perfect and onhypostatic Idea of God, can commune mutually; and it is upon this logically possible communication that the reality of the incarnation of the substantive Idea
of God, in the perfect Man, our Lord Jesus Christ, is based and
supported. The Substance of the Logos of God can commune, or
enter into communion, with the nature of the perfect man and
become incarnate; accordingly, the hypostasis of man can commune with the nature of God and become deified. Moreover, this
which is logically possible also really occurred; and the reality
of it already has become manifest to our eyes. The Logos of God
became a perfect man, became visible to us as a God—man, as a
perfect God and a perfect human being; and the perfect human
being became a God, was deified, and became equalized to God.
The Logos in His divine and infinite and sempiternal hypostasis
assumed the nature of the perfect man and deified it; man, on
the other hand, in his finite and temporal hypostasis assumes the
nature of God and becomes deified. The Logos deifies the perfect
man. The perfect man personifies and images God in creation.
Hence it is evident that every perfect human being is a God—man,
because he images God and himself. But in particular it is Jesus
Christ that is the God—man, because He images God in point of
essence, possessing a divine and sempiternal and infinite hypostasis, whereas the perfect human being images God in point of
nature, as having his hypostasis contingent and made in time,
come to be such and finite.

The constant law of the unchangeability of hypostasis is
also the law of their unimpartability. For this reason neither can
the hypostasis of the Eternal Being be imparted to the fact, nor
can the hypostasis of the fact be imparted to the Eternal Being.
The identity is their eternal character; and the contradiction is

their eternal law. Neither can the Eternal Being become a fact, nor can the fact become Eternal Being. The Eternal Being, however, can partake, or have a common share, of the nature, or, more expressly, of the attributes, of the fact; and the fact can partake, or have a share, of the Eternal Being's nature likewise. The impartability of the nature does not imply an impartability of the hypostasis. Nor does the unimpartability of the hypostasis imply an umimpartability of the nature. The nature can be imparted, but the substance is unimpartable. But it is to be noted that the impartation of the nature is a different thing from its unchangeability. Natures, we said further above, are unchangeable, and they cannot become unlike themselves or become something different. The nature of a human being cannot deteriorate into that of an ass, nor can the nature of an ass become that of a human being, according to the principle of identity, to the effect that natures are ever the same, being peculiar to the substances of which they are predicated. The relationship between substances and natures is the law of their consonance and analogy and purposefulness. Thus the divine nature cannot become human, nor can the human nature become divine. But the substance of the God Logos can assume a human nature, and can make His appearance in the world as a human being. Likewise the hypostasis of a human being can assume the nature of God, and present him as a God before the eyes of God. This possibility of occurrence is also logically possible, and it really occurred. For the incarnation of the Logos is nothing else than a revelation of God in the form of a human being. It was an assumption, or taking on, of human nature in connection with the divine substance of the Logos. The deification of man, on the other hand, is an assumption, or taking on, of divine nature, in connection with the human hypostasis, and is the rational, moral, and spiritual exaltation of man. The nature of God belongs to the substance of God and to the substance of man. And the nature of man likewise belongs to the hypostasis of man and to the hypostasis of God. In other words: The substance of the Logos is capable of receiving the nature of a human being, because the Logos is the standard or measure of man. But the hypostasis of man, on the other hand, is capable of receiving the nature of the Logos, because man is an image of the Logos. It follows, therefore, that as between like natures there is a law of mutual communication; but as between unlike and contrary natures there exists an incommunicability and an unapproachability. A man cannot impart his nature to another and different being, unlike him, but can impart it only to one like him, to a rational and free being. But both God and man are rational and free beings.

Therefore it is evident that human nature can be imparted to both God and man. Moreover, God does impart His nature to those who are beings like Him. But every rational and free being is like God. Hence it is evident that God imparts His own nature to rational and free beings, among whom is man. But as between a nature and a hypostasis there obtains the law of contradiction, and that of identity, of likeness, and of analogy — there exists the relationship cognized between them. The law of the communication of natures, of those which are alike, the same, and analogous. The same comes from the same — like comes from like — what is analogous is produced out of what is analogous. Every substance is capable of receiving some nature. The natures, on the other hand, are analogous to the worthiness and order of the hypostasis.

Hypostasis — Relationship — Nature.

The lower hypostasis possesses a lower nature. Natures are graduated, or graded, according to their hypostases, and the latter according to their natures. The hypostasis of a mineral is lower than that of a plant; and the latter than the hypostasis of an animal or human being. Hence it is evident that their natures are graduated likewise. But above and over these hypostases is the first and perfect and absolute hypostasis of the Eternal Being, which has a perfect and absolute nature, together with a perfect and absolute relationship. From this hypostasis it was that all the hypostases of beings received beinghood creatively; and it was in accordance with the hypostatic Idea of the first substance of the Eternal Being that the higher hypostasis in the fact was formed structurally, and received its own nature; this refers to man. The perfect hypostasis of the Eternal Being, cognizing Itself perfectly, begets another hypostasis out of Itself, equal to It and the very image of It; and with this second hypostasis it becomes related in point of equality through a third hypostasis emanated out of the first. And thus God's sempiternal Essence comprises: 1) the first and chief sempiternal hypostasis. 2) the sempiternal hypostatic Idea; 3) the sempiternal substantive Relationship. Hence it is evident that there are three hypostases to be distinguished in the Godhead, namely: that of the Being, that of the Truth, and that of the Cognition. The first and chief hypostasis is the productive and creative cause of beings. The second is formative and mundificative (or «world — creative») of them. The third hypostasis is cohesive, conservative, and regulative of them. The hypostases of beings are images of the absolute Being. Their natures are images of the absolute and hypostatic Idea of God. Their relationships are images of the absolute and hypostatic Relationship of the Being. Hence the Eternal Being is an absolute Existence, and an absolute Idea, and an absolute Relationship. One God essentially, in three Substances. These divine Substances, as being alike, have a common Nature; and on this account and for this reason they are said to be co—essential, or homoousian, meaning of the same Essence. Thus from the notion of the relationship between contigent and finite hypostases and natures we have been led back up to cognition of the one absolute and necessary hypostatic Relationship of the Eternal Being, subsisting between the hypostasis and His hypostatic Idea. We therefore can now cognize the absolute Essence as an absolute Beinghood, as an absolute Idea, and as an absolute Relationship. We can cognize the possibility of impartation of the divine Nature to the substance of man, the substance of man being capable of receiving it; and we can also cognize the possibility of impartation of the human nature to the hypostasis of God. We can cognize the possibility of the birth of the God—man. Accordingly, we are going to proceed to prove this logically in the following manner. What is logically possible is what also actually occurred. Accordingly, it is to be pointed out that the incarnation of the Logos in the person of Christ is the reality of this logical possibility of the divine incarnation of the Logos in man.

EXTENSION

Extension is the space which each being occupies in the order of beings; space is that which contains the beings, which are the contents of it —it is the immense expanse in which beings exist and move and act, and the ends or bounds of which elude our percipience. We observe that each being occupies a certain region, or portion of space. And we can extend this observation of ours inductively to all beings in general, judging that every being occupies some space or other, and that every space is occupied by some being or other. Therefore we conceive space as a whole to be suitable for the beings, and the beings to be sufficient to fill it. Hence we also judge that there is nowhere any empty space, or any being that lacks and is outside of space. Whatever is, is in space and time; and there is no being that is in lack of space and outside of space. Consequently we can cognize the fact that space is one of the conditions for the existence of a being; for this reason we also cognize the notion of space as an element of the idea of a being. Space is a bounded extension. Every being occupies a certain bounded extension. All beings as a whole occupy the whole of extension. But between extension and beings there is observed a proportion and an analogy. For there exists as much extension as there are beings, and space is as extensive as beings. Every space of a finite being is finite. Taken together the spaces of finite beings are finite even in their totality. Finite beings are what constitute the fact. Hence it is evident that even finite space is a fact, having commenced existing when the beings received their beginning. But before the fact what was there? The infinite Being, and the consequently infinite space, the infinite extension. But this infinite extension is the infinite Spirit in which the infinite Being exists. Hence it may be said that everything that is a fact exists in a part of finite space, while the Eternal Being exists in the infinite Spirit. But what is this infinite Being and the infinite Spirit? Can it be said, however, that we have attained to an understanding of what the finite being is, of what the fact is? or can it be said that we have surveyed finite space so as to be able to cognize or understand what the infinite Being is, and what the infinite Spirit is? If when we are finite and in finite space we not yet succeded in gaining a knowledge of that which is finite, how can we expect to gain a knowledge of that which is infinite, which can be comprehended only through and in an infinite Being? We know that there is an infinite Being and an infinite Spirit, by contrast with what is finite and the fact, and with finite space. For we can cognize the fact that above and over the fact and what is finite there cannot be cognized or conceived any other finite being, or anything else but one absolute Being in an infinite Spirit. One absolute Essence, sempiternal, cognitive, and volitive, cognizing in a perfect and infinite Spirit, and having the Idea of It sempiternal. The creative source of finite space is the infinite Spirit, in which the infinite Being exists. Its end and bound is the infinite Spirit, which contains the infinite Being, and is contained in the infinite Being. If we abstract the bounds of space, we abstract that which is finite and conceive everything in the infinite to be infinite. But by means of reason and spirit we can conceive and cognize the infinite Being and the infinite Spirit; and in this cognition and conception we are communing with the infinite, aiming at it, and earnestly wishing to get out of what is finite. Were there within us no cognitive spirit, nor a law to cognize the infinite, we could not have any Idea of the infinite, nor the ability to look towards It. Our tendency towards the infinite arises from our meeting with it in discourse, and through reason, whereby we can cognize the perfect, and absolute, and sempiternal existence of it. Nevertheless, the cognition we have of the infinite

Being is imperfect and slight. What this infinite is we cannot understand except in so far as we commune with the infinite and become initiated into its mysteries. Cognition of the infinite demands an infinite spirit. So if we know the beings roundabout us very imperfectly, how much more we shall know the infinite Being! The more we know the perfect man, the more we attain to a conception of God and knowledge of the infinite. Perfect knowledge of the perfect man is tantamount to perfect knowledge of God, for the perfect man is a perfect image of God. The perfect man exists in the infinite Spirit, in which He lives, acts, thinks, and moves. So, then, it may be said that everything that is a fact is in finite space and in finite extension. But the Eternal Being is in the infinite Spirit, in which He lives, and thinks, and exercises His will and power. The infinite, indeed, is the efficient and final cause of finite space, as the Eternal Being is the efficient and creative cause of the fact. The infinite is the sempiternal and necessary space of the Eternal Being. Finite space, on the other hand, is the contingent region of contingent beings. As it came into being, so it may also go out of existence. Abolishment of contingent space is abolishment of the finiteness of beings, and their introduction into the infinite. In the perfect man finiteness is abolished, for His cognition cognizes and comprehends the infinite infinitely. The instrument for cognizing the infinite is the Spirit, which in the perfect man is infinite. But after we receive the Spirit of God infinitely, we shall also cognize the infinite infinitely. Infinite cognition, be it noted, takes us out of the finite, and at the same time imbues us with an infinite nature, and makes us be, and live, and think in the infinite.

DURATION

The duration of a being is the length of time and of the life which it leads and during which it lasts. Every being has a beginning and an end of existence. From its beginning and on until it reaches its end it traverses a straight line, and covers a distance called the duration of the being or its time. Time, like space, co-exists together with a being; accordingly, as there is no being that does not reside in a region of space, so is there no being that does not persist during an interval of time. As a result of observation of numerous beings that have a duration, we judge inductively that every being has a beginning, and a duration, and an end of existence.

> Beginning — duration — end.

Time contains everything; accordingly, every being has a duration and a time, and there is no being without and outside of time. But if every being has a duration, all beings taken together — the sum - total of beings, which we call the world — have a duration and a time, in which and during which they persist or last. But inasmuch as the sum - total of beings which constitute the world are of a finite nature, are the fact, their time is also of a finite nature, is a fact. Hence from the notion of particular time we have been led back up to the notion of finite time, to the general idea of finite duration; and from this idea we are logically led back, or reduced, to a conception of sempiternal eternity, and of sempiternal duration, which is the time of the absolute Being. Finite time begins, lasts, and terminates. The bounds of it are eternity. It starts from eternity, and ends at eternity. Its duration, conceived as a straight line, is trisected into a past, a present, and a future. The beginning of time is the instant when nonbeing is entified and receives a hypostasis. The end of it is the instant when the fact and being matures and acquires whatever goes to make up its nature. The beginning of time is the incomplete existence of the fact; the end of it is the finish or maturity of the latter. Duration and time proper is a s e r i e s   i n   t h e   f o r m   o f   a   s u c - c e s s i v e   s e q u e n c e   o f   v a r i o u s   t r a n s m u t a t i o n s   o f   a n d   c h a n g e s   i n   t h e   f a c t . This successive sequence of changes begins with the entification of the fact and terminates with its finish or maturity. If we abstract the beginning and the end of time, we abstract therewith the duration of beings, and instead of time we then have eternity, which is the efficient and final cause of time. For whence comes time? From eternity! But why, then, was time given? In order that we might be perfected, or attain to maturity, in it and enter upon eternity. But what is eternity? If we are unable to comprehend the vast sea of finite time, how shall we be able to comprehend eternity? What do we know out of the past of time? And what out of the present, and out of the future? We barely even imperfectly know the past of time, as we do also the present of it. As for the future of it, we know it from our knowledge of the past and of the present as though through an image. Eternity is the sempiternal duration of the Eternal Being. The duration of the Eternal Being endures as long as He does. Sempiternal and perpetual existence. Sempiternal and perpetual life. Sempiternal and perpetual cognition, volition, and power. A sempiternal and perpetual Mind, Logos (or Reason), and Spirit, and endless sempiternity constitute the eternity of the infinite and perfect and absolute Being. In God there is no past and future, but, on the contrary, in His eyes everything is present, and by means of His cognition God beholds everything at an immediate, momentary, and instantaneous, so to speak, glance. His cognition pervades everything, and for this reason it penetrates into all things at the same time and together, immediately and contemporaneously. In the sight of the infinite Being's infinite cognition, the universe stands nude and revealed, and God stands a beholder of all things and a governor thereof, everywhere present and pervading all things. He is present everywhere because He is in the infinite Spirit, through which He cognizes everything infinitely. He pervades all things because He is contained in the infinite and contains the infinite. But as He is in the infinite, so too does He behold things in the infinite, and there is nothing that is hidden from His cognition. God is in the infinite and in eternity, as an infinite and eternal Being. If we had no rational cognition, how could we cognize eternity and acquire an idea of it? Through consciousness and perception experience furnishes us the idea of finite time, as well as the idea of finite space. But as for the idea of eternity and of infinity, we have these ideas from reason and rational cognition, whereby we are led back up to cognition of eternity and of infinity. And it cannot be otherwise. For if we can logically cognize the necessary existence of an absolute Being, as the cause of the numerous beings in existence, yet we cannot cognize this Being without absolute time and absolute space, or, in other words, without eternity and infinity.

Infinity — — Eternal Being — — Eternity.

But we know neither what the Eternal Being is in depth, nor consequently what His infinity and eternity are. The knowledge we now possess concerning the Eternal Being, as concerning His infinity and eternity, differs from the knowledge which we seek concerning the nature of the Eternal Being and concerning His infinity and eternity. We know through reason that the Eternal Being is necessarily in infinity and eternity, but we are ignorant of what this Eternal Being is, and of what His infinity and eternity are. These matters are problems awaiting solution. They can be solved and proved [through the spirit and right reason. Hence it is evident that it is from Reason — i. e.,

the Logos — and through Reason that we ought to expect the
solution and proof of them : for the Logos is well aware of what
the Eternal Being is, and of what His infinity and eternity are.
Through the Logos, or Reason, when our cognition is guided
like a child being led by the hand, we are led up to contemplation and comprehension of the infinite, and are enabled to enter
upon the infinite.

The fact is outside of the Eternal Being. Therefore it may
be said to be outside of infinity and eternity also. But the Eternal
Being is also in the fact. Therefore it may be said that He is
also in finite space and time. For the fact received its beinghood
from the Eternal Being, and also received its duration from
eternity, and its extension from infinity. The bounds of the fact
are time and space, within which the fact begins, progresses, and
matures, or come to perfection. This work is work that is done
in time and space. For this reason the means for performing
this work are proportionate and analogous to the accomplishment
of the work, which is being performed and continues through
the sequence of the ages and in suitable space. But after the work
being performed has been consummated in space and time, and
the seal of perfection has been placed on it by the Creator of the
universe, the bounds of the fact shall be abolished, i.e., space
and time shall be done away with, and the fact will thereupon
enter within the infinite Spirit and come into eternity, thenceforth being infinite and eternal and remaining forever in a state
of imperishability. But until the fact actually matures and attains
to a state of perfection, the existence of time and space is necessary; and so are the instruments and means needed for the
purpose of perfecting it and bringing it to maturity, which,
however, are necessarily abolished and done away with as soon
as the work is finished and terminated. The instruments and
means for the purpose of perfecting the fact are the laws governing it and prescribing how it is to be constructed, arranged, regulated, and perfected. The laws governing the fact are the law
of birth and death, of generation und decay. When the birth and
generation of beings is done away with and abolished, the introduction of new beings into the world will cease. With the abolishment of decay and death, the beings that have been perfected
will become inperishable, and all living beings will become immortal. Hence it is evident that imperishability, life, and immortality, these attributes of the infinite Spirit, will then prevail.
Moreover, all the spiritual means whereby the ego becomes perfected will also be abolished, as well as the spiritual modes of
cognition. Only one of our cognitive and spiritual abilities will
remain perpetually and eternally, to wit, the ability to contem-

plate immediately the Eternal Being and all the beings in Him, a contemplation which is accomplished through the immediate glance of the Spirit. Everything, and even the infinite itself, will then stand revealed before the eyes of the cognizing ego, and will be immediately and directly cognizable, without reflections and reasonings and memory, as it is cognized now, but, instead, will be perceptually cognizable in the infinite Spirit. In cognizing the infinite in the infinite Spirit, the e g o will become likewise infinite. But now, being in finite time and space, we cognize the Eternal Being imperfectly through right reason, and through logical cognition we contact Him while aiming at the infinite, for which an ardent wish and vehement desire is engendered within us as a result of this cognition of the infinite. But then, when the fact shall have been perfected, we shall cognize the infinite as it is, as if looking at face to face, and no longer amid shadows, and in parables, and in riddles, and in a mirror : we shall cognize it immediately and directly, perceptually, not conceptually, and the wish, the yearning, and the vehement desire within us to enjoy the infinite Being shall be fullfilled. In the face of this perfectness there will be the eternal consciousness of our former imperfectness, with which we started and have been brought to perfection, and the cognition of our perfectness, which is the perfect work of God. Between the perfected ego and the perfect God there will be the eternal partition of the work of the ego finished in time from the sempiternally existent perfect God. It is evident, therefore, that we shall retain eternal consciousness of the being perfected in time, namely, the ego, and of the eternally perfect Being. But now, while we are situated in the realm of space and time, and are being worked up by God for the purpose of our being perfected, it is our obligation to be plastic material in the hands of God, by conforming to His will as moral and free beings, and diligently obeying His commandments. We ought to listen to His words and do whatever He enjoins upon us, with the awareness that our progress and perfection depend upon heeding and executing the words of God and consist in strict observance of His commandments. In walking the way of the Lord, we are walking the way of our progress and of our perfection, are availing ourselves of the time allotted to us for this purpose, and are being perfected in virtue, which is also the viaticum of eternity, and the chief attribute of the perfect and infinite Being. By thus preparing ourselves we gain admission to the eternity and infinity of God, being, and living, and thinking, and exercising power infinitely and eternally in God.

PERFECT BEINGHOOD = A BEING

We naturally aim at perfetion, at what is perfect, which precludes any want or excess and possesses everything that it ought to have, being complete and self - sufficient and in need of nothing. Our yearning is perfect, because it is filled by acquisition and possession of what is perfect. What is perfect is nowise identical with the essence of me, the one aiming at it. For if it were the same as I, I myself should be the perfect one. Every yearning in me after the perfect is an obvious contradiction. For, if I were the perfect one or what is perfect, how could I be yearning after what is perfect? My yearning after it is patent testimony offered by experience, which testifies that our entire life is a certain tendency or trend towards progress. But neither is what is perfect identical with the world. For, if the world were the same as what is perfect, it would therefore be perfect. Therefore all of its parts would also be perfect. In that case I should find in the world that which is perfect. For example, I should find it in the acquisition and possession of material goods, in my living in accordance with the laws of nature. But, as I learn from experience, material goods cannot satisfy the infinite yearning in me after what is perfect, nor can the laws of nature secure the wish I have for life. Wealth, glory, beauty, strength, are apparent goods that only cheer me for the time being, not being able to make me happy forever and eternally blissful. Hense it is to be inferred that the world and the goods of the world have not what is perfect, nor are perfect themselves, because they too become, unbecome, turn into something else, are transmuted, and are changed. But what is transmuted and chanّ ged is progressing and is not perfect. For what is perfect does not progress, nor consequently is it transmuted or changed. Hence it follows that the world and I, as imperfect beings, are progressing while being transmuted and changed and aiming at what is perfect, which is the efficient and final condition and reason of my existence. Between our imperfect nature and the nature of what is perfect — a nature which is complete and self-sufficient and wantless — there may be cognized the existence of progress, which is effected through transmutation and change as a result of the influence of what is perfect upon us imperfect beings.

Imperfectness — Wantfulness—Progress — Perfectness

What is perfect, being nowise identical with the essence of me and of the world, is not identical with both either. Accordingly, it may be said that Pantheism is a tragelaphic system refuted by right reason as stupidity and as a grievous error, into which fell Fichte, Spinoza, and Hegel, these three advocates of Pantheism, who identified what is perfect with the imperfect ego and world, and idolatrously deified creation instead of the Creator, or confused the Creator with His creatures and took the creatures to be modes and forms and representations of the Being that are sempiternal and necessary. Hence it is evident that what is perfect lies outside of me and the world and is something else than the essence of the ego and of the world, or, in other words, it is something of a different essence than they are, and not of the same essence. What is perfect obtains as the final condition of the existence of both me and the world at which we are aiming through progress, which joins our imperfectness with the perfectness of the perfect Being. That which is perfect, being something of a different essence than we are, is also immutable and unchangeable and unalterable, nowise progressing, but, on the contrary, being ever the same and maintaining the same habitude forever. From it begins and at it aims what is imperfect; what is imperfect progresses through and is perfected in it. In thus being conceived what is perfect is conceived as a being, and not as a becoming (or occurrence in time), as a being in itself and as an eternal being, and not as a being come through another and derived from another, as something that has become and is a thing existing in time. Being perfect, it is the possessor of everything in repletion and perfection, whatever is considered a being and regarded as existing in the fact. Now in the fact and being there are: 1) the beinghood of every being; 2) the process of living; 3) the process of thinking and exercising cognition; 4) the process of exercising power. The hypostasis, or beinghood; the nature; the relationship; the extension; the duration. For in regard to every being in the fact we observe these same things, but in a state of imperfection and progressive action. The beinghood of every being is its beginning and the center towards which the circumference of its nature and attributes turns. The beinghood of the fact, and its essence when it is denuded of every attribute, is the primordial matter out of which the genera and species of the beings were formed and the world of beings and of essences was made. Matter is whatever is in ignorance of its own existence. It is beinghood without awareness. The primordial

hypostasis of the fact is the most imperfect beinghood whereof
the efficient and final condition of existence is that which is
perfect, the perfect Essence. It is said to be efficient because
matter could not have become of itself, nor could it have been
entified spontaneously. It is said to be final because, after being
entified by the will and power of the perfect Being, it aims at
having perfection bestowed upon it by the perfect Being, in
conformity with the law of gradual progress, owing to its being
imperfect. Thus the perfect Being, as creative, through entification
of matter out of nothing, as formative, and effigiative and con-
figurative of the beings, and as conservative and gubernative of
the world in accordance with the common law of the progress
and gradual development and perfection of beings from imperfect
to perfect, is conclusively shown to be a being having both life
and volition and power and extension and duration, in perfect
measure, and in contrast to the imperfectness of the fact, with
which it is related by a perfect relationship, as we shall see.
Having in Himself life and cognition and perfectness sempiternally, the perfect Being lives and thinks and wills (or exercises
volition) sempiternally. Being and living and thinking and exercising power infinitely, He resides outside of space and every
other region, just as He is, and lives, and thinks, and exercises
power outside of all time, in eternity. Being and living and
thinking sempiternally and infinitely. He possesses an infinite
and sempiternal nature and power, and relationship between His
beinghood and His nature ; and He is a source of self-entity, of
self-vitality, and of self-cognitivity. He is the source of everything that exists, in the fact and the being. Cognizing sempiternally and infinitely, He is a being that is sempiternally and
infinitely cognitive. A self-knowing and all-knowing Mind,
overseeing all things and knowing all things, superintending and
supervising everything, cognizing the nonbeing and the being in
perfect measure. Thus the Essence of the perfect Being, His beinghood, is found to be a Spirit, because He knows that He is
existent and because He has perfect consciousness of Himself, of
the Being and of the fact, and is conscious of being a self-knowing and all-knowing being. That is why the God-man defined
God as a Spirit, by saying : «God is a Spirit; and they who pay
him adoration ought to pay adoration in spirit and truth» (John
4 : 24). The perfect Being, as a perfect Mind, cognizes perfectly
what is perfect, or, more expressly, Himself. But in this perfect
cognition, which is sempiternal and infinite, and which is one in
which the infinite cognizes itself infinitely, He begets the perfect
and sempiternal and infinite Idea of Himself through which He
cognizes Himself and the fact, the Being and the contingent. The

perfect Idea of the Being, moreover, is an express image of Him, portraying and representing the hypostasis of the Being, His nature, relationship, extension, and duration. The Idea of the Being, as an image of His perfect hypostasis is a hypostasis out of a hypostasis a beinghood out of a beinghood, an essence out of an essence, one who is of the same essence as the Being Himself; He is indeed an infinite and sempiternal offspring of the beinghood of the Being. Being a hypostasis out of a hypostasis He possesses a beinghood distinct from that of the Being. But His beinghood is also an awareness that He is the sempiternal and infinite principle of awareness, because it is through Him that the perfect Being cognizes and knows Himself. Thus the Being may be said to be the sempiternal and infinite principle of beinghood, since it is from Him that the beinghood of awareness originates. The Idea, that is to say, is the sempiternal and infinite principle of awareness, because all cognition and knowledge comes through the Idea. But the cognizing Mind, cognizing Himself through Himself, and begetting the sempiternal and infinite Idea which is equal to Him, cognizes through a perfect cognitive ability, through a perfect Spirit. This cognition is the living of the Being; wherefore the Spirit is Life, and for this reason is called life - creative (in Greek: z o o p i o s). This perfect Life of the Spirit is both sempiternal and infinite being emanated out of the Being, and reposing in His Idea, and through the latter being transmited to all intelligent and rational creation. As equal to the hypostasis of the Being and to His Idea, it is a hypostasis out of a hypostasis emanated sempiternally and infinitely, having the nature of the Being and of His Idea, of the same essence as the Being and His Idea. As a self - lived and self - conscious hypostasis it is the principle of living and of consciousness, the principle of the metaphysical light of cognition and of consciousness, because from and through it result the living and the thinking of the Being and of His Idea. The Spirit in the perfect Being is the means of living and of thinking, and the principle of Life and of Cognition. His Idea is the means by which He cognizes Himself, and is the principle of awareness. The Being, on the other hand, is the absolute principle of the existence of His perfect Idea and of the perfect Spirit. The Idea of the Being is the absolute principle of awareness, and not of beinghood — the absolute principle of awareness and the source of every idea and knowledge. The Spirit, on the other hand, or, more explicitly speaking, the Life of the perfect Being, is the absolute principle of living, and consequently the source of life and of immortality. These three absolute principles of beinghood, of awareness, and of living are three Existences having the same nature. They are three distinct hypostases sempiternal and infinite personalities, identifiable as the Mind, the Logos, and the Spirit; or as the Being, the Idea, and the Cognition (or Thought); or as the Father, the Son, and the Holy Spirit, according to the diction of Holy Writ and the words of the Logos of God who became incarnate as a human being. These three hypostases or perfect sonalities, are three Beings distinct from each other in one Essence, because they possess in common a single nature, predicated of them all. Thus, while they are distinguishable by their peculiar character into three hypostases from the common predicament involved in all the hypostases they constitute one single Essence that is simple, and incomposite, and indivisible, the Essence of the Deity, which Essence is otherwise referred to as the perfect Spirit. Hence it is evident that the perfect Being is a Mind, a Logos, and a Spirit, infinite and sempiternal — a Trinity in a Unity, and a Unity in a Trinity of persons; or, in other words, a God Mind, a God Logos, a God Spirit — not three Gods of a different essence, but three personalities of the same essence—omoousios— one God, the Creator of heaven and earth, and of all things visible and invisible.

THE PERFECT NATURE OF THE BEING

The perfect Being has a perfect nature, equal and analogous to His existence and hypostasis. But let us proceed to reflect upon the question of what the perfect nature of the Being is. In saying «nature» we mean the sum - total of the attributes of the Being with which He co - exists and through which He is known and distinguished from other beings. The perfect Being is a perfect Spirit. Consequently He has a spiritual nature. It is sempiternal and infinite cognition and volition and sensation. The Being's cognition cognizes everything, and there is nothing that escapes it; for this reason the attribute of universal knowledge, of omniscience, belongs to God alone. In this omniscience God knows the beginning and end of beings and the means by which they can fulfill their destiny. Hence it is evident that He possesses the attribute of all - wiseness, because wisdom consists in conceiving a design and end in being aware of means whereby this may be actualized. But in His wisdom God distributes and grants to each and every being that which is analogous to it and which belongs to it. Hence it is evident that He is just, acting and proceeding with equality and justice. But in the process of distributing goods with justice, God prevails and predominates in power, and there is no one that can frustrate His design or obstruct His activity. Hence it is evident that He is powerful enough to be able to do all things. He possesses, in other words, the attribute of omnipotence. But in His activity God acts and proceeds of His own accord, having His goodness, benevolence, and morality as His motive, as a result of which He does all things, such, for instance, as is to be seen in the fact that He creates matter out of nothing, which matter is the substance (hypostasis) of the world : He molds and forms it in accordance with His will ; He governs and conserves the beings and directs them to their best end. Hence it is evident that He possesses all - goodness and all - holiness ; for in whatever He thinks, wills, and acts, and feels, He never thinks mistakenly, neither does He will or do anything wicked, but always what is good. In His omnipotence by which He always does what is good and never what is wicked, being prevented by His goodness and holiness, God is conscious that He Himself is supreme over all, the sovereign of all, and master over all. Therefore it is evident that God possesses also the attribute of sovereignty and of absolute authority over all, because He is the Creator and Governor of everything. Evidently, therefore, God is a Being in His Essence and hypostasis that is triune, all - wise, all - powerful, all - good, all - holy, just, sovereign, self - knowing, and all - knowing, creative, and the creator and conserver of the world. A perfect Being that is blissful, both ever - living and immortal. That, however, which distinguishes the Essence of God from the essence of the ego and of the world is His perfectness, or more expressly speaking, the sempiternity of His Existence, Life, and Cognition, His infiniteness and His absoluteness. God is a sempiternal Spirit, whereas the ego of a human being is in the beginning a nonbeing, an unsubstantiated idea in the intellect of the perfect Being. In being produced out of nonbeing as matter, it receives an existence and substance outside of the Being: it receives beingness without aliveness and awareness, and is a simple atom and particle of matter, which through the process of physical birth receives cognition and consciousness of itself by virtue of God's Spirit. Between the Being, the ego, and the world there subsists the limit of eternalness and of becomingness, which distinguishes the one and multiple sempiternal and infinite nature of the perfect Being from the nature of the fact, a nature which becomes, unbecomes, turns into something else, is transmuted and changed, until it becomes fully developed and mature and equal to the perfect nature of the Being. Overlooking this distinction, the objective Pantheism of Spinoza identified the fact with the Being, and took the ego and the world to be modes, forms, and representations of the Essence of God, thus abnegating the freedom and self - authority of the ego. But the subjective Pantheism of

Fichte and of Hegel identified the Being with the fact and deified the fact, thus abnegating God's objective existence as distinct from the existence of the ego and of the world. Nevertheless this distinction between the Being and the fact kills Pantheism and establishes Philosophy on solid ground because it opens to it a wide range of activity for the quest and discovery of the truth. The sempiternal and infinite nature of the Being together with the sempiternal and infinite hypostasis of the Mind, of the Logos, and of the Spirit, are the sempiternal and infinite Being, the efficient and final cause of finite beings, the source of all existence, of all life, and of all cognition. The sempiternal and infinite nature of the Being is impartable to beings which God endowed with the ability to be and to live and to cognize and to think. But the beingness of the Being, the hypostasis of the Mind, of the Logos, and of the Spirit, is unimpartable, just as the sempiternity is by nature unimpartable. Though partaking of the nature of the Being, because it cognizes through God's sempiternal Spirit, the ego does not partake of the Essence and of the hypostasis of the Being — a thing which otherwise inclines to Pantheism, which teaches that the Substance of the Being is the same as the hypostasis of the fact, and thus confuses things that are by nature distinct and unconfusable. Being by nature capable of receiving and assuming God's perfect nature upon itself, the ego by nature becomes enamored of perfectness. The perfectness, however, is the impartation of God's perfect nature to the ego's substance. For any beings that do not yearn after infinite perfection, like plants and animals, are incapable of receiving a share of God's perfect nature and of entering into communication with God. Man alone, by nature aiming at what is perfect, and craving for perfection, is receptive of God's infinite nature. Hence it is evident that he is receptive of equality to God. Just as man is receptive of the divine nature, because of his being an image thereof, so too is God receptive of the human nature, because of its being an image of Him. But man, as one who is imperfect, and by nature inclined to aim at what is perfect, by nature yearns after God's perfect nature; whereas God, who out of His goodness aims at finishing man by enabling him to develop to maturity and perfection, being Himself perfect, by nature yearns after man's perfectness, and condescends by way of economy to assume the human nature for the purpose of perfecting it. This communication of natures presupposes a likeness, but not an identity of substances; for the substance of a human being, or what is called his beingness, is capable of receiving aliveness and awareness, which are possessed also by the perfect beingness of the Being, the three sempiternal Substances of the Deity, the Mind, the Logos, and the Spirit. But where there is a likeness of hypostases there is also a likeness of natures. The ego's nature is like the Being's nature, for, whatever God's nature possesses in perfect measure the ego's nature possesses in an imperfect measure, and it is perfected in accordance with the law of progress. Between unlike natures, which presuppose an unlikeness of hypostases, there is no communication, and for this reason God's nature is unimpartable to plants and animals, and impartable only to rational beings. But rationality, morality, freedom, are attributes of the divine nature and essence, being impartable to hypostasis that are like those of God. But that man's hypostasis is like the divine hypostasis is proved a p o s- t e r i o r i, and not a p r i o r i, or, in other words, it is attested by experience. For although it has an imperfect nature, yet it is like God's nature. In craving after perfetness, man is craving after the divine nature, at which he is aiming and towards which he is drawn by civilization; but his perfectness consists in complete acquisition and possession of the divine nature, without which he is bound to be unhappy and miserable, whereas with it he will be happy and blissful. Omniscience, all-goodness, and omnipotence are what is definable as the final condition of man's existence and of man's life. It is here that all progress forward ends, and motion is succeeded by an eternal standstill, time is succeeded by eternity, and imperfectness by perfectness. As God is the efficient reason of the existence of beings, so is He also their final reason; that is why all things begin, or receive their start, from God, and are steered towards God, and are brought to maturity and completion in God. God's perfect nature will become man's perfect nature, and man will become equalized to God, after becoming a man-god, in the same that God after taking on a human nature became a God-man.

The nature of every being is its specific form and its structural form, without which it can be neither distinguished nor known. Beings are known by their nature. Being underneath the nature, the hypostasis of a being is imperceptible and eludes observation, but it becomes manifest through the nature, because the nature is an image of the being. The perfect Being has a perfect nature, and this is the perfect form and image of Him. From the perfectness of His nature we judge also about the perfectness of the Being, drawing our conclusions about Him by a law of cognition. The hypostasis of the Being is invisible, but it can be seen indirectly through His nature, and not immediately and directly. God, the perfect Being, is imperceptible and invisible to us, but He can be seen through His structural form and through His specific form, through His attributes and His nature, which is an image

of Him. Being an all - wise, all - good, and all - powerful being,
God exists, because God is a being that is all - wise, all - good,
and all - powerful. All - wiseness, all - goodness, and all - powerfulness constitute the divine natute ; anyone that has this is a
God. But we can see God's all - wiseness through creation and
revelation through Christ. For creation and divine revelation
through the Savior are purposeful works and fruits of infinite
wisdom and power. We can see likewise His all - goodness
through creation and revelation, because both of these bear
witness that they are works of a good will which has taken
thought to impart of its perfectness to other beings. We can see
the all - powerfulness of God through creation and revelation,
because these bear witness that they are work of a Being who is
absolutely mighty, and are products of an infinite power. But the
work of God in the revelation of Him through His Logos, being
higher, shows, much more than does creation, God's all - wiseness,
all - goodness, and all - powerfulness, as well as God's perfect
nature. Accordingly, whoever studies and knows God through
the Gospel, studies and knows His perfect nature. For there
is no other explanation of God's nature that is more perfect or
more complete than that which is to be found in the Gospel.
This explanation is followed by a perceptual view or contemplation of God, which we cannot obtain in this life and which is
reserved for the future,when man shall be gladdened at the sight
of God's glory : «I shall rejoice when I have seen thy glory» (PS. 17).

THE PERFECT RELATIONSHIP OF THE BEING

The hypostasis with the nature maintain a relationship of
equality and analogy. Perfect relationship is the association of a
perfect hypostasis with a perfect nature. This exists in God's
most perfect Essence. God's Essence has been shown to contain
or comprise three distinct hypostases, that of the Mind, that of the
Logos, and that of the Spirit, between all of which there subsists
a perfect relationship, which exists also between them and the
perfect nature of God's Essence. Let us proceed to consider this
relationship. The relationship of the Mind to the Logos is one
that is generative, or one that involves generation or begettal.
For the Mind naturally begets out of its essence a Logos that is
depictive and representative of it. This generative relationship is
sempiternal and infinite, like some constant and immutable law
between the Mind and the Logos, between the Being and His Idea.
This relationship is one that is perfect ; that is why both the
begetter and the begotten are perfect. The relationship to the

Spirit, on the other hand, i. e., of the Mind to Cognition, is a relationship that is emanative, sempiternal, and infinite, and perfect, because both the one who emanates and the one who is emanated are perfect. The generation, or begettal, of the Logos out of the Mind, and the emanation of the Spirit out of the Mind alone, and not also out of the Logos, as the theologians of the West erroneously contend, are two modes of relationship that produces the Logos and the Spirit out of the sempiternal and infinite substance of the Mind, out of one and the same principle of beingness. The relationship holds also as between the Three hypostases and the single indivisible nature of the Being, because between these there subsists a sempiternal and infinite association and an immutable and perfect bond; for whatever can be predicated of the Mind can be prepicated also of the Logos and of the Spirit, as common attributes, as a constant and immutable nature. The relationship is equal to the ones related, to the hypostases and to the divine nature, and it is immutable and unchangeable, sempiternal and infinite.

But in being related to Himself God is related also to the potential being and to the contingent being. This relationship, however, is one that is creative and not generative of beings. For out of nonbeings it produces beings creatively; and whatever it creates is neither begotten nor emanated, but is created. It creates beings by His will and power; accordingly, He is related to them as Creator. The creative relationship of God to beings is a mode of producing beings out of nothing, by the power of God; but, being creative, it is at the same time also conservative and perfective of beings. A perfect, sempiternal, and infinite relationship joining the Eternal Being with the eternal potential being: an Idea knowing God, itself, and the potential being: an Idea equal to God when substantiated, and equal to man when unsubstantiated, and which is being produced creatively in time by the will and power of the Being. This relationship, sempiternally in God, on the one hand, hypostatic images God, but, on the other hand, unsubstantively it images man, the most perfect of God's works. Temporally, however, outside of God, it images God and man in the hypostasis of the sempiternal Deity, which is the relationship between the Being and the fact, between God and His work. When we seek the perfect relationship of the Being to the fact, we discover it in the incarnation of the Logos as a human being, revealed in the God - man, and actualized in the union of divinity with humanity in the hypostasis of the Logos. Being related to God through Christ, we have the most perfect relationship, are lifted up Godwards, and become equal to God. Equality to God, therefore, is the fruit of our most perfect relationship to God.

THE ETERNITY OF THE BEING

The perfect Being is not restricted or limited by any region of space, but neither does He exist in time, for He is infinite and sempiternal. As an Eternal Being He is eternal, and the eternity coexists with His sempiternal Essence as some constant and unchangeable duration having neither a past nor a future but ever and at all times a present only. Eternity is a condition of perfectness, just as time is a condition of imperfectness. But into the eternity of the perfect Being under no circumstances can there be introduced an imperfect being before it has been brought to maturity and completely developed and has acquired the nature of the perfect Being. Time is judged by the transmutation and change and motion of the occurrence. For, Beings having an imperfect nature and being subject to the law of progress and of gradual perfection, the beings move, are transmuted, become, turn into something else, and unbecome. Eternity is judged by the immutableness, and unchangeableness, and immovableness of beings, by their perfectness. God, on the other hand, is the perfect Being, the being who is not subject to any transmutation or change or alteration. Hence it is evident that He exists and lives and thinks sempiternally and eternally, and that His duration is eternity. In cognizing the Being, we at the same time cognize also His eternal beingness, aliveness, and awareness; and we are unable to cognize the contrary of this. But in cognizing the imperfect being, the fact, we cognize it with time and in time; and if we mentally abstract time from it, we abstract its imperfectness, and either we conceive it as an unsubstantiated idea, as a nonbeing, or else we conceive it as perfectly developed and finished, and consequently sempiternal. In cognizing the fact in its perfectness, as something sempiternal, we cognize it as having received a beginning of beingness, but as an endless or interminable being, i. e., as a being that endures forever and without end. But just as the perfect Being is the condition of the existence of the fact, so and in like manner may it be said that eternity is the end of time, or, at any rate, of its changes and variations, resulting in the abolishment of the law of progress of beings to a state of perfection. In aiming at perfectness we are aiming at eternity, and are being irresistibly swept towards it through progress and the agencies of civilization.

THE INFINITENESS OF THE BEING

The perfect Being is also infinite. But that which is infinite is the extension of the infinite Being, an extension without limits and restrictions, without bounds or an end. That which is infinite is the space of the Being; and since there is nothing else than the Spirit that is infinite, therefore God dwells in the Spirit, being himself a Spirit too. But in order to be able to cognize the infinite extent of the Spirit of the Being, let us consider the nature of our own spirit, which aims at what is infinite. The spirit in us knows the things within us and those which are outside of us through consciousness and perception; and through rational and logical cognition it extends cognition to as far as the perfect Being, to whose beingness it bears witness, and it seeks a way to learn all about Him. This cognition, or thought, which reaches from us up to the perfect Being through the ideas of speech, affords us some sort of image, so to speak, of the infinite Spirit of the Being, of whom we too have some ray or other of light whereby we think, and of the infinite cognitivity of God. For by one immediate glance of the Spirit God beholds Himself and the things outside of Him, the Being and the nonbeing; and by no manner of means can any time intervene in God's cognition. That is why God is said to be everywhere present, or ubiquitous, thanks to the Spirit, and to fill all things. Before God's infinite cognition everything is visible, nude, and stark, and there is nothing can escape its notice. Hence the infinity of the Being is His perfect cognition, His perfect Spirit. It is at this infinite that we too are aiming, because it is the final condition of our existence. The fact, as an imperfect being, is also extensive, occupying space that has bounds. In proportion to its perfection it also partakes of the infinity of the Being as its bounded extension is done away with. By acquiring the perfect cognition of God and of His infinite Spirit it will acquire also infiniteness, and through infiniteness it will become infinite. This is accomplished through impartation of God's Spirit to man's substance — a result which is is being brought about gradually and in accordance with the law of his birth and regeneration, or rebirth, as we explained about him in our work entitled H u m a n   N a t u r e .   In the beginning by means of His inbreathing God imparted a vital and cognitive spirit to man, and brought him from his unconscious state to the sphere of spiritituality — from extensive matter to inextensive spirit; and through regeneration in Christ is accomplished this great work of the transition of man, through gradual impartation of the Spirit, from time to eternity, and from extension to infinitude. But when man adds to his ego all the infinite nature of God's Spirit, though not also His unimpartable and incommunicable hypostasis, man will become infinite, being and living and cognizing like God in the infinite Spirit, as a separate personality distinct from the divine Substances, in accordance with the relationship which we considered previously. Thus man's ego from its simple and unconscious existence becomes conscious and cognitive thanks to God's Spirit, which is the third consituent of the man who has been made in the image and likeness of God and who is passing into His life and cognition in the infinite, into a state which represents the ego's perfectness and deification — a state in which man co-exists together with the perfect Being. Just as time is the process in which beings are changed and altered, so and in like manner it may be said that space is the condition of boundedness of beings. When change and boundedness are done away with as a result of the perfection and cognitivity of beings, time and space are also abolished, as well as duration and extension, and there prevail thenceforth eternity and infinity. But the perfect Being, as outside of all change and ignorance, is also outside of time, of duration, and of extension.

THE ABSOLUTE

What is the absolute? The absolute is that which exists by itself and contains the cause of its own existence, and does not depend upon anything else for its existence. For whatever does not exist by itself, but depends upon something else, is that which is relatively existent, the fact. Admittedly the being which exists by itself as self-caused and self-existent, is neither the world nor man, for both of these become and unbecome, and are altered ; instead it is a being above every other being, a perfect being, an eternal being, and one that ever maintains the same habitude, a being which undergoes no alteration or change and which we are wont to call God. The absolute cannot be imperfect. For, if it were imperfect, it would have to have an efficient cause outside of itself—it would have to be the work and product of some other being. Consequently it would be neither infinite nor sempiternal, nor unalterable and unchangeable, nor an eternal being. It would therefore have to be relative and a fact. For, all the attributes of sempiternity, of infinity, of unalterability, are attributes of the absolute Being. But if, on the contrary, it is perfect, it follows that it must also have all the attributes of perfection in a perfect and absolute degree. There exists, however, but one absolute Being ; and it is impossible for there to be two or more absolutes, for these would either have to depend upon one another and could not exist by themselves, and consequently would not be absolute, or they would have to exist by themselves independently of one another, but be beings of the same essence, and consequently essentially one, the absolute. For, two or more absolutes of different essences cannot co-exist, because each one of them would know that outside of it and independent of its will there exists an omnipotent being against which nothing can prevail. It would know that it itself is not an omnipotent being; and therefore it could not be said to be absolute. All the other supposedly absolute beings would also know this very same thing too. In supposing the existence of a number of absolutes we are supposing the existence of a number of Gods; accordingly, we ought to acknowledge either that the several absolutes have the same essence, and consequently that they are co-essential, or that they differ in their mode of being or in some one or more of the divine attributes, that they are superior and inferior to one another, and consequently that they are not absolutes, that they have a beginning and end of existence. The first supposition of numerous co-essential absolutes implies a common characteristic that exists among them, and precludes distinction, and consequently precludes numerosity. Numerous beings not distinguished by any peculiar characteristic cannot be many, but, on the contrary, can be only one. Numerosity obtains only where there is distinctness of beings. So, in order to be able to say that there are one, two, or three absolute beings, we must have that number of absolute essences which are distinct from each other. The second supposition of many absolute beings in the sence of being of different essences, of being superior and inferior, contradicts the conception of unity which we conceive before the conception of plurality. Admittedly it is naturally impossible for us to conceive (cognize) plurality before unity, to conceive (cognize) two before we do one. We first conceive (cognize) one, and afterwards two and other numbers. We cannot conceive (cognize) a plural number before unity—many absolutes before conceiving (cognizing) one absolute. Consequently we cannot lay down as the first principle a plurality without a unity. It is impossible, therefore, to admit the existence of a plural number of absolutes; one and only one absolute is admissible. Moreover, just as the many beings depend on the existence of the absolute Being, so and in like manner all ideas depend on the conception of Him which is in us. Just as the ontological world is founded upon the absolute Being, so and in like manner the ideal and ideological world is founded upon the absolute Idea of Him Thus it may be said that the absolute dominates and rules and governs everwhere.

The absolute, being one, and it being impossible for there

to be many absolutes, owing to the perfectness of its essence and
to its being complete and self-sufficient and in need of nothing,
is a Mind which begets an absolute Logos (or Reason) which is
perfect and equal to It; and that Mind is a projector of an absolute and perfect Spirit which is equal to both the Mind and
the Logos. But both the Mind, the Logos, and the Spirit are all
three beings in a single essence, that of the one God, as we previously have clearly stated. Before the infinite our cognitive
spirit stands aghast and cannot conceive (cognize) anything higher than the absolute, because there is no such thing. Consequently it conceives the idea of the absolute and posits this idea
as the principle and foundation of all its ideas. The ego learns
also about the world, and from its knowledge of both it is reduced
(brought), or led back up, to cognition of a being outside of the
essence of the ego and that of the world, the creative (efficient) and
final principle of every being. In other words, it is enabled to
ascend to the self-existent Being, and before the Idea of Him it
stands still, being unable to conceive (cognize) anything higher
than Him, nor even desiring to ascend higher than the absolute,
because no such higher thing exists. Our cognition and yearning
are satisfied before the Idea of the absolute Being, because in the
absolute is the perfect, which is not subject to want or excess.
But if it is true that we yearn for the infinite, it follows that we
also conceive it and cognize it, and our cognition aims at it,
struggling to comprehend it and to know it more fully. But,
our will has the absolute as a law and rule of its action; and
before it as the absolute Good, it stops willing, performing and
doing everything that the absolute Good wills, in accordance with
the latter's perfect volition. The absolute perfectly and completely
satisfies our yearning, cognition, and volition, and imbues us with
perfect and complete joy over its perfectness and its communication with us. Whatever we are seeking, that is the absolute. We
seek after the absolute in cognition. We seek after the absolute in
volition. We seek after the absolute in affection. For, from the
relationship of our cognition to the absolute we learn and come
to know the absolute Truth. From the relationship of our volition
and of our affection to it we acquire and come into possession of
the moral Good as a possession of our own. We entify within us
the moral good, and become good ourselves, like God, and feel
the ineffable joy which is interminable for evermore and which
ushers in the dominion of blissfulness within us. In this relationship of ours with God, as a result of the Truth and of the Good,
it is or lies the kingdom of God, the kingdom of heaven,
concerning which we wish by saying «Let thy kingdom come»
(Matt. 6:10).

THE IDEA OF THE BEING

We have previously shown the elements forming the idea of a being, the hypostasis, the nature, the relation, the extension, and the duration. We also showed the cognitive manner modes and laws in accordance with which the idea of a being together with its elements (i. e., the elements of the idea in question) can be cognized. We distinguished b e i n g n e s s into sempiternal beingness and beingness consisting in a fact that has occurred or has become such in time; and we learned that sempiternal beingness is perfect, whereas the fact which has occurred and is in time is imperfect, being advanced and perfected in the course of time. But since the sempiternal Being is both before and after the fact which has occurred and is in time, and is that from which the latter has received and has its beingness, through the latter we are led back up to cognition of the Eternal Being logically, and as through an appearance and an effect through reason we conceive the idea of the Eternal Being, and of the absolute Cause; therefore and on this account we call the fact an appearance, or phenomenon, not as something lacking existence and hypostasis, but as a work and product of the Being, indicative of the latter's existence. In observing the fact, we observe the phenomenon, or appearance, of the Being by means of consciousness and perception, and can behold immediately and perspicuously His beingness and existence. Our consciousness clearly and perspicuously reveals within us the phenomenon of the ego; and our percipience likewise with the same perspicuity reveals to us the phenomenon of the world. The perspicuity of the phenomenon informs us with certitude, so that we have no need of any proof to assure us that the fact exists. The perspicuity of the consciousness and perception is sufficient evidence of the existence of the phenomenon; the ideas of the existence of the ego and of the nonego are the matter of the cognition of the phenomenon. The ideas of the beingness of the ego and of the nonego are the primary knowledge, (first knowledge) what is known to begin with, but are not real knowledge, what is known by itself. For the ego and the world are the fact, the phenomenon of the Being, and not the Being proper, the Being by and in Himself. But we are seeking to cognize the real Being, the self-existent and self-hypostatic Being. Hence it may be said that we are seeking the idea of the real Being, of the Being who is self-existent and self-hypostatic. This means that we are seeking the concrete Idea of the Being, and not the mere abstract idea of beingness. For we seek to cognize, nor most imperfect matter, but the most perfect Being, and the most perfect Spirit. And true enough. Knowledge of the Being is worthy of and analogous to the perfect yearning to know which is felt within us. In cognizing the perfect Being we fulfill our yearning to know, and therefore we thereupon cease seeking, for beyond the perfect there is nothing more perfect, and beyond the infinite Being there is nothing more infinite, and beyond the eternal and sempiternal there is nothing more eternal and more sempiternal. The satisfaction or complement of right reason is the necessary, the absolute, the sempiternal, the real Being, the eternal, and the infinite character of the Being. That is why right reason is said to be the eternal law, the absolute, and universal, and eternal, and infinite law. For by means thereof we can cognize the infinite and absolute Being, and in it lies the cognition of the universality, of the necessariness, of the sempiternity, of the infinity, and of the sempiternal attributes of the Being. So where should we find the first Idea and first Principle that is analogous to the infinite yearning to know which we have within us ; In the phenomena? No. For the phenomena, being of a finite nature, are unable to fulfill our infinite yearning to know. In the ego? No. For this is a particular phenomenon, and unable to fulfill an infinite yearning. Well, then in the nonego? But if an analogy and proportionality between the fact and the yearning to know is not to be found in the totality of things and in all the phenomenon and fact, how can it be expected to be found in the parts thereof? Hence it follows that the satisfaction of the yearning within us to know is to be found neither in the parts nor in the whole of the phenomena. I observe the phenomenon before me, and seek to become acquainted with it. They explain to me the various phenomena of the ego and of the world, and they interpret to me the mysteries of nature, do the psychologists, the naturalists, the anthropologists, and the cosmologists (i.e., the physical scientists), and they discover for me the causes of phenomena as respects nature and the fact. I gladly learn whatever I wished to learn, and feel still more eager the passionate love within me for knowledge. While I am learning I desire and demand all the more eagerly to learn more ; and, being thus carried onward from knowledge to knowledge and from learning to learning, I come into contact with a certain Idea that is universal, necessary, and absolute, the absolute, and universal, and necessary Being, the chief and primary and first Idea, on which all the ideas of phenomena depend, as the phenomenon depends on the Being. Above the phenomenon my cognition conceives the real Being. Above the temporal and finite it conceives the eternal and infinite. Above the possible and contingent and mutable it conceives the idea of the necessary and immutable Being. Above the particular and relative identity of the fact it conceives the idea of the general and absolute identity, and above the finite cause and purpose of the facts it conceives the idea of the absolute Cause and of the absolute purpose of everything. In the Idea of the Being is contained everything that is absolute, universal, and necessary, that which is immutable and unchangeable.

In being led back up to the Idea of the Being we cognize the infinite, necessary, absolute, and universal b e i n g n e s s of the Being. But what we are ignorant of in the very beginning and what we are yearning to learn is what the Being is in His Essence. Hence it follows that in the beginning we have but an imperfect idea of the Being. By being perfected in the Idea of God we acquire a more perfect idea of the Being. This perfection of us in the Idea of God is equal and analogous and proportionate: 1) to our yearning to know; 2) to the Essence of God. But since the yearning within us to know is infinite and God is likewise an infinite being, the perfection of us is infinite too, terminating in the infinite; accordingly it is only, through the Idea of the infinite that it can be attained and achieved. Hence it follows that through the Idea of the Being: 1) the yearning within us to know is fulfilled; 2) God is revealed to us and becomes fully comprehended. For this reason the chief and primary Idea, which we are seeking after as the one corresponding to the chief and primary idea within us to know is the Idea of the chief and primary and first and highest Being — and this Idea is the chief and first and primary one, the necessary and universal and absolute Idea. We are seeking the Idea of the Being because It fulfills the infinite void of the yearning within us to know, and reveals to us the nature of the Being and the nature of the fact, which we cannot learn without the Idea of the Being. For the fact became such and partakes of the beingness of the Being. Hence it follows that it is through the Idea of the Being that it becomes possible to learn what the fact is, and what its efficient and final reason is. We find this Idea of the Being in the Cognition and in the Spirit of the Being objectively, and in our own cognition and spirit subjectively, as we shall see.

A SUBJECTIVE
CONTEMPLATION OF THE IDEA OF THE BEING

The subject of cognition is the ego; the object thereof is that which is cognized by the ego. In cognizing the fact the ego cognizes itself and the world, or, in other words, the phenomenon of the Being. It cognizes the Being by cognizing the phenomenon and the fact. Cognition of the fact is the immediate idea of the ego and of the nonego, whereas cognition of the Being through the phenomenon is the immediate idea of the Being. Cognition of the ego results from consciousness. Cognition of the nonego results from perception. Cognition of the Being results from the exercise of right reason. Consciousness, perception, and reason are three laws of cognition of one and the same spirit, in which and through which the ego cognizes and thinks. Consciousness is immediate and direct and perspicuous cognition. Perception is likewise cognition that is immediate, and perspicuous, and direct. Right reason is likewise cognition that is immediate, perspicuous, and direct. Consciousness testifies to the identity of the ego. Perception, to the identity of the nonego. Right reason, to the identity of the Eternal Being. Perception presupposes consciousness, for without consciousness there can be no perception ; just as consciousness presupposes the existence of the spirit, because without a spirit there can be neither consciousness nor perception. Right reason presupposes the existence of consciousness and of perception. So, in order to cognize the fact we have to confirm its identity through consciousness and perception. Then, relying upon the certainty of its identity, we are led back up to cognition of the being in accordance with right reason, and can verify its identity. Hence it can be seen that we cognize the Being in His Idea and through His Idea, and have an objective view of His Idea.

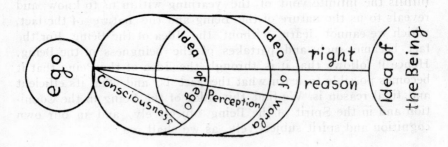

The above diagram represents the cognizing ego, the laws of cognition, and the primary ideas of thought, and is an image of the ego's cognition. But the three laws of cognition constitute a single law, the primary law of the spirit, denoted by a straight line, and also called right reason.

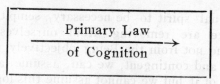

The primary law of cognition is : 1) the law of contradiction and of identity, confirming the beingness of the Being; 2) the law of causality, confirming the identity, of the cause by the identity of the effect; 3) the law of purposefulness and of aimfulness, confirming the purpose and aim of beings by the identity of the beings, or, in other words, attesting the identity of the teleological order of everything. Hence it is in accordance with the primary law of cognition that we cognize the beingness, the efficient and final cause of beings, and can verify every item of knowledge that we have in us. This primary law of cognition is the essence of right reason, the universal principle in our spirit, by means whereof we cognize everything that we do cognize, and without which we cannot cognize any thing rightly. (*)

---

*) The diagram following this is denotative of the ego cognizing in the fact by means of the abilities of the spirit, itself, the world, and God, who is outside of the ego and of the world, and who is revealed in the ego through right reason. Thus F represents the fact ; E represents the ego. CC represents conscious cognition, by which the ego is cognized. W denotes the world cognized through perceptive cognition, which is designated by the letters PC. The straight line extends beyond the ego and the world, the fact, and indicating the Eternal Being above the letters LC, is the logical cognition of the spirit. The line RR which meets it and touches it in the cognition of the Eternal Being outside of the fact, is the law of the spirit, right reason, from which originate all the laws of cognition of what is absolute, necessary, and universal.

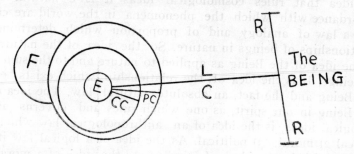

By hypothetically removing the fact, we remove the subject of cognition, the ego. But we do not remove cognition, for the latter is a property of the spirit, which in turn is eternal necessary, and sempiternal. Hence we conceive the primary law of cognition in the eternal spirit to be necessary, sempiternal, and absolute. Hence we are removing from ourselves the cognition subjectively, and not from the Being objectively. But since the fact is possible and contingent, we can assume also the removal and inexistence of it, but we cannot assume this logically in regard to the necessary and sempiternal Being. For the Being could not have not existed, and exists because He necessarily exists. He is selfexistent existence that subsists of itself and is without a cause. At the time when, though existent, we cannot cognize anything, it is obvious that we have no cognitive spirit, nor any knowledge of the primary law of cognition, which is in the spirit, as a law of the spirit. But after the sempiternal spirit accrues within us initially, like some ray of a metaphysical light, we immediately cognize the fact in accordance with the primary law of cognition, and through or by means of it the real Being, the Being Himself, and we thus possess ourselves of the primary knowledge and idea concerning the fact and the Being. This is what is known to begin with, the basis of all knowledge, and the supporting prop of all science and learning. Thus within ourselves initially there is given the knowledge of the fact and of the Being — knowledge which is primary and first, conscious, perceptual, and logical, knowledge accruing through the primary law of cognition.

The idea of a being which is in us is initially imperfect, but contains the elements of beingness, the nature, the relationship, the extension, and the duration of the being. There is in us the first and highest of ideas, before which all the other ideas of a possible and contingent being are the phenomenon. Without it all other ideas are as nothing, for they cannot exist without the necessary and absolute Idea of the Being. All other ideas depend on it, and are because it is. It, indeed, is the criterion of every idea. As an idea that rules cosmological ideas it is a natural law in accordance with which the phenomena in the world are carried out, a law of analogy and of proportion which determines the relationships of beings in nature. So the idea of the natural law is the idea of the Being as applied to nature and to the sum-total of beings. It is the idea of the relationship which exists between the Being and the fact, an absolute natural law. The idea of the the Being in our spirit, as one which rules and governs anthropological ideas, is the idea of an anthropological law which is 1) logical 2) moral; 3) political. As the idea of a logical law it is to be met with in the ideas of science. As the idea of a moral law, in ethics. As the idea of a political law, in political and social ideas. The idea of truth and falsehood without the idea within us of the Being is nowise distinguishable. Likewise the idea of virtue and vice, and the idea of right and wrong. Hence it follows that the idea of the Being is an infallible, unfailing, and legitimate criterion of all the ideas in us. Without it we are utterly ignorant of the idea of law and of the relationship of the fact ; for the idea of the Being is the idea of law by which idea the Being is related and connected with the fact, and without which we are ignorant of everything, or, as we might say, of the Being and of the fact.

Fact — Law — Being

But the idea within us of the Being, in the beginning being imperfect, is developed and perfected. The standard measure of it is the Being, whom it images. Hence until it has matured within us, it is imperfect : 1) as idea of the natural law ; 2) as an idea of the logical law ; 3) as an idea of the moral law ; 4) as an idea of the political law. On this account we know all things imperfectly, as long as we know the idea of the Being imperfectly. But we also do our work in life imperfectly. Thus are to be explained : 1) imperfect scientific knowledge ; 2) imperfect moral knowledge and acts ; 3) imperfect forms of government and acts of legislation, the imperfect theories of positive right, and imperfect civil life. But as the idea becomes perfected within us, or is revealed, so is the scientific, and moral, and political knowledge perfected, and the truth, what is good, virtue, and what is right in the world are revealed through reason and practice. But the idea within us of the Being, as one capable of being perfected, may be developed incorrectly and falsely because of defective and unmethodical teaching ; it may be perverted or distorted in the cognitive faculty, and by it the ego may be cognized as God, and so may the world, or both the ego and the world together. A perversion or distortion, however, of the primary idea of the Being is not a denial of His existence ; for one who (cognizes) conceives matter and the fact to be God is not denying the existence of God, but confusing God with matter, the Being with the fact, and is cognizing illogically and falsely. One who falsely cognizes (conceives) matter to be a God, cognizes it as infinite, as absolute, and as necessarily existing. As a result of this false conception (cognition) he forms within himself a false idea of the Being and consequently conceives (cognizes) beings to be the reverse of what they really are : he conceives (cognizes) falsehood to be truth, and truth to be falsehood ; he conceives (cognizes) virtue to be vice, and what is good to be what is bad, what is right to be what is wrong, and he takes the phenomenon to be a Being. But a society of human beings having a false idea of God is a true Babylon, because there is neither truth nor virtue nor justice in it. On the other hand, a society having a true idea of God is a society that is divine, and divinely established, and provided with good laws, because sciences, virtues, and wise legislation flourish therein. For this reason and on this account a true and correct idea of God is the basis and foundation of science, of virtue, and of social life in general. Yet how neglectful individuals and societies are nowadays as respects the formation of a correct and true idea of God! For this reason it is that so much error flourishes among men, as well as so many vices, and the subsisting caconomy (the opposite of eunomy) and bad government. Education ought before every other idea to implant in the souls of men from the time of their childhood the idea of God, and to develop and cultivate it correctly and truly, for upon the development and perfection of it depend the development, progress, and perfection of our social life in general. For this reason the first task of education and of pedagogy and of bringing up is that of teaching knowledge of God, and respect for Him. For, according to the wise man (i. e., Solomon) «the beginning of wisdom is fear of the Lord». Knowledge of God begets respect for Him in the soul ; and a soul knowing God is the one that is godly and pious, doing whatever is pleasing in the eyes of the Lord, and shunning whatever is bad. A society that knows God both respects Him and is pious, and does what is good, and keeps aloof from things that are bad.

When we cognize a man who has been brought up and instructed in the Idea of God from the start, and who has come to know God to perfection, and who has a perfect idea of Him, we cognize him to be exceedingly godly, and exceedingly pious, and impeccable, loving justice and righteousness, and hating lawlessness and iniquity, and doing what is good, but repelling evil altogether. We cognize him to be perfect as respects power of cognition, because the perfect Idea of God is cognized through a perfect Spirit. We cognize him to be perfect as respects the ability to exercise power, because the power of cognition leads to the ability to exercise power. We cognize him to be perfect as respects the matter of living, because perfect cognition leads to perfect life ; for cognition is in reality life and immortality. We cognize him to have a perfect preference for what is good, or, in other words, to prefer everlastingly what is good, and to refuse and repel everlastingly what is bad from himself and from others. For anyone that has been matured and finished in the Idea of God becomes an equal of God, and is naturally entitled to become an unerring teacher of the truth, a perfect example of moral virtue, and the social and political s t a n d a r d, the social and political principle and authority, in both its legislative, its executive, and its judicial aspect. When we cognize a society of human beings according to the idea of this one man, formed in the Idea of the Being, we cognize a society of God - equal men : we cognize on earth the kingdom of the t r u t h, of w h a t i s g o o d, and of w h a t i s r i g h t — the kingdom of God. This notion and idea of the perfect man is the ideal of society as a whole, and the destiny of man taken individually and socially. This is the perfect formative type of a human being. In comparing these two ideas — the idea of the Being, with the idea of the perfect man — we can contemplate their equality and agreement and see it to be full and perfect.

The Idea of the Being — The Idea of the Perfect man.

Such a perfect man is initially Jesus Christ. He is followed by all those who think and act and feel as He does. A society formed and refined after the manner of Christ is a society living in the truth, in what is good, and in what is right. Concerning it we shall have something to say in the proper place.

THE OBJECTIVE
CONTEMPLATION OF THE IDEA OF THE BEING

After the subjective contemplation of the idea of the Being, in accordance with the idea of the Being that has become known to us, as our cognition can perceive it, we now enter upon the objective contemplation of it, or, in other words, upon the view of it in the absolute Mind, as the latter can perceive it. We cognize the idea of the Being imperfectly, because we ourselves are imperfect ; in fact we often cognize it in a way that perverts or distorts it, because of false teaching respecting the Being, by confusing the Being with the fact, and predicating His attributes of the latter. Imperfectness and (delution) error — the former dissuades our intellect from cognizing the Being perfectly ; the latter obscures it so as to cause it to cognize the Being falsely and mistakenly, and to have a false and mistaken idea of Him. But God, being a perfect Mind, cannot cognize the Idea of the Being either imperfectly or mistakenly. What is perfect abolishes and does away with imperfection and (delution) error. In cognizing God as a perfect Mind, therefore, we are cognizing Him as the Being who cognizes perfectly and truly. God, being a perfect Mind, cognizes Himself perfectly and truly. Hence it is evident that He has within Himself a perfect and true conception of Himself, the Idea of the Being, which is representative of the perfect existence, nature, relationship, extension, and duration or the Being. The Being is God ; the Idea of God, on the other hand, is the hypostatic Idea of the Being is a perfect image and likeness of His perfect hypostasis equal to and exactly like Him. The Idea of the Being, as His image, depicts and represents : 1) His beingness and hypostasis hence it may be seen that it is a Being itself ; 2) the nature of the Being ; hence it may be seen to have a nature ; 3) His relationship ; hence it bears a relationship to the Being ; 4) His extension ; hence it partakes of the infinity of the Being ; 5) the duration of the Being ; hence it may be seen to partake of the infinity of the Being ; it is therefore infinite itself ; 5) the duration of the Being ; hence it may be seen to partake of His eternalness ; it is therefore eternal itself. The Idea, therefore, of the Being may be distinguished, as an Idea, with respect to its beingness, from the hypostasis of the Being. But though this Idea is distinguishable from the hypostasis of the Being, it is not also independent thereof, but, on the contrary, is conjoined and correlated therewith, as an Idea of the Being. Between the hypostasis of the Being and the hypostasis of His Idea there exists the difference that logically the Being is pre - existent to His Idea, whereas actually He coexists with the latter ; for, the Being and the Idea of Him are together at the same time, both of them, co - beginningless, and sempiternal, and co - essential. The Idea of the Being is equal to the Being, whose idea it is. But inasmuch as It is equal to Him, It cannot help representing Him in accordance with His beingness, i.e., substantially (or, to employ the corresponding Greek term, h y p o s t a t i c a l l y). For, an idea of a perfect being, cognized through a perfect spirit and through a perfect cognition, yet unhypostatical (i.e., substanceless), is impossible. If God cognizes Himself perfectly, as the perfect Being, He necessarily must beget out of Himself an idea of Himself, perfect and equal to Himself, that is, hypostatic, having the beingness, the nature, and all the attributes of the Being. The Idea of the Being, as an idea of the absolute and necessary Being, is absolute, and necessarily is (real) ; for it is impossible for the Being to cognize Himself without His Idea. The Idea of the Being, through which the latter cognizes Himself in a perfect Spirit, which in turn is a third Substance (or Hypostasis) in the Deity, equal to the Being and to His Idea, is an image of the Being's beingness, aliveness, and power to exercise volition and ability to do things. Hence it is evident that It is a living, thinking, volitive, and potent substance (hypostasis), in the same way and to the same extent as the Being lives, thinks, exercises will and has the ability to do things. It exists, because the Being Himself exists necessarily and absolutely. Thus the Idea of the Being can be cognized objectively ; and It cannot be cognized otherwise.

God being necessarily existent, and being logically evidenced as a perfect Mind, the existence of the perfect Idea of Him is necessarily also admitted and proved logically ; because the Mind, and the Idea thereof, and the Spirit are together at the same time. For these three constitute Cognition. But inasmuch as God is the most perfect Cognition, it may be logically concluded that He is the perfect Mind, the perfect Idea, and the perfect Spirit. In denying the Idea of the Being we are denying the Mind of the Being, and are falling into Materialism. If we deny the Mind, we cannot explain Creation, which is plain evidence in itself that it is the product of a supreme Wisdom and Power ; in that case we should be at a loss to solve the problem we are discussing, the problem concerning everything taken together. If, while admitting the existence of the absolute Mind, we admit that He has no substantial (or hypostatic) Idea of Himself, we are denying the perfectness of His Idea, and are admitting that the Mind does not cognize Himself perfectly, nor possess, consequently, an exact and perfect Idea of Himself. But in cognizing Himself imperfectly, He would be suffering ignorance and would not be aware of Himself. Hence it would follow that He Himself is not the cause of His own cognition. For if He were the cause of His own cognition, He could cognize Himself perfectly, and could moreover represent Himself perfectly in the process of thinking. Hence it would follow that He is not an absolute Mind, though we necessarily must ascend to the idea of the existence of a perfect mind cognizing itself perfectly through (i. e., by means of) a perfect idea and a perfect spirit: a selfcognitive mind, a source of cognition. Hence we conceive the Mind to be perfect, to think through a perfect Spirit and a perfect Idea. But perfectness of cognition necessarily implies three principles, of which one is that of the Being Mind, another that of the Idea of the Being, and a third that of the Cognition of the Being. Hence it follows that Being, Idea, and Spirit are three Beings in the Deity — or three primary and absolute existences, sempiternal, perfect, co-essential, and necessary. The Idea of the Being does not exist of Itself, but, on the contrary, has the cause of Its existence in the Being Himself. It is a sempiternal offspring (or generation) of the Being, sempiternally co-existing together with the latter—a Substance (Hypostasis) begotten out of a Substance (Hypostasis), and a co-essential Essence out of an Essence. Being equal to God, the first and absolute Idea of the Being possesses sempiternalness and universality, and necessariness, and leads all the sempiternal ideas in the Spirit of God, of the possible and contingent being. In cognizing Himself God cognizes also the other, the nonego. Since He sempiternally cognizes Himself, He sempiternally cognizes also the other. The other, of God, which He cognizes sempiternally, is the nonbeing, or that which is not and which God cognizes as possible and contingent. Hence it follows that the cognition of God is cognition of the Being, as of that which is necessary; whereas the cognition of the nonbeing is cognition of what can contingently and possibly become a being.

Idea		Idea
—	Eternal Being	—
of the Being		of the nonbeing.

The Idea of the Being is one that is infinite and universal, whereas the ideas of what is possible are finite, individual, and general. God cognizes the nonbeing because He cognizes Himself, or, more explicitly speaking, His ego. If He did not cognize Himself, neither could He cognize the nonbeing. Being unable to cognize the nonbeing, neither could He create and substantiate it. But since God does cognize Himself, it follows that He cognizes the nonbeing; and by cognizing the latter as a being, He can substantiate and actualize it, and bring into being outside of Himself the Creation of existent beings, and image Himself, and reveal Himself through it. Being the first among all ideas of what is contingent and possible, and being itself the criterion of the reality and substance (hypostasis) of every idea, the Idea of God is the object at which they aim, the center of the ideal world in God. Roundabout the first and necessary and universal Idea of God, one may say, circles, or revolves, the world of contingent ideas, which receives substance (hypostasis) in time, and is in time, and on this account is temporal, and extensive, and finite, and contingent. The ideal world of the nonbeing is founded upon the enypostatic and perfect Idea of the Being, and through the perfect Idea of the Being God cognizes Himself and the nonbeing. Contemplation of the ideal world in God is effected through the Idea of the Being, at which Idea the ideal world aims, or has regard. God cognizes the ideal world through His Idea, the fact through the Being.

Eternal Being — Idea — Ideal world.

But the ideal world, however, also has reference to God through and by virtue of God's first and chief Idea, being in relation to God, through and by virtue of His Idea. Nevertheless, this cognition of God's is immediate, and simultaneous, and sempiternal, because it is at the same time cognition of Himself and cognition of the ideal world. The cognition of the ideal world is a cognition in the Idea of the Being. Hence it follows that the bond, or nexus, between the cognition of the Being and that of the nonbeing is the Idea of the Being.

$$\text{Being — Idea — nonbeing}$$

Wherefore, and since the Being does not cognize the nonbeing without the Idea of Himself, therefore and on this account He cannot even entify it without His Idea and Logos (or Reason). Hence it follows as a matter of logic that the Idea of the Being is a bond, or nexus, of the Being with the nonbeing, or, more expressly speaking, with the contingent being, and is at the same time also the bond, or nexus, of the Being with the fact, or more expressly speaking, with the Creation of the nonbeing.

$$\text{Being — Idea — fact}$$

The contingent being the fact, having received beingness, or beinghood, and substance (hypostasis) through the Idea of the Eternal Being, is connected with Him through this Idea in such a fashion as to partake of beingness, of aliveness, of awareness, and of potency (or ability to do things), out of the Being who sempiternally is, lives, has awareness, and exercises power; accordingly, it becomes a being, alive, thinking, and exercising power too. This impartation and partaking of advantages (called «goods» in Greek) is effected through and by virtue of the Idea of the Being, which Idea possesses sempiternal beingness, aliveness, cognitive power, and ability to do things. The Idea of the Being, being the criterion of every contingent idea in God, is the law of God's cognition, the law in accordance with which God thinks or cognizes the ideas of contingent beings. God cognizes Himself as a real being, and cannot cognize Himself at the same time also as a nonbeing. He cognizes the nonbeing as a contingent being, and cannot cognize it as at the same time both a nonbeing and an eternal being. Hence it is evident that He thinks and cognizes what is rational and logical, and not what is self-contradictory and antinomic. The Idea of God is the law and principle of the Being's identity. But in cognizing Himself God cognizes in Himself the cause of His own existence. He cognizes the truth of the statement that He is self - existent, an uncaused cause. He cognizes furthermore the truth of the statement that He is the end and purpose of Himself. In other words, He cognizes that He Himself is the efficient and final cause, because the efficient and final reason of the existence both of Himself and of all the contingent worlds resides in Him. The Idea of God is the law and principle of causality and of purposefulness. But since God's cognition is an immediate and intuitive contemplation of Himself as of a real Being, and is a cognition of everything that is a possible and contingent being, therefore and on this account it may be said that God cognizes everything through a simple cognitive process. This cognitive process, or mode of thinking, is the primary law of the Spirit, usually called r i g h t   r e a s o n. The Logos (or Reason) enypostatic in God is the absolute identity, the absolute causality, and the absolute purposefulness. It is in these aspects that the essence of the Logos consists, wherein the Logos is manifested as the absolute and universal law.

The Idea of the Being, being one, i.e., a simple, and indivisible, and perfect unit, can be contemplated from many points of view, or under many aspects, in relation to the activities and spiritual movements (or operations) of the Being, which it now behooves us to consider. The Being, being a single and essentially simple being, contemplates and considers Himself under many aspects, or from many points of view, to wit : 1) as a thinking, or intellectual, being ; 2) as a willing, or volitive, being ; 3) as a feeling, or sentient, being. Hence it is that the Idea of the Being can be regarded : 1) as an idea and law and principle of the intellect ; 2) as an idea and law and principle of the will ; and 3) as an idea and law and principle of feelings. The cognition of the Being sempiternally cognizes what is consonant and consistent with the principle and law called right reason. His will wills, performs, and executes things sempiternally in accordance with the law and principle of volition, the moral law. His feeling, or sentience, is pleased or displeased, and analogously disposed, in accordance with its law and principle, in accordance with the law of what is really fine and beautiful. Hence God may be said to contemplate and consinder in Himself through His own hypostatic Idea whatever is true, whatever is fine and beautiful, as opposed to what is false, what is bad, and what is shameful and ugly. Accordingly, He thinks and cognizes, or, in other words, He approves, what is true ; He wills and executes what is good ; and is pleased and is favorably disposed in regard to what is fine and beautiful and good He cognizes what is true as true, and what is false as false, through Right Reason ; and He accordingly divides the light from the darkness. This means that He wills and does what is good, and refuses and repels what is bad, following the moral law ; and He feels pleased as a result of doing what is good and feels sorry as a result of doing what is bad following the primary law of benefit. But since God is perfect, therefore He sempiternally thinks and cognizes in accordance with the sempiternal law in Him of thought and of cognition ; that is to say, in accordance with the universal Logos, the truth. He sempiternally wills and does what is good, in accordance with the moral law. And He sempiternally feels joy and pleasure, because He sempiternally wills and does what is good. But truth, what is good, what is beneficial, and what is fine and beautiful are the sempiternal offspring, or generation (i.e., the begotten or generated product) of God's cognition (or thought), volition (or will), and affection (or sensibility). In sum, truth, and goodness, and beneficialness, and beauty, and consonance, and analogy (or proportion) are the produce of Right Reason, which is the supreme and universal and necessary law of cognition and of thought. But the Essence of God includes the perfect Mind, the perfect Logos (or Reason), and the perfect Spirit, each of which is a distinct Principle ; and on this account each of them is obliged to think (or cognize), to will (or exercise volition), and to feel (or entertain affections) mutually together with the others, for sempiternal preservation of the sempiternal harmony and order in God. The Being, as the Principle of beingness, imparts b e i n g n e s s to the Logos (or Reason) and to the Spirit. The Logos imparts a w a r e n e s s, or the idea and knowledge of the Being to the latter. The Spirit imparts aliveness and power to do things to the Being, being the Principle of these ; and it sempiternally acquires from the Being b e i n g n e s s and existence ; and from the Logos, the idea and knowledge of the Being and of the Truth — a w a r e n e s s. For this reason it may be said that the sempiternal Principles in God — namely, that of beingness, that of aliveness, and that of awareness — are three principles, distinct from each other, but also united together in a single Essence and Nature ; each indeed of which Principles performs its own function ; and the three together make the whole and everything. It is in the performance by each of its own function and duty, consonantly with the Logos (or Reason), that j u s t i c e and r i g-h t e o u s n e s consist ; and it is out of these latter characters that what is really r i g h t is begotten, in accordance with which all the outer acts of free beings are judged. In such a case the Logos is what is really R i g h t ; and every act consistent therewith is right and just ; and its consonance with what is R i g h t is what constitutes r i g h t e o u s n e s s and j u s t i c e.

The Idea of the Being in a logical and abstract sense is the absolute identity, the absolute causality, and the absolute purposefulness. But in the ontological and concrete sense it is the Truth, that which is morally Good, Right, Fine, and Beautiful — or, in a word, the Being, proving and exhibiting the identity of the Being, His truth; exhibiting the causality and purposefulness of the Being, and proving it — or, in other words, exhibiting the first and necessary and highest Cause and End of beings. Hence it follows that He is a being who comprises in Himself the absolute knowledge of the absolute identity, causality, and purposefulness. Through the Idea of the Being God cognizes His identity as a sempiternal unalterable entity — cognizes Himself as the uncaused cause of every possible and contingent being — cognizes Himself as the end and as the purpose of everything. The Idea of God in God is the intestine discourse, the law of cognition, the moral law. But outside of God It is the oral discourse, the law of thought, and the moral and physical law. For, if God is aware of Himself through His Idea as the Eternal Being, He must also know the fact through this same Idea, because it is through His Idea that He sempiternally cognizes in Himself the ideal world, the contingent being which is not yet become a being. If in the cognition of the ideal world God cognizes in accordance with His perfect Idea, it is also true that in both His volition and His decision for the entification and creation of the nonbeing, or, more expressly, of the ideal world, He operates and acts in accordance with His Idea. But just as the ideal world could not exist without the Idea of the Being, so could it it neither receive substance (hypostasis) outside of God were it not for the perfect Idea of God. So it may be said that the Idea of the Being is a law in God's perfect cognition, and in His volition and action. God cognizes in accordance with His perfect Idea, in accordance with the primary law of cognition. God wills and acts in accordance with His perfect Idea, in accordance with the primary law of His operation and action, the moral law. Perfect rationality and morality reign in the cognitive and volitive nature of the Being. Whatever God makes or creates bears the seal of His rationality and morality as Creator.

Philosophy being science of the necessary, sempiternal, and universal being, it is the science of the perfect Idea of God in which are the sempiternal and absolute Principles of thought, or, in other words, the laws of the Spirit. Accordingly, it is this necessary, and universal, and sempiternal, and absolute Idea that Philosophy is seeking to comprehend. Logically from the necessary existence of the Being Philosophy regards this Idea as necessary for a comprehension of both the Being and the fact. Philosophy seeks to comprehend the Idea of the Being logically and ontologically, as the first Truth, through which every truth may be known, and as the primary law of cognition and volition of the Being — as the absolute Truth ; as the perfect moral Good ; as Right ; as Truth Itself ; as the Good Being Himself ; as Right Itself ; and as what is Fine and Beautiful Itself ; as the perfect Image of the absolute Being, of the absolute Good, of the absolute Right, and of the absolute Fine and Beautiful. In ascending to the Idea of the Being by means of Philosophy, the intellect can survey the ideal world and the real world, can know the Being and the fact as they actually are, can gain possession of the key to knowledge of everything, open the gates of learning, and enter the adytum of knowledge, and explain the mystery of the universe. Omniscience is nothing but the contemplation of everything through the Idea of the Being. God contemplates everything through His Idea, without which He would be ignorant of it, for He would be ignorant of Himself. But we shall contemplate everything through the Idea of the Eternal Being ; and for this reason we have a tendency to attain to full knowledge and comprehension of it, without which we cannot learn anything. Omniscience will accrue to us through the Idea of the Being, through which God too knows everything. Hence it follows that the same law of cognition is in us as the one which is in God. For, as God knows everything through His Idea, so and in like manner we too shall know it through the same Idea. But after we have considered the Idea of the Being in the infinite Cognition of God as the Truth and as the primary law of cognition and of volition of the Being, let us proceed to consider it also outside of God, in His external act of creation.

CONSIDERATION
OF THE IDEA OF THE BEING IN HIS WORK

God cognizes what is contingent and not yet a being through His Idea, whereby He also knows Himself. He cognizes the ideal world through which He also cognizes Himself. He cognizes the nonbeing as a contingent being. Between cognition of the nonbeing but contingent and possible to be made something, and the execution and actualization of it there are : 1) the will to execute it ; 2) the power to execute and actualize it. In willing to create what is cognized to be right through the Idea of the Being, the will of the Being wills this of its own accord, spontaneously, and as a result of the goodness and morality it possesses. That is why rationality and morality are combined in volition, in order that they may co-operate. The will of the Being wills and decides to entify and substantiate the nonbeing, and to actualize and realize the ideal world. It wishes to create this as a result of its own goodness and free will in accordance with the primary law of cognition, the law of morality, which makes it a law that anyone who wills and does anything ought to will and do what is good for the sake of the one who is good. The law of thought is identical with the law of volition and action, and it is the primary law of the Spirit. The executive power of the Being has power to carry out and realize the decision of the will in accordance with the primary law of action, in accordance with what is right, and what is analogous, and what is proper and meet. For God does not create all the things that He can think of, but only those things which He considers to be more in keeping with His perfect Design and with His great Plan. What does God cognize in the beginning? He sempiternally cognizes in Himself through His Idea the ideal world. He cognizes the nonbeing as something that is contingent and can become something (real). He sempiternally wills through His Idea to realize the ideal world which is consistent with His Idea; accordingly, in the course of time, outside Himself, He entifies the ideal world by His power, and endows it with existence and substantiality (hypostasis). Hence we ought to distinguish the sempiternal cognition of the ideal world, and His sempiternal will, from the creation and entification of it in time. Being strong enough to cognize the nonbeing as a contingent being, being strong enough to will it sempiternally as something to be realized in the future, He is necessarily also strong enough to substantiate and entify the nonbeing in accordance with His sempiternal cognition and design. The beginning of His entification of it is the beginning of time. In all the activities of the Being, His Idea is the first and immediate instrument.

The Being cognizes Himself sempiternally through His Idea.

The Being cognizes the ideal world through His Idea.

The Being sempiternally wills to create the ideal world through His Idea.

The Being sempiternally has power to create the ideal world through His Idea.

The Being creates in the course of time through His Idea that which He has cognized, willed, and had the power to create.

Externally the Being realizes His sempiternal conception, or thought, and wish, or design, through the creation of beings. But the realization of it comes about in the course of time through the first, necessary, universal Idea of the Being.

Eternal Being — Idea — Creation of beings.

If the Being had not a perfect Idea of Himself, He could not cognize Himself perfectly and the ideal world perfectly. Consequently neither could He exercise volition without making a mistake, nor could He act justly. His work would be confused and appear to be unwise, to be produce of imperfect cognition and volition, a product of disorder and of want of learning. Absence of the Idea of the Being spells absence of His cognition, volition, and power. Any imperfectness of it is imperfectness of the power to cognize, to do things, and to exercise volition correctly. But a work of an imperfect intellect neither bears the seal of logicality and rationality and of purposefulness, nor is it a product of perfect wisdom and perfect power. Consequently it cannot be conserved and exist. Hence it follows that creation could not be effected nor even exist without God's perfect Idea. Materialism is left speechless and without a leg to stand on in the face of this argument. For it cannot deny the wisdom which is beheld in nature, nor the order and harmony of beings, and their power and their relationships, but illogically ascribes these to unintelligent and irrational matter and its forces. But O materialist, why dost thou take the wisdom and order in the world to be a product of matter and its forces, yet dost not suppose the wisdom and order in human affairs to be a product of men's bodies, but, on the contrary, by means of the terms m i n d, t h o u g h t, w i l l thou dost involuntarily distinguish the mind from the body, as thou dost also the artisan from his tool? Why dost thou not ascribe the works of the intellect and of the will of men to their heads, to their hands, and to their whole body, and dost neither praise nor blame their heads, hands, or body for good or bad, logical or illogical conception and action? If the soul were a force due to matter, and not an essence distinct from the body, it would necessarily be inferior to and lower than matter, as a property belonging to an essence; consequently it would be analogous to the substance of matter in accordance with the all-prevalent law of likeness and of analogy. The soul, as a property of matter and as one of its forces would have to be material, possessing no cognition and spirit, nor being cognitive, volitive, and passive or affective. Cognition cannot be a property of matter on account of its being unlike matter. So for this reason the cognizing ego is something other than unintelligent matter, an essence distinct from the essence of the body. The works of the cognizing ego, on the other hand, bear the seal of its rationality and logicality and of its morality, and through them we can behold the cognition and volition of the ego and the power of the ego. Moreover we can behold the cognition, the volition, and the power of God through Creation, and can cognize the world to be a work of God, bearing the seal of God's rationality, logicality, morality, and power, without foolishly, like the meterialists, confusing Spirit with matter, the Being with the fact, the workman with his work the artisan with the tool of his art.

God's perfect Idea is the basis and foundation of Creation. Creation is the manifestation and revelation of the Idea of the Being. In entifying the contingent being, the ideal world, God reveals Himself in Creation; that is to say, He reveals His Idea. The first revelation of God is entification, in the course of which the nonbeing receives substance (hypostasis) and becomes a being, namely, matter. This matter images the beingness of God. A second revelation of the Idea of the Being is the creation of the world, during which matter acquires a specific form and a structural form, and a nature, and makes its appearance in nature dressed in the garb and nature of a mineral, of a plant, of an animal, or of a human being — of an inorganic or organic, of an inanimate or animate, of an irrational or rational being — the specific form distinguishing the primary genera and species of beings. In the creation of matter in accordance with the law of progress God advances beings according to primary genera and species in order, ascending from the most imperfect to the most perfect, from existence to life, and from the latter to cognition. Hence it is that the scale of beings is divided into three primary genera, namely: 1) that of mere beings; 2) that of living beings; 3) that of thinking beings. The most imperfect of these is the mere being; the most perfect, the thinking being. In the scale of the gradual creation of the world of matter, on the other hand, there is revealed the Idea of the Being: 1) with respect to its beingness in the order of beings universally, as for instance, in that of minerals and that of plants; 2) with respect to its life in the order of living beings particularly, as, for instance, in that of animals; 3) with respect to its cognition or thought in the order of rational beings, as, for instance, in that of angels and human beings. The order of mere beings includes everything that is not alive, nor possessed of cognitivity, i.e., minerals and plants. The order of living beings includes everything that is a living being but incapable of thought, i.e., animals in general. The order of thinking beings includes every being that lives and thinks, i.e., rational and free beings, angels and men. The entification of matter and the creation of the world may be exhibited by means of the following figure :

Eternal Being — Idea — $\begin{cases} \text{not being, not living, not thinking} \\ \text{being, but not living or thinking} \\ \text{being, living, but not thinking} \\ \text{being, living, thinking.} \end{cases}$

The nonbeing is an absolute negation. The being but nonliving and nonthinking being is a relative position and negation combined. The being and living but nonthinking being is a position and negation combined. The position is more complete than that of the nonliving and nonthinking being; the negation is more imperfect than this, because the more attributes and characteristics a being receives the more positive it becomes in the order of beings, and the fewer the attributes it lacks for its perfection. The being that lives and thinks is an absolute position as compared with beings below it, because it is the most perfect being in the Creation of beings — a relative negation in comparison with the Supreme Being, God, the Creator of everything, because it images Him with respect to its beingness, aliveness, and awareness, but non perfectly. In order that it may image God perfectly it must take on perfect existence, life, and cognition, and become a perfect being, like God. Hence a being that lives and thinks is the most perfect one in the lower order of beings, but very imperfect in comparison with the Eternal Being who lives forever and thinks forever. The Idea of the Being is revealed in creation through the rational and free being that is endowed with beingness, aliveness, and awareness; and it is because of this that we can discern in him the traces of the Idea of the Being, though very imperfectly. Hence it may be said that the rational and moral creation is imperfect. The Idea of God is revealed through the natural creation of beings as a natural law governing nature, as a constant and invariable law, as a primary law of nature in accordance with which all occurrences and phenomena in the natural creation are carried out. For everything that occurs in nature occurs in accordance with some natural law, in accordance with or after an image of the Idea of the Being and of the sempiternal laws of the Spirit. As works and images of the Idea of the Being the natural laws are based on the Idea of the Being and on the good will of the Being. For creation is not a product of necessity, but of the Being's most benevolent and free will. So it turns out that the intrinsic reason of creation is the Being's good will, while the extrinsic reason of it is the revelation of the Idea of the Being. Natural creation commenced with entification and terminated in the creation of man, who is the foundation, and the starting — point of rational and moral creation, which

God is making outside of Himself, but equal to Himself, or, in other words, after His own image and likeness. But since man is the most perfect of the beings in creation, though a very imperfect representation of the Idea of the Being, it is plain that the Idea of the Being has been revealed in natural creation, but in due season will be revealed also in moral and rational creation, whose foundation is the perfect man. In the natural creation It was revealed as the natural law of existence and of life, whereas in the rational and moral creation it will be revealed as the law of cognition, of volition, and of action. If God is revealing Himself to us through creation, it follows of necessity that He must reveal Himself in all aspects and in accordance with its requirement. Hence it is evident that the revelation of God in creation is a work of His most benevolent will, and a requirement of creation, which out of benevolence He made an actuality when the fullness of time came.

THE IDEA OF THE BEING
IN THE NATURAL CREATION OF BEINGS

Whatever God makes, He makes it in accordance with His Idea. But the natural world is a creature and work of God. Hence it is evident that it has been made in accordance with God's Idea; accordingly, we may seek therein God's idea and mind. The universal order of beings, from molecules of matter to men, the more perfect beings, is a revelation of the Being's Idea; for all beings bear witness that they are products of the sempiternal Being, and that they have been endowed with beingness. The order of beings with life, from the humblest animalcule up to the strongest animal, is a revelation of the Being's Idea, as of a supreme life; for all living things bear witness that they are products of the sempiternal living God, and that they received and possess life. But existence and life are maintained in accordance with laws which are the revelation of God's sempiternal laws. The laws of the natural creation are natural and analogous to their nature and destiny. The motion, life, and balance and harmony of beings are the result of the operation of the natural laws in accordance with which natural creation moves and operates while harmoniously preserving its balance, which, be it noted, is a product of the natural law of universal gravitation. Every material being exists and lives together with others, so that the totality of material beings form a certain general concatenation, and, taken all together, they tend towards the universal center of matter, by dint of the mutual attraction of the lesser for the greater, and of the weaken for the stronger. But the uni-.

versal center of the material world towards which the whole material world is being attracted, is the Being's Idea, on which the universe is founded and supported. The law, therefore, of balance, of gravitation, and of analogy of the material world is an image of the sempiternal laws of the Spirit. Outside of these laws the material world cannot exist : it is by means of them that it functions and performs its part, and is truly a representation of the Being's Idea and of the Spirit's sempiternal laws. But the revelation in the natural world of the Being's Idea is very imperfect, because this world is also most imperfect, though complete and analogous to its nature and destiny. This first revelation of the Being's Idea in the material world affords us our first knowledge of it Thus by studying nature we are enabled to ascend in thought to the Being's Idea and to the Spirit's sempiternal laws. Hence we must by no means hold aloof from the study of nature, because it is therein that we get first knowledge concerning the Being, and it is thereby that we are led back up to a more perfect knowledge and notion of Him. Nature is the starting - point of the science of the Being, and the more we know about it the more we know about the Being : from the fact we can ascend and reach up to Him. The world of material beings does not provide us merely with food for the nourishment of our bodies, but also with theory and knowledge for the perfection of our spirit.

THE IDEA OF THE BEING
IN THE RATIONAL AND MORAL CREATION

Man is the most perfect of the beings in the natural creation, but the most imperfect in the rational and moral order of beings. His perfectness consists in his a w a r e n e s s, of which the inferior beings in creation are destitute. By means of his awareness man rules and governs nature, and by means of science he subjects nature's forces to himself ; accordingly, he exists as another God in the natural creation, or as a representative of God. His imperfectness, on the other hand, consists in the imperfect awareness which he has received from God, and which implies imperfectness of ability and of beingness. Man is the capital, or principal, being of the natural world, and is the foundation, or groundwork, of a new creation and of a new rational and moral world. Because of this, besides beingness and aliveness, which are common to all living beings, he possesses also awareness, which is unique in man. Man's beingness, aliveness, and awareness are depictive and representative of the Being's Idea, of God's existence, life, and cognition. But man in the beginning is imperfect in respect of beingness, aliveness, and awareness. Consequently he can only imperfectly represent the Being's Idea ; and therefore in imperfect man the revelation of God's Idea perfectly is impossible. Yet by contemplating man we can cognize the Being's Idea more or less shadowily — i. e., we can adumbrate to some extent the Being's Idea. The Being's Idea can be cognized through an infinite Spirit and in an infinite Being. But, possessing a limited cognition, how can imperfect man cognize the infinite Idea of the Being! Or how can he depict and represent It perfectly in rational and moral creation when he cognizes the truth unerringly, sets his will in all things upon what is good, and does what is right ? If creation is a perfect revelation of the Being's Idea, a perfect work therein ought to depict the Being's Idea perfectly. But it is plainly manifest that man was not made perfect from the beginning, but capable of becoming perfect. Hence it follows that imperfect man is an imperfect image of the Being's Idea, and not a perfect image thereof. But the revelation of the Being's Idea is a requirement of creation. Indeed, since what is more imperfect naturally precedes what is more perfect, as in the natural creation, while in the moral creation the more imperfect being is imperfect man, who possesses imperfect cognition and power, for this reason we infer that God's perfect work is the making of the perfect man. But this more imperfect being is by nature adapted to become perfect; wherefore it is true that he is intended to become perfect. His becoming perfect means his becoming aware of all things. Hence is logically evident that the perfect man is the perfect work, the image and perfect representation of the Being's Idea. But imperfect man does not know what his beginning is and what his end is. Moreover, he is subject to much error and delusion; and all the cases of men's going astray on the highway of their scientific and moral and social life are due to ignorance of man's origin, end, and purpose, and of the means leading thereto. His limited cognitivity, though having an initial conception of man's destiny and end, is unable to comprehend it in detail, nor can it comprehend the means leading thereto. Evidently, therefore, it is in need of an unerring guide who knows everything. But since everything can be learned through the Being's Idea, and nothing without It, we draw the conclusion that it behooved the Being's Idea to become humanified, i. e., to become incarnate in man, in order to be become revealed perfectly in the moral world, that Idea Itself becoming the guide and teacher of imperfect men yearning after perfection. The incarnation of the Being's Idea, of the Logos (or Reason), is a requirement of human nature, and it is logically possible for it to be fulfilled. But if creation is the revelation of the Being's Idea, it behooved the Logos to become incarnate for the purpose of a perfect and complete revelation of God's Design. This revelation, however, has been but a partial one, because the Logos of God assumed human nature and was seen in the world as a perfect human being begotten in time, though being sempiternal God. He was called J e s u s C h r i s t . The partial revelation of the Logos, however, was preceded by the general and universal revelation of Him among men, which is our next subject of discussion.

THE GENERAL REVELATION OF THE LOGOS

The emergence in every human being of the idea of the Being as a result of contemplation of the fact by virtue of the primary law of cognition, is the revelation thereof in our spirit, by virtue of which revelation we come to know about the Being imperfectly, having but an imperfect idea of Him. This revelation of the idea of the Being is a general one, because it is observed in every human being. Every human being cognizes the Eternal Being as a result of his idea of the fact. He cognizes that which is infinite and absolute as a result of his idea of that which is finite and relative. He cognizes that which is necessary on the basis of his idea of that which is contingent. Hence it follows that every human being cognizes the idea of the Being, and this idea is revealed in every human being. But in the perfect human being it is revealed perfectly, because he is become equal to the Idea of the Being, and between them both there is a complete equality and analogy.

> The perfect man = The perfect Idea of the Being

The Idea of the Being is revealed in the natural world as a natural law, but in the rational and moral world it is revealed as a rational and moral law, as the primary law of cognition and of volition, as the law of external action and practice. As a rational law it shows man the sameness and the beingness of a being. The cause and the end of it. The identity of a being, the cause and the purpose of it, constitute the essence of the primary law of cognition. For in regard to any object we naturally cognize its sameness, in distinction from the other, its cause and its end. That is why our questions about it are : 1) whether it is anything; for it is impossible for it to be and not to be the same at the same time ; 2) what the being actually is ; 3) why it is. The first question, because of its being of a hypothetical nature, is not permissible in regard to the existence of the ego, of the world, and of God, because the ideas of these beings are primary, and immediate, and positive ideas. For this reason the questions whether the ego actually exists, whether there really is a world, whether there really is a God, are absurd on the face of them. Principles are positions, and not suppositions. But more particularly and properly speaking, the principle of the Logos is a position, and so is the Idea of the Being. For we never ask whether there is a Being. Because any question asking whether there is any such thing as this or that presupposes a being who is asking the question, and one to whom the question is addressed. I exist because the eternally existent God exists. The only safe answer to the question whether there is a God is one that traces the reason for a belief in the existence of God to knowledge of the existence of the ego and of the world at large. There exists a God because both I (the ego) and the world at large exist. But God is self-existent and uncaused, and exists necessarily. But in respect to mediate principles the hypothetical proposition w h e t h e r t h e r e i s, has a reason, because it is one which asks for proof of the existence of something which is questionable. What may be questioned is the existence of things that are not perspicuously presented to our spirit, but can be proved by means of other perspicuous principles and positions. In this way a supposition may be nullified by a position and be converted into a position (i.e., a positive assertion) asseverating t h e r e i s or t h e r e i s n o t. Everything that is, is, and everything that is not, is not. But first and immediate principles are positions, and as such cannot be proved, but are shown immediately and perspicuously to the spirit. Therefore when I say that t h e r e i s a G o d, I am asseverating an absolute position, because God is an absolute being, and His Idea is an absolute principle. I asseverate the sameness of the Being, and cannot at the same time cognize or conceive the contrary thereof. I cannot cognize or conceive at the same time in respect to the Being that He is and that He is not — that He exists and that He does not exist, because either He is or He is not. There is no middle way. Here the principle of contradiction is obvious to all. Those who deny the existence of God are really foolish ; and those who question it are illogical and absurd, and are making a supposition of a position, by considering whether there is a God, contrary to the perspicuity of the position that t h e r e i s a G o d, which exists in our spirit. The supposition w h e t h e r t h e r e i s is one that arises only in our imperfect cognition : in a perfect cognition it cannot arise ; but, instead of it, there arises the position t h a t t h e r e is. Therefore the contradiction does not consist in the supposition, but in the position. The contradiction occurs between two propositions of which one excludes the other : t h e r e i s, t h e r e i s n o t. The proposition t h e r e i s is a position. The proposition t h e r e i s n o t is a counterposition. So both of these propositions cannot stand together at the same time, because they are opposite and contradictory.

Next after the principle of contradiction there exists in our spirit another called the principle of causality. For in cognizing a being we cognize it either as an effect or as a cause. We cognize it as a fact or as a being. In cognizing it as an effect, as a fact, we cognize it as being in some order and as having been made with regard to some purpose, and as being intended for its end. The sameness of the Being, the cause and the end of Him, these three cognitions of our spirit, constitute a single cognition, or one conception, the conception of the Idea of the Being. For the Being possesses beingness necessarily and sempiternally. It is the efficient and final cause in God of all things. Through His Logos God created and made the natural world and governs it. Through His Logos He created the rational and moral world. Through His Logos He formed it and perfected it and governs it, and leads it to its blissful and supreme end. «All things,» as John the Theologian says, «were made through the Logos, and without him not even one thing was made that was made» (John 1 : 3, translated directly from the Greek original). The principle of the spirit is rational cognition and right reason, through which we can cognize the Being and His sempiternal Idea. This cognition is a revelation within us of the Idea of the Being — a cognition which contacts the infinite and the absolute, and the necessary, and which is itself characterized as infinite. This cognition, moreover, is the metaphysical light of the spirit, the true light, which was in the moral world from the beginning ever since the formation of man, having been given to him by God for the purpose of enlightening every human being that comes into the world by being born into it, i.e., through the process of being begotten (John 1 : 9). This revelation of the Idea of the Being is a rational and metaphysical revelation of the truth of the Being which is imperfect but capable of being perfected. Under the dominating influence of this revelation the human will, though imperfectly cognizing what is good, regulates itself in accordance with the idea of what is good, and becomes formed and refined in accordance therewith in the matter of its motives and designs. But as the revelation of the truth is imperfect, yet capable of being perfected, so and in like manner is the assertion of the idea of what is good imperfect in us, yet capable of being perfected. The imperfect revelation of the truth is what institutes the imperfect logic in vogue among human beings, while the imperfect assertion of what is good institutes the imperfect ethics in vogue among human beings. The perfect Logic, on the other hand, and the perfect Ethics are products of perfect cognition and of benevolent volition. The imperfectly cognized truth, and the imperfectly actualized idea of what is good, are imperfectly externalized in the relations of life with our fellow men, and what institutes imperfect law (i.e., the body of jurisprudence), and they produce and promote the imperfect laws in society. Imperfect logic and ethics, jurisprudence and nomology, are what institutes the system of imperfect society. But when what is imperfect becomes perverted and gets mixed up with what is false, then are formed the false systems of logic and of ethics, of jurisprudence and of nomology which falsely and tragelaphically introduce and reveal the Idea of the Being. In such a situation a different statement and revelation of the Idea of the Being is necessary to purge man of falsehood, of the evil resulting from injustice and iniquity, and of his social corruption. The correction and reformation and regeneration of humanity necessarily requires the immediate intervention of God, and the revelation of the Idea of the Being through incarnation for the salvation of corrupt man who is being led to perdition. Thus do we cognize the necessity of the incarnation of the Logos for salvation from evils, return to the natural life of simplicity and innocence, and progress towards the perfection of man by means of a social system worthy of God's nature and of man's original nature. Here is founded the dominion of religious laws, of educational, and of moral, and of political laws; and here is established and consolidated the new state of Christocracy, in which the Logos incarnate has been appointed by God and is recognized by human society as the absolute Principle of religion, of education, of philosophy, and of the political state. On this account the task of the humanified Logos is: 1) one of saving men; 2) one of refining men; 3) one of perfecting men. Concerning these matters we shall have something to say in the proper place. Thus do we cognize the imperfect revelation of the Idea of the Being in imperfect man, and the necessity, engendered by corrupt man, of a revelation of the Logos for his salvation and reformation and return from evil ways, through incarnation and humanification. In the perfect man, on the other hand, we cognize revelation of the Idea of the Being as having been entirely finished; and we proclaim the perfect man to be perfectly rational, perfectly moral, and perfectly just, to be truly able to guide others to truth, virtue, and justice, — i. e., to righteousnesss. But when it came to pass that man was corrupted and could not be perfected in the contemplation of the Idea of the Being, it behooved the Being's Idea Himself to become humanified, to take on the imperfection of human nature, and to become the savior and unerring guide of corrupt man, regenerating him and reforming him by means of religion, and perfecting him by means of ethics and justice. Whatever had become impossible to man owing to sin, preventing him from comprehending the Idea of the Being by means of the original metaphysical light which had become dimmed in him, was precisely what was possible for the Idea of the Being to actualize through partial incarnation in the person of Christ, and for It Itself to become the object of man's contemplation and practice. Thus do we cognize the condescension of the Logos in man's weakness and powerlessness, and His great humiliation for the exaltation of man. Hence it may be seen that even right reason declares categorically that it is impossible for sinful man to be perfected unless he is first saved by being freed from evils. But in order to be saved he stands in need of a Savior, and such a Savior is Jesus Christ. Since all human beings are sinners, it follows that all of them therefore require salvation and are in need of the Savior. Hence the salvation of men had to be effected through the Logos, and so did their reformation and rehabilitation and perfection, because, as has been said, all things were made through the Logos. For Logos makes a being out of nothing. Logos endows it with a specific form and imparts to it a stractural form. Logos conserves and preserves it. Logos makes man and initially creates and preserves and perfects him. When he has fallen from rectitude Logos again helps him up and raises him back to his feet, and cleanses him of the sin, and heals the wound. Logos makes laws for him, and judges, and tries, and chastises him judicially, and guides him through the wilderness of life to the spiritual land of promise, while safeguarding him from every evil. Logos perfects and deifies him, and advances him in the eyes of the God of Truth, of Love, and of Justice. Logos is the beginning and end of creation. That is why everything that has been done and is being done by the Logos is logical and rational, moral and ethical, and just and righteous. Let us bow our head before the Logos, and let us take off our hat to His unlimited knowledge, goodness, and power ; and let us learn what He thinks, speaks, wills, and does, in order that we too may think, speak, will, and do like Him.

THE PERFECT REVELATION
OF THE IDEA OF THE BEING

The revelation of the Idea of the Being through the natural creation and its natural laws, or, in other words, through the relationship of beings, is imperfect, that is, proportionate to the worth and order of the natural world — an unconscious revelation, because the natural world has no consciousness and knowledge of the revelation of the Idea of the Being. But even the revelation of the Idea of the Being which is unfolded through the rational and moral laws and relationships is proportionate to his imperfectness, though it is a conscious revelation, because the moral and rational world is conscious of the Idea of the Being and of the revelation of It in its cognition and volition, as of a rational and moral law. It is naturally impossible for a perfect revelation of the Idea of the Being to be effected in an imperfect being and through an imperfect being or even through a work unequal to Him. For how could it ever be possible for that which is mindless, senseless, and unconscious to represent the perfectly conscious and rational Being perfectly? How can a being that thinks imperfectly and cognizes imperfectly succeed in cognizing and representing the perfect Idea of the Being? Therefore it is true that like represents like, and equal depicts equal. For this reason in creation we ought to discover a perfect Being perfectly depicting the perfect Idea of the Being — a conscious and perfectly cognitive Being, the key to beings and to all creation. For if creation is a revelation of the Idea of the Being, the Idea of the Being must be revealed through a Being equal and analogous thereto. The natural world, and imperfect man, is the first revelation of the Idea of the Being, the one that is imperfect. Naturally all works begin in a state of imperfection, and attain to perfection (later); and this law of gradual progress and perfection of creation is one that is general and universal. The simpler and more imperfect being is the basis of the more perfect and more composite. Matter supports plants, and plants support animals; both of them support man, the more perfect being of the natural creation. Afterwards the imperfect man serves as the abbozzo or ébauche in the making of the perfect man; that is why imperfectness precedes perfectness in point of order. The perfect man is the most perfect work and product of God, and in him is to be found the perfect revelation of the Idea of the Being. For he knows God as He is, with respect to truth, and in perfectness, as God knows Himself. He is therefore equalized to the Idea of the Being. For he wants what is good, like God, in perfectness. He is therefore equalized to the Design of the Being, which is What is Good. For he does and practices what is right like God in strictness and rigor. He is therefore equalized to the law of volition and of practice of the Being. It is precisely this, in fact, that every man should aim at; accordingly, the ideal of man is perfect knowledge of the Idea of the Being, perfect acquisition of moral virtue, and perfect exercise of justice. It is in these things that the essence of the perfect man consists; and this is the ideal of man in general. The yearning within us for perfectness is a yearning for these goods (i. e., for these good advantages): it is a yearning for deification. Deification means the equalization of man to God. That which is perfect exists inherently in God and His perfect Idea. For perfect knowledge, perfect moral virtue, and perfect justice are possessions of God that are inalienable. To learn perfectly and to do justice and virtue betokens possession of that which is perfect and coming into immediate contact with the Idea of the Being. God, being perfect in respect of knowledge, virtue, and justice, cognizes the Truth immediately and directly, and is related immediately and directly to what is morally Good and Right, through His perfect cognition, volition, and power. This relation is direct and immediate, and sempiternal, because God sempiternally cognizes the Truth, wills what is Good, and does what is Right. He coexists sempiternally together with His perfect Idea, which is the Truth, What is Good, and What is Right. So the perfectness of God resides in His perfect Idea. The Idea, therefore, of the Being is the Ideal of man; accordingly, the consequence of man's immediate and direct relation thereto is man's perfection. For through his relation to the Idea of the Being man learns and knows the Truth, and wills, or desires, What is Good, and does What is Right and Just. He possesses, therefore, the Idea of the Being. This shows that in yearning after the ideal of perfection we are yearning after the Idea of the Being, becoming immediately related to the Idea of the Being, and are enjoying perfection. The perfect man, therefore, is equal to the Idea of the Being, and consequently equal to God, or, in a word, is God - equal (in Greek: i s o t h e o s). He is related to God through the Idea of God, and resides with God in the same point of perfectness, cognizing the Truth, like God, willing what is Good, like God, and doing what is Just and Right, like God. The Idea of God is thus the common bond, and the common relationship between the perfect man and God.

| The perfect man God - equal | = | The Idea of the Perfect Being | = | The perfect Being | = GOD. |

THE PERFECT MAN

Perfectness being sempiternally in the Eternal Being who eternally cognizes Himself, it exists potentially also in the nature of imperfect man as an infinite and perfect yearning. For to yearn after that which is perfect signifies to contact perfectness through feeling. This feeling, in fact, is a feeling of our being in want and imperfect, and a conviction that what is perfect exists outside of us. The feeling speaks to us and says that we are wantful and in need of many good things, and that we ought to get out of the ego and the world, get out of what is finite, and seek what is perfect, whose existence is indubitable, for unless it actually existed we should not be yearning after it. The yearning is an indisputable and indubitable proof that what is perfect actually exists outside of us, because it is reasonable, and it is roused within us by reason, and it urges the ego to seek the perfect Being outside of itself and outside of the world. The yearning after what is perfect is a conscious conviction that we are imperfect, and is evidence supplied by right reason that what is perfect exists outside of us, but is able to enter into us and become a possession of ours. The dwelling and lingering within us of that which is perfect makes us perfect and equal to the perfect Being. But can what is perfect become a possession of ours? We yearn after what is perfect, and aim at it, as at the universal center of the rational and moral world, but it is to be wondered whether this which is perfect can contact us — i.e., whether we can get in actual touch with it. If the possibility of perfectness is in us by nature, it must at all events reside also in the nature of the perfect Being. For, if we ourselves long for what is perfect, that which actually is perfect must at all events long for us, because otherwise, as imperfect works of the perfect Being, having a view to perfectness, how could we get within hailing distance of perfectness? While longing for that which is perfect, but being pushed away by it contrary to our innate longing, how could we get near it? But is not to long for what is perfect and not succeed in attaining to it, or to be repelled by it, tantamount to a contradiction in our nature? But this contradiction nullifies our nature, because it belies it. Hence it is logically evident that the possibility of enjoying what is perfect inheres in our nature and in the nature of the perfect

Being. The perfect Being longs for a being that is capable of becoming perfect, as much as the being that is capable of becoming
perfect longs for that which is perfect. The longing is common to both and is equal on both sides. God longs to impart His
perfectness to man, as much as man longs to acquire it. But in
order for the perfectness to be communicated or transmitted to
man, and for man to become a possessor of it, what is required
is : 1) the exaltation of man in the Idea of the Being, in the
Logos ; 2) the condescension of the Idea of the Being in man, the
perfect revelation of the Logos in man. The exaltation of man in
the Logos is the acquirement of the perfect neture of the Logos.
The condescension and perfect revelation of the Logos in man is
the acquirement of man's imperfect nature. The exaltation of
imperfect man in the perfect Logos follows in the wake of the
condescension of the Logos in imperfect man, and of the revelation of Him. In condescending to the imperfectness of man, and
assuming it in Himself, the Logos, being a perfect Being, does
this out of extreme love and philanthropy, and for the purpose
of revealing God. For this reason, on the one hand He reveals
the design of God perfectly, while on the other hand He actualizes it Himself in Himself by being the first to become the
Teacher of both the theory and the practice at the same time of
the truth, of moral virtue, and of justice. So in the Logos both
the temporal and imperfect nature of man and the sempiternal
and perfect nature of God come together and coincide. The Logos
is the subject and center of them both. The Logos, being sempiternally a perfect Being, assumes the imperfect human nature
«economically» (i.e., as a m o d u s v i v e n t i or matter of
accomodation) with the purpose of exalting and perfecting man,
and perfects it by equating it to God's perfect nature. This equa-
tion takes place in the Logos and through the Logos. The Logos
is the Idea of the Being.

Imperfect human nature	— LOGOS —	Perfect divine nature

By thus perfecting human nature in Himself, the Logos
equates it to divine nature, and perfect God becomes perfect man,
as perfect man becomes and is perfect God.

Human nature perfect	— LOGOS —	Divine nature perfect

The revelation of the Logos in man, in perfectness, is a historical fact. We have received a philosophical and logical idea of this fact from preceding discussions; for we have learned that the perfect man becomes such by virtue of the Idea of the Being, which is his ideal at which he aims, and that between the Idea of the Being and the perfect man there exist an equality and consonance. Christ is the perfect God and the perfect man, because in Christ God combined human nature with His own nature, and made the perfect man. For in Him the Substance (or Hypostasis) of the perfect and sempiternal Logos is the subject, or substratum, of God's nature and of man's nature. Jesus Christ is a t h e a n t h r o p e , or God - man.

CONCERNING FIRST PRINCIPLES
A SUBJECTIVE CONSIDERATION OF THEM

We are seeking the first ideas and first principles of science, the primary laws of the spirit, by means whereof the grand and wonderful edifice of the first science is being built. And as the first idea we have found the Idea of the Being together with its elements, namely, its substance, (or hypostasis), its nature, its relationship, its extensity, and its protensity (i. e., quality of duration) — an ontological and concrete idea, as distinguished from the general and abstract idea of being. As first principles, on the other hand, we have found the primary laws themselves of the perfect Spirit, which exercises cognition, or thinks, by means of a perfect Idea of a perfect Being, by means of an ontological idea. Inasmuch then, as we have reserved the subject of first principles in order to treat of it in a special chapter, we now undertake to examine it by asking, What are the first principles of science?

In every science there are immediate and mediate principles, which are also called consequences of the immediate premises, or secondary principles. These primary principles of which we are now speaking are self - evident, perspicuous, and plain, needing no interpretation to explain them; whereas the secondary principles are cognized and understood by means of the primary, and are interpreted by means of the latter, as is done also in the case of primitive and derived ideas. Each proof forms a new principle; and thus by proceeding from proof to proof we pass from principle to principle — or, by means of the first principles we create second principles; and by means of these, third principles, and so on; and in this fashion we convert all scientific generalizations (called p o r i s m a t a in Greek, or p o r i s m s in English) into scientific principles. Yet this multitude of principles has come from the existence and combination of the first principles of science, which are self - evident, self - proved, and self - interpreted, and on this account certain and perspicuous. But the first principles of all particular sciences are particular principles, and on this account are consequences of more general first and absolute principles. The relative consequences presuppose the existence of relative principles from which they have been derived. Relative principles presuppose the existence of absolute first principles of which they are the consequences. But what we are now in quest of is not the first principles of any particular science, or the principles of all particular sciences, but the first principles of the first and highest science, called Philosophy ; these principles are absolute principles, and are the source from which all the principles of the particular sciences are derived. But in order to discover the first principles we must observe the principles of the particular sciences first. Each science is the science of some being, and its purpose or object is to ascertain and comprehend its subject - matter (called its «object», i. e., object - matter, in Greek) a) with reference to its nature and essence ; b) with reference to the efficient cause of it ; c) with reference to the final cause. On this account it may be said that all the generalizations, or results, of science are generalizations and proofs of the nature, of the efficient and final cause, of its subject - matter. W h a t i s e a c h o f t h e b e i n g s? W h a t i s i t s e f f i c i e n t a n d f i n a l c a u s e? W h a t i s e a c h b e i n g f o r? On these pivots turns all our knowledge, which is knowledge of the nature, of the origin, and of the end of beings. We observe that in each of the particular sciences the precise thing that is being sought is this knowledge of the nature, of the origin, and of the end of the being whereof it is the science. Inductively we extend this cognition to every particular science, meaning that in every particular science, what is being sought is the nature, the origin, and the end of its subject - matter, i. e.. of its object of study. From this general observation we are led back up to cognition of the absolute first science of the Idea of the Being, which science is seeking to comprehend and learn all about the Idea of the Being as respects Its nature, origin, and end. What is the Idea of the Being ? What is Its efficient and final reason ? Here, behold, is where the knowledge of the first science is staked out, and enclosed in a circle demarcating it from all other sciences.

In cognizing that a being exists our cognitive spirit cognizes it with respect to its nature as well as its efficient and final cause. But outside of the circle of this cognition it is impossible for it to extravagate. In the cognition, or thought, What is the being? the spirit cognizes the being with respect to its primary and elementary attributes, and cannot at the same time cognize it both as being and as not being, i.e., both as a being and as a nonbeing. This limitation of the spirit whereby it is rendered naturally incapable of cognizing a being at the same time both as existent and as inexistent in the realm of reality — that is to say, both as a being and as a nonbeing — is the immediate relationship of the subject to the object — a necessary relationship, and a necessary law of the spirit, according to which the spirit necessarily cognizes that a being is a being, and that a living being is living, or alive, and that a thinking being is thinking, or intelligent. This immediate relationship of the cognitive spirit to the cognizable object is what constitutes the principle of identity and of contradiction, a logical and scientific principle. Moreover, since this principle is an immediate relationship of the cognizer to the object cognized (i. e., of the thinker to the object thought of), wherein the cognizing subject is assured of its identity, it constitutes the all — dominating and universal law oi contradiction, which may be illustrated diagrammatically as follows ;

Principle	
Ego ——————————————— Ego	
of contradiction	

The principle of contradiction when applied to particular beings acquires a particular character. But when applied to the Absolute Being it is characterized as an absolute principle. For in cognizing the Idea of the Being we are cognizing His beingness, and it is impossible for us to cognize at the same time His beingness and His nonbeingness. When we are cognizing the Being, we cognize Him as something absolute, and as ever the same, unchangeable and immutable, as an absolute identity. This cognition of our spirit is a cognition of every cognitive spirit. Therefore also of God. For this reason it is an all - dominating and universal law. God as a perfect Spirit knows Himself perfectly, and any being contingently outside of Him : as for Him Himself, He cognizes Himself as an absolute and necessary identity, but as for the fact, He cognizes it as a contingent and relative identity. The first principle, therefore, of the spirit is that of contradiction, a logical and scientific principle.

But every thing that is cognized as a being is cognized either as a principle, or as the consequence of another principle. It is cognized either as a cause, or as the effect of another cause. Any cause that is the effect of another cause is relative, because it has its reason of existence in its productive cause. For instance; Joachim was a descendant of David was a descendant of Judah ; Judah was a descendant of Abraham ; Abraham was a descendant of Shem ; Shem was the son of Noah ; Noah was a descendant of Seth ; Seth was a son of Adam ; and Adam was a work of God. Joachim, as a descendant of David and the father of the Theotoke (more usually called the Virgin Mary in English ; but Theotoke is the usual appellation in Greek and is more appropriate as signifying «the woman who gave birth to God»), is therefore a cause and an effect, not taken contradictorily, but from another point of view. For he was the father of the Theotoke, but a descendant of David. David was the cause of the birth of Joachim ; the cause of the latter was Judah, ond of Judah again the cause was Abraham. Abraham was an effect due to Shem, the cause of whom was Noah ; and the cause of Noah was Seth. The cause of Seth was Adam. By following this chain of reasoning through one becomes logically convinced, therefore, that Adam was the first cause of human beings, because all human beings, including both men and women, were begotten of his loins. But was Adam also the first cause of himself ? Had he, that is to say, the cause of his own existence in himself, and was he a self - existent being ? Certainly not. For Adam was a work of God ; therefore he was an effect. God, on the other hand, as having the cause of His own existence in Himself, as being a self - caused being, is a self - existent and absolute Cause. In order to cognize the first and absolute Cause we must first cognize the particular effects and their particular causes. From the cognition of these we must lift ourselves up to cognition of the absolute Cause, on whom depend all particular causes as effects of Him. Because this cognition involves a relationship between the effect and its productive cause it constitutes the principle of causality — a heuristic principle, because it enables us to discover the cause of every being. The relationship between the cause and its effect is the constant law of causality, which we formulate as follows :

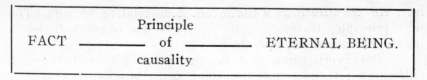

The principle of causality when applied to particular and contingent causes and effects possesses a particular and contingent character. But when applied to the absolute Cause it is characterized as an absolute principle. For in congizing a being we cognize it either as the cause of another being or as the effect of something, or else as both an effect and the cause of some other being at the same time. B is the cause of C, and an effect of A. The latter is the first letter, uncaused and absolute. B and C together are effects of A — i.e., B+C←A. The cognition of causality is an all - dominating (i.e., universally valid) cognition, and a universal law of the spirit. In the perfect Spirit the cognition of this law is perfect.

Everything when cognized as a being, however, as an effect or as a cause, is cognized also as having some purpose, as aiming at or being aimed at some end. What is this or that being for? What final reason has it? We deduce this general cognition (or conception) from observation of the particular purposes which particular beings have. Every being among the sum - total of beings aims at or is aimed at the existence and maintenance of another being; and all beings together concur mutually in promoting the effectuation and accomplishment of some universal or general purpose. For instance : plants are intended to maintain the life of animals; both of them are intended to maintain the life of man. This is the natural purpose. But when a human being derives sustenance from plants and animals, he maintains his life with a view to some purpose that is higher than matter — a moral and spiritual purpose which he is pursuing. Hence from the partial purposefulness of beings we gather the general and universal principle of purpose and of order — a legal and legislative principle — by conceiving that every being has some final reason of its existence. Thus it may be said that since beings are adapted to themselves in accordance with the order and purpose of each and of all together, and to the Being of beings, they form the particular purposes and the one absolute purpose which creation aims at. This purpose has been discovered in the absolute existence of the Being, as an absolute purpose, which we may formulate in somewhat the following fashion :

General	Principle	Absolute
	of	
purpose	purposefulness	purpose

The principle of purposefulness when applied to the case of particular and contingent beings is a particular and contingent principle; but in reference to the absolute purpose of the Being it is an absolute principle. For in cognizing each and every being as benefiting and at the same time being benefited by others in the universal order of beings, we cognize the relative purpose of beings. But in cognizing the Being who benefits but is not benefited by others, we cognize the perfect Being, who has in Himself the final reason of His existence. Why does a plant exist? In order to benefit an animal. Why then does an animal exist? In order to benefit man. But why does man exist? In order to be made a God who is being benefited by God. The plant and the animal were made for man, but man was made for God, who is the end of creation. But it is in this benefit which the plant and the animal confer upon man that their beneficialness is to be found; for all finite beings are benefited mutually, because they are particular and relative goods (or «good things»), whereas God, as the highest Being, and the absolute Good, benefits all things, and, because He is perfect and wantless, is benefited by none. Because He is the perfect Being, God is also the perfect and really good Being, the one who is complete and self - sufficient and in need of nothing. But the purpose of benefit is a different one from the purpose of perfectness. Benefit consists in the purposeful use of a being. The perfectness of a being, on the other hand, consists in the acquirement of all things whereof its imperfect nature has need. Being begotten as infants, we need food for the perfection of our body (i.e., in order to enable our body to grow to maturity); and we need instruction and teaching for the perfection of our souls. The naked body requires clothing; and a mindless (i. e., «senseless») soul requires cognition and knowledge. Bread, teaching, clothing, cognition are goods of benefit to our bodies and souls. The purpose of benefiting them is the nourishment and growth of the body and of the soul. But what sort of end are the body and the soul intended for? Manhood is the age during which our body acquires whatever it needs to acquire in order to serve as the means of a higher purpose. Deification is that state of the soul in which the latter has acquired everything that it had need of, has fulfilled its yearnings, and yearns for nothing, because it has acquired what it needed, and needs nothing, having now become self - sufficient and perfect. Thus do we cognize the distinction of the purpose of benefit from the purpose of perfectness, whereof the former becomes the means of the latter, because all beings concur in the effectuation and accomplishment of a certain supreme purpose, the deification of man, and the immediate consequence of the accomplishment thereof is imperishability and immortality, as the highest benefit of creation.

AN OBJECTIVE CONSIDERATION OF FIRST PRINCIPLES

The laws of the spirit are connate to the spirit; accordingly, we cannot cognize the existence of the spirit without also cognizing the coexistence of them together with the latter. Since, therefore, the ego acquires its spirit from another source, and does not project it out of itself like God, it acquires along with the spirit also the laws of the latter, and cognizes things in accordance therewith, notwithstanding that in the beginning the ego is ignorant of their nature and significance. An infant, having its sense organs, because it has a body in which there are located, eats by means of its mouth, hears by means of its ears, and feels by means of its touch, and sees by means of its eyes. Yet it is ignorant of the significance and nature of sense organs, notwithstanding that it possesses such, since it has acquired a body. By analogy we cognize a similar predicament as respects the spirit, in which, though it is true that there are laws of cognition, the ego is ignorant of them to begin with so far as concerns their significance and nature, although possesing them, since it has acquired a cognitive spirit. The laws and the first principles of the spirit immediately regulate cognition, and relate the latter to the cognizable object, and connect it therewith as by means of a bond. But since the necessary and sempiternal Being is a single being (i. e., a s o l e being), the cognitive principle is a single one too, though likewise a necessary and sempiternal principle, a universal, absolute, and first principle. Hence therefore God in cognizing Himself as a sempiternal being who is not only necessary but also universal, as a being who contains all existence. God exercises cognition in accordance with a certain principle and sempiternal, necessary, absolute, and universal law, which is the sempiternal and necessary law of the Spirit. Everything that God cognizes He cognizes it directly and immediately by means of His perfect Idea, in which is contained every idea of every contingent and possible being. This immediate and direct cognition is the law of cognition, an absolute and sempiternal law, be-

cause the Spirit of God too is absolute and sempiternal. The law
of cognition, though a single law (i. e., one in point of number),
has a threefold nature, resulting from the variety of objects cognized, to wit : 1) the Law of contradiction ; 2) the Law of causality; 3) the Law of purposefulness. God cognizes Himself as well
as the contingent being outside of Him. In other words, He cognizes the Being and the fact. In the cognition of Himself He
begets the Idea, who is equal and like unto Him, as a perfect
image of Him, possessing perfect beingness, perfect aliveness,
and perfect awareness ; and through It He sempiternally contemplates Himself, as He is, being unable at the same time to cognize Himself as he is not. God cognizes Himself as one who is
perfect, and He cannot at the same time also cognize Himself as
one who is imperfect. He cognizes Himself as a necessary and
sempiternal being, and He cannot at the same time also cognize
Himself as contingent being and as a fact. Diagrammatically :

Eternal beingness Necessary beingness Sempiternal beingness Perfect beingness	Law of contradiction	Eternal nonbeingness Necessary nonbeingness Sempiternal nonbeingness Perfect nonbeingness

This cognition of the Being is a) absolute, b) necessary, c)
universal. It is absolute because it has in itself the reason of its
existence, and has no cause of itself : it is self — caused and self
—existent cognition. It is necessary because it cannot help existing — that of which the inexistence is impossible, and whose
existence we can perspicuously and immediately cognize, and
cannot deny, is said to be necessary. It is universal because it
has every cognition within it, because it is the universality and
totality of cognition, and out of it arises, or is formed, every
cognition. On this account the principle of contradiction in the
Idea of the Being is analogous to the Spirit of God and to His
Idea : it is an absolute, necessary, and universal principle. The
absolute contradiction is an absolute principle and law of the
Spirit connecting the subject of cognition — the Eternal Being
— with its object — with the Eternal Being, and with the contingent and possible being : a) as with an eternal idea, and b) as
with a (real) being, and a fact in time. Diagrammatically :

| Law |
| Eternal Being   —   of   —   Eternal Being—Eternal Nonbeing. |
| Contradiction |

But God cognizes Himself and what is outside of Him — Himself, as a necessary and absolute cause ; what is outside Him, both before entifying it and after entifying it, as something contingent and possible, and relative and causate, capable of being or not being, depending on the Being's will. As an absolute cause, in cognizing Himself God begets the Idea of His absolute cause of every possible and contingent thing, being perfectly able to bestow existence, life, thought, according to His own free and independent will, voluntarily and after His own bent, and to nullify it freely, should He care to do so, in the idea of His omniscience and justice. In cognizing Himself as an absolute cause, He cognizes the product thereof to be causate, while in His Idea he connects the cognition of the cause and of the effect ; accordingly it may be said that the Idea of the Being is at the same time also an idea of the fact. By nature it is an Idea of the Being ; but by position it is an idea of the fact, because it depicts the fact, which it contains and comprises in itself, as an idea that possibly might actually receive existence and hypostasis outside of the Being, through the operation of the Being's will. Hence it may be asserted that through the law of causality God cognizes in His own Idea of Himself the truth that He is the absolute cause of every possible and contingent being, of every potential and actual being the necessary cause.

Absolute	Law	Absolute
	— of —	
Cause	causality	Causate

This cognition of God's is a) absolute, b) necessary, c) universal. It is absolute because it is a first cognition of the absolute and first Cause, and has in itself the reason of its existence. It is necessary because God cognizes Himself and what is outside of Him necessarily as a cause and (causate) effect. He cognizes the (causate) effect sempiternally, as a hypostasis (i. e., unsubstantiated) idea, whose hypostasis is possible and contingent in time.

Hence it may be said that God necessarily cognizes the cognition of the unsubstantiated (i. e., substanceless) idea of the nonbeing, because in cognizing Himself He cannot help cognizing also t h e o t h e r (i. e., His nonself). In cognizing the Being He cannot help cognizing also the nonbeing. It is the cognition of the Being as a being, and of the nonbeing as a nonbeing, that the necessary principle of causality really resides. That which is contingent, on the other hand, exists in the entification of the nonbeing, in creation, and not in the cognition of the nonbeing, because God necessarily cognizes the nonbeing.

	Law	
ETERNAL BEING —	of —	FACT
	causality	

The necessary cognition of the Being as of a cause is also a necessary cognition of the contingent being as of a causate effect. For this reason we say that the law of causality is a necessary and sempiternal law. The cognition of the cause is universal, because it contains in itself every cognition of every cause and of every causate effect, cognition both of that which is necessary and of that which is contingent, because it is the totality and universality of cause and effect. The absolute causality is an absolute principle and law of cognition connecting the effect with its cause, the principle with its consequence, and the Being with the fact, eternity with time, the infinite, the necessary, the immutable with that which is finite, contingent, mutable — the perfect with the imperfect. Hence it is evident that this law is the link connecting the cause with its effect.

A necessary consequence of the cognition of the nonbeing in God is the cognition of the nonbeing. Hence it is logically to be inferred that the cognition of the Being is the principle. For this reason just as the cognition of the Being as of the cause is necessary and absolute, so and in like manner the cognition of the nonbeing is necessary and absolute likewise. By hypothetically nullifying, or doing away with, the cognition of the Idea of the Being, in conjunction therewith we are nullifying, or doing away with, the necessary laws of the Spirit as well as the existence of the cognitive Spirit. For this reason we say that the necessary cognition of the nonbeing is a consequence of the necessary cognition of the Being. The nonbeing is cognized through the Being. For this reason it is that the perfect Idea of the Being which necessarily is, has in itself eternal and necessary beingness, as well as possible and contingent and temporal beingness. Hence it follows that the Idea of the Being conjoins in Itself the Being and the fact, the cause with the (causate) effect. Accordingly, as It is sempiternally the Idea indicative of the Being and of the nonbeing, It can receive hypostasis even outside of the Being, in the fact, and can reveal Itself also as the perfect idea of the fact. This possibility of revelation of the Idea of the Being in the fact, is not a denial of the Being, nor a contradiction, because the revelation of the Idea of the Being in the fact, is an assumption of the fact, and not a degeneration or modification of the sempiternal Idea of the Being into a hypostasis of the fact. For the Eternal Being, being an absolute, and necessary, and immutable, and sempiternal being, it is naturally impossible for Him to be modified and to degenerate into a temporal, contingent, mutable, and transformable being. But the Eternal Being can assume the nature of the fact without nullifying His own immutable nature. The perfect Being can assume the imperfect nature of the fact in order to perfect it therein. The recognition of this possibility is based upon the principle that the fact in no wise nullifies the Being, what is imperfect does not nullify or do away with what is perfect, but, instead, the eternal and perfect Being makes and makes perfect the fact and that which is imperfect. The impossibility exists in the contradiction, whereas the possibility exists in the consonance and nature of the truth. Whatever does not contradict itself or anything else is something that can be actualized or realized. The revelation and incarnation of the Idea of God is logically possible, because it contains in itself no contradiction. Hence it is evidently possible for it to be actualized. Accordingly, this matter is a question of history, as to whether it has been actualized. The Eternal Being cognizes the nonbeing and what may contingently become something of a being by virtue of the Idea of the Being. Hence He cognizes it in His Idea as a privation, as an imperfection, and not as a contradiction, because in a logical idea there can be no contradiction. Through His perfect Idea God can cognize the imperfect idea of a contingent being. But He cannot cognize beingness and nonbeingness of Himself through His Idea at the same time, because this would be a logically impossible contradiction. A contradiction both posits and negates the same thing at the same time, which is absurd. Hence it is logically evident that God can make the nonbeing through the perfect Being, an imperfect being capable of being perfected, because the imperfectness of the work nowise contradicts the perfectness of the one who made it, because He can make it perfect. An imperfect being nowise contradicts the perfect being, but is a defect of the latter, yet capable of being perfected and of casting off the defect. God made an imperfect being capable of progress and of being perfected. Moreover, just as through His Idea He conceived and made the imperfectness and defect of the fact, through His Idea He has conceived, and has revealed, also the means whereby it can be perfected. Accordingly, the revelation of the Idea of the Being in the fact purposes the bringing of the fact to perfection; and for this reason it is also possible, and reasonable, because of its being a requirement of the fact. Hence it may be said that in revealing Himself God is doing a deed or work which is reasonable and proper, and the omission of which would be tantamount to a deadening of creation and destruction of the divine work. The denial of Him or of the declaration that He is the author of the work is tantamount to a denial of the Being's wisdom and providence. It would be a denial of God's existence. All those persons who deny the possibility and the actualizability of the revelation and incarnation of the Logos in the world for the purpose of perfecting creation, and for the fulfillment of God's sempiternal Design, are atheists (i. e. , «men without a God», according to the etymology of the word). Further, the revelation of the Idea of the Being is a declaration of the absolute Cause of beings, the revelation of the Entity Himself, of the Truth Himself, of the Causality Himself, of the Endfulness Himself the expression of the eternal laws of the Spirit.

But God cognizes Himself as the reason for benefiting beings, as the end of their existence, as the law of the essence of their existence, life, and thought. In this cognition He begets, or generates, His Idea depictive and representative of the Purpose of beings a) of Himself as purposefulness itself ; b) of things outside of Him as contingent. But why does God exist? Because it were impossible for Him not to exist. Hence it is evident that He has in Himself the efficient and final cause of His own existence. But why do beings exist? Because God, the Supreme Being, exists, and without Him they could not exist. Hence it is evident that the end of beings is the Being of beings, God. As for the purpose of beings, it is their law. For this reason it may be said that purposefulness is a legislative principle. This principle in God is a law connecting God as the highest end of beings with the latter, the purpose with the nature of the being, the destiny with the attributes of the being, by means whereof the latter can achieve it.

Imperfect	Law	Perfect
—	of	—
being	purposefulness	Being

The imperfect being aims at the perfect Being, who is its law. Life completes and supplements existence; and imperfect cognition completes and supplements life and existence. Perfect cognition, on the other hand, supplements and perfects imperfect cognition by means of the perfect Idea of the Being, by means of the absolute Truth. Hence it may be said that the perfect Idea of the Being is the perfect and absolute Purpose of beings. The perfect cognition of the absolute Purpose of beings is the cognition of the perfect Design of Being, and of His perfect Law which issues out of God's perfect volition. This cognition is a) absolute, because there is none other higher than it; b) necessary, because it cannot help being such, on account of God's sempiternally cognizing Himself as the universal and necessary Purpose of beings; c) universal, because it comprises every cognition of a particular purpose. The perfect Design, of God, because of its being the end of beings and their destiny, is consonant and analogous to their nature. For if God made the beings, necessarily these aim at or are aimed at Him, i.e., are intended for Him; accordingly, they demand of Him a law for their perfectness. This means, therefore, that He is the law of their existence, life, and thought, because He is also their Maker. Hence it may be said that a declaration of God's perfect Design in creation is a possible and reasonable demand of the beings, involving no contradiction. This indeed is declared in creation by a work that is perfect and able to represent it perfectly, and to become itself the Principle of God's works and the Law of beings. This revelation of God's Design in the perfect work involves in itself no contradiction; for God's Design itself in the perfect work does not become a work and product essentially modified, nor can it be identified with the essence of the work, but, on the contrary, continues to be an eternal Design of God that is perfect, assuming the fact in time in order to perfect it and equalize it to Itself. Assumption, however, differs from degeneration and modification of a being, which is as impossible in the nature of things as assumption is possible. For this reason we say that the Being made the fact, and not that He degenerated into the essence of the fact, because this would be contradictory. So, in sum, it may be asserted that the creation of the perfect work is a perfect revelation and incarnation of God's s u b s t a n t i v e (otherwise spoken of as «subsistential» and «hypostatic» — in English) Design, or, in a word, the Good.

⊙ THE ESSENCE OF THE LOGOS

The three principles of cognition (i. e., of thought) — namely, that of contradiction, that of causality, and that of purposefulness — constitute the essence of the Logos, because the Logos indicates this to be a) the beingness of the Being and His essence as distinguished from the beingness and essence of the contigent and of the fact; b) the truth that He is the first and absolute cause of all beings; c) the truth that He is the end and purpose at which all creation aims. The indication of these truths is complete and perfect; and, accordingly, the Logos is a complete and perfect expression and explanation of the Being's essence and nature. In looking at the Logos we are looking at the identity, the causality, and the purposefulness of the Being, in whom all beings are, from whom they have received their beingness, and at whom they aim as at a final purpose, or target. The absolute identity of the Being is also the absolute identity of the Logos, because the Logos possesses entity, as a perfect image and exact expression and representation of the Being. The absolute causality of the Being is also the absolute causality of the Logos, because the Logos, as an image of the Being's causility, cannot help being the original cause. The absolute purposefulness of the Being is also the absolute purposefulness of the Logos, because the latter is the express image of the Being's purposefulness. Through the Logos the Being cognizes His identity, causality, and purposefulness. Hence it may be said that the Logos in God is an image of the Being's absolute identity, purposefulness, and causality. He is a Being who is the same essentially with the Being, being distinguished from the Eternal Being as being the latter's sempiternal offspring, as the cause, and as the Purpose, of creation. He is, in addition, the efficient and final reason of beings. In order, therefore, to learn the origin and end and nature of beings we must cognize the absolute Logos of the universe, or, more plainly speaking, its efficient and final cause. In the essence of the Logos resides the identity, the causality, and the purposefulness of the absolute Being and of every contingent being. He explains the essence of the Being, and reveals the efficient and final cause of beings, God. He connects the fact with the Being, God with creation, the cognizer with the cognized, the infinite with the finite, the divine with the human, and serves as the bond between them. It was through the Logos that all things were made, and it is through the Logos that they progress and are perfected. Things that bear the seal of Logos are approved as «exceedingly good» (Gen. 1 : 31 ; the ordinary English versions of the Bible have it translated as «very good», but the foregoing phrase is closer to the sence of the original text. — N o t e   o f   t h e   T r a n s l a t o r) . Furthermore, the Logos, being the primary law of God's perfect cognition, is like-wise the primary law of His volition, and action, and power, and feeling. He is an absolute and universal law, sempiternally exi-sting and sempiternally being begotten out of the Being's cogni-tion. In short, God sempiternally cognizes, exercises will and power, acts, and feels in accordance with Him. Diagrammatically:

```
                              RIGHT
Eternal  Being — (called  the  Logos) —  Fact
                              REASON
```

The Logos is the eternal and necessary law of the Spirit. Accordingly, the application and prevalence of the Logos in all cognition is their relationship and communication with God's absolute cognition, which sempiternally cognizes in accordance with the necessary Principle of the Logos, i.e., the Truth. In the Logos the cognitions of finite beings coincide and meet with God's infinite cognition, communing with the infiniteness of the Being, and being equalized through the Truth to God's infinite cognition. This indeed is the end at which all cognition aims. The Logos is the mountain of cognition, and the intellect that climbs it beholds the Being and the Truth, and has a scientific knowledge and understanding of the origin and of the end of beings. In the Logos is the limit of the most advanced and perfect knowledge, because in Him is to be found the notion of the uni-versality, of the infinity, of the eternity, of the necessariness, of the identity, of the purposefulness, and of the causality of beings. The Logos is the limit of the absolute s c i b i l e. Accordingly, upon Him is founded Philosophy, the highest and chief of the sciences, whose purpose and end is comprehension of the Logos, as the Idea of the Being, and as the absolute and primary Law of the Spirit ; and, furthermore, the application and domination thereof in every act of volition, whereby beings enter into relationship and communication with the perfect volition of God, which sempiternally wills, in accordance with the Principle of the Logos, what is Good. In the Logos volitions coinciding with God's infinite volition become equalized thereto in the volition of what is Good, which is their goal. The Logos is the limit of the will's free activity; and in the Logos the will succeeds in actualizing what is Good, and accomplishes its purpose. In the Logos exists the notion of morality and of perfect virtue. Accordingly, the will which climbs up in the Logos acquires perfect morality and virtue. Upon the Logos, moreover, is founded true Ethics, the object of which is the performance of what is good. The Logos is the necessary law of the Spirit. In the application of it to any external act the external act of God coincides with the acts of rational and free beings. Thus these acts become equalized to a perfect act of God through the operation of what is Right and Just. Every power that performs its own function in the Logos, is acting rightly and justly, and is a free power. In the Logos are to be found the notions of rightness, of justice, of freedom, and of equality; accordingly, whoever acts in the Logos, is exercising justice and is really free. The Logos is the law of the Spirit and the law of the feeling of the Being. In feeling in accordance with the Logos all the feeling of beings coincide with God in what is Fine and Beautiful; accordingly, they feel glad and rejoice in the enjoyment of what is good and in the contemplation of the truth. What is true, what is good, what is right, what is Just, what is fine and beautiful, are all harmoniously compined in the Logos and the Idea of the Being; and they form the harmonious world of eternity and immortality, the blisful kingdom of God. When thus conceived (cognized) as the absolute Idea of the Being, and as the absolute and necessary and primary Law of His cognition, the Logos is the substantial (or substantiated) image of the Being, the efficient creative and final Reason (or Logos) of beings, the absolute identity, causality, and purposefulness, the Truth, what is Good, what is Right and Just, the Fine and Beautiful feature of the absolute Being, the object proper of Philosophy, and the first Principle of the science of Logic, of Ethics, of Aesthetics, of Jurisprudence, and of Political Science.

THE UNITY OF PRINCIPLES

The three logical principles, that of contradiction, that of causality, and that of purposefulness, which constitute the essence of the Logos, are united in the notion of the absolute Being, in the absolute Idea, in which they are characterized as absolute, because in the process of cognizing the Idea of the Being the ego applies the logical principles in an absolute sense. But we cognize the Idea of the Being from the idea of the fact, in accordance with the principle of absolute causality as correlating therewith. Hence it follows that the unity of logical principles exists in the rela-

tionship between the fact and the Eternal Being, in cognition of
the absolute cause, in the absolute Idea. So that the principle of
causality, being a heuristic and philosophic principle, is the main
principle which Philosophy is seeking after as a first and universal principle, as a primary law of cognition. In this principle
are comprised also the two other logical principles in their absolute sense. These three principles of reason together constitute an
essentially single principle, that of causality, in accordance with
which we cognize what is absolute from what is relative, the
Eternal Being from the fact, that which is necessary from that
which is contingent, what is infinite and eternal from what is
finite and temporal. For how can we determine the impossibility
of there being or not being a Being from the impossibility of
there being or not being the fact, unless it be through the principle of causality? How can we cognize the absolute principle of
contradiction without being led back up in accordance with the
principle of causality to cognition of the absolute Being? Moreover, we cognize the principle of purposefulness in an absolute
sense through the principle of absolute causality. For how can
we cognize the absolute purposefulness of beings from the beingness of particular purposes, unless it be through the logical
principle of causality? On this account we say that in the principle of absolute causality are involved the principles of absolute
contradiction and of absolute purposefulness. For the absolute
cause exists absolutely, and cannot at the same time not exist
absolutely, as the efficient (or creative) cause and as the absolute
final purpose of being. On this account, in seeking the first Principle and the first Law of cognition Philosophy is seeking the
principle of absolute causality, which may be formulated as follows:

Eternal	Law	the
———	of	———
Being	causality	fact

But even in regard to the fact the three principles of reason
are united in the principle of causality. Because in the fact we
observe occurrences past and present, of which some are the
results of the others. Hence it follows that they are effects of
other causes, which likewise are effects of still other causes; and
for this reason it may be said that are relative causes producing
relative effects. But since relative causes cannot be said to proceed without limit — i.e., be multiplied infinitely — we conclude
that before them there was an infinite cause productive of them,

namely, God. The relative effects and the relative causes which we discover or trace by applying the principle of causality in the process of induction, present themselves perspicuously in our spirit, and it is impossible for us to conceive of their inexistence. The impossibility of their being and not being, in accordance with the principle of contradiction, presupposes cognition of the cause and of the effect. Logically, therefore, this presupposes the principle of causality. But even any particular purpose of a being depends on some other more general one; and this more general one, in turn, depends on one that is universal and absolute. But we have the conception of the more general purpose from a conception of the particular purpose. Hence it follows that in order to cognize any general purpose, and therefrom the universal purpose, we have to apply the principle of causality. So, then, we reach the conclusion that in general the three principles of contradiction, of causality, and of purposefulness in both their relative and their absolute sense and application, depend on the principle of causality, which is the first principle of Philosophy, the relationship and bond of the Being to the fact. The Idea of the Being comprises in itself also the idea of the fact, as the principle of cognition is one that comprises every logical principle. In seeking the Idea of the Being, Philosophy is seeking to cognize everything. In seeking the first and absolute Principle of cognition, it is engaged in seeking the Law of the Spirit through which the Being and the fact are comprehended, and not merely cognized. The discovery and comprehension of them fulfills Philosophy and satisfies the yearning to know. God cognizes Himself as self - existent, as a self - caused being, in accordance with the principle of causality, by which the cause is sought. He cognizes Himself as a being itself, and cannot cognize Himself also as a nonbeing itself, in accordance with the principle of contradiction. He cognizes Himself as complete in Himself, as perfect in and by Himself, in accordance with the principle of purposefulness. His Idea, on the other hand, is representative of His perfectness, of His essence, of His self - causality, self - perfectness, and self - entity. This means that the Idea of the Being is also the idea of the principles of cognition, and that the Idea of God is at the same time also the idea of His Law of cognition. Consequently the ontological Logos is the Idea of the Being, and is the bond, or nexus, of the Being to the fact. In the cognition of the Idea of the Being is the cognition of the Logos; and in the cognition of the Logos is the cognition of the Idea of Being. Therefore it may be said that in seeking to comprehend the Idea of the Being, Philosophy is seeking to comprehend the Logos and the application of Him in all cognition. In seeking to comprehend and apply the Logos it is seeking to comprehend the Idea of the Being. The absolute Idea of the Being and the absolute Principle of cognition, together are the object of Philosophy. By ascending upon the principle of absolute causality we are enabled to cognize causality itself, entity itself, and perfectness itself — we are enabled to cognize the perfect Idea of the Being. This principle, in which are included also the other principles of reason, are the ontological Logos, who reveals to us the perfectness of the Being. A philosophy supported upon this unshakable Principle is true and unshakable. Such is the Christian Philosophy, whose truth and principles we now intend to point out in the following pages; and it is being taught in our Philosophical College of the Logos, in which we too have been taught it.

THE PRIMARY LAW OF THE SPIRIT

The ego, a cognitive being, cognizes a) itself as the subject of cognition; b) the other as the object of cognition. In the process of cognizing the subject and the object it prescribes the primary law of cognition, which it also formulates as an absolute and universal law of the Spirit. For the ego, in cognizing itself as subject and at the same time object, cognizes itself as a contnigency and as a fact, as having a relative existence, as an effect. Thus it also cognizes what is outside of itself - its body and the beings roundabout it. It can cognize that which is c a u s a t e, which is the first condition of logical cognition. By conjoining and combining the relative cognition of the ego with the relative cognition of the sum - total of the beings roundabout us — the world — through the logical principle of causality, in which are comprised also the two other principles of contradiction and of purposefulness, it is enabled to ascend to a conception of their cause and to connection of them therewith, through the principle of reason, which defines the relationship between effects and their causes. In the conjunction of the idea of the ego and that of the world, the idea of the finite and of the fact with the idea of their efficient (or creative) cause, is to be seen the primary law of cognition, whereby we are led back from the effect up to the cause, and from the latter we are let down to the effect and the fact. From relative contradiction and relative purposefulness we are led back up to absolute contradiction and purposefulness, to the real Being, the First Cause and the final purpose of the existence of beings. We formulate the primary law of the Spirit as follows:

Relative contradictions	: :	Absolute contradiction
Relative causes	: :	Absolute cause
Relative purposes	: :	Absolute purpose.

But in order to cognize absolute contradiction from relative contradictions, the absolute purpose from the relative purposes, and the absolute cause from the relative causes, we need right reason, the primary law of cognition, the principle of causality. The relative contradiction is the contradiction of the fact; and the relative purpose is one dependent upon the universal purpose. The relative contradiction depends on the absolute contradiction, as an effect depending on its cause. The absolute contradiction, the absolute purpose, and the absolute cause logically are the absolute entity, the absolute causality, and the absolute purposefulness — the essence of the unsubstantiated right reason within us. Ontologically, on the other hand, — or, more explicitly speaking, in the perfect Spirit of the perfect Being, God — they are the absolute Truth, the perfect and absolute moral Good; the absolute cause, or, in other words, the essence of the ontological Logos, through whom the First Being, God, can be known perfectly. The perfect Being, exercising cognition in a perfect Spirit through a perfect Logos (or Reason), cognizes Himself as the absolute Truth, the absolute Good, and the absolute end of beings. But in cognizing also what is not — i.e., nonbeing — yet is able to become something. He cognizes it perfectly as a nonbeing, as capable of becoming something, as relative, as causate, and as an effect. He cognizes it through the ontological Logos, through whom He also cognizes Himself; for in the Logos are to be found all the ideas of all possible and contingent beings, which are cognized through the Logos, and through the Logos are created and entified outside of God.

The perfect Being, God, cognizes Himself as a self - existent, and self - caused, and self - perfect Being, through the primary law of cognition, the ontological Logos, through whom He cognizes and creates the fact out of nonbeing. Between the Being and His Idea operates the cognitive Spirit, as a bond uniting the Idea with the Being. In the perfect cognitive Spirit of the Being resides the perfect Law of cognition a necessary and sempiternal law, an absolute and uviversal canon of thought, of volition, and of external activity of rational and moral beings. In the primary Law of cognition the relative coincides with the absolute, the phenomenon with the being, the fact with the Eternal Being, that which is temporal with that which is sempiternal and everlasting, that which is contingent with the necessary Being, that which is finite with that which is infinite, that which is imperfect with that which is perfect, the many with the one, that which is alterable with that which is unalterable : and the fact is united with the Being with resulting imperishability and immortality and perfectness. In the primary Law of cognition the cognition of what is finite coincides with the cognition of what is infinite ; the volition and activity of the fact with the volition and activity of the Eternal Being : and through it the cognition of the Infinite, His volition and activity is transmitted in the cognition, the volition, and the activity of that which is finite. which is thus transmitted into the sphere of the Infinite, and exercises cognition and volition, and acts and moves, in the Infinite. Thus through the primary Law of cognition, from the relative notion of contradiction, we pass to the notion of the truly existent Being : from relative causality we can ascend to the idea of absolute causality, of self—causality ; from the relative notion of self—perfectness. The acceptance of the primary Law of the Spirit results in acceptance of every cognitive law regulating our spiritual, moral, social, and physical activities. The denial of it is naturally followed by a denial of every logical, moral, physical, and social law, because it is the source of all kinds of relative laws. But if we deny the principle, we must deny also the consequence flowing out of it, in order for us to be thus consequent, because it is impossible to cognize any consequences without a principle. If there are any laws, these necessarily have a first and absolute Principle, of Whom are the consequences. Therefore the admission of the consequences is also the admission of the principle whereby these proceed. Whereas then we necessarily admit the eternal existence of the primary law of cognition, whereby emanates every law, the question rises. Who is then this law, and how is it formulated, and by what form does it appear and manifest itself to us ? The primary law of the Spirit is common to every cognition, as being declaratory and expressive of the cause and the being. By means of this is cognized the being and the truth, the efficient and final cause of beings. Being therefore a primary law of volition and action it is common to every volition and activity, it is a moral and social law, declarative and expressive of truth and of that which is good and just ; it is a law according to which is tried and judged every cognition and judgement, every volition, and resolution and action ; it is a criterion of Philosophy, of Ethics, and of the political and legal science. The existence of such a primary law within the Spirit, whereby is cognized the eternal Being and the relation of the fact with the Being, the Truth and the Being, is the existence of the road whereby is cognized the Being and the Truth, and without this road the Being could have not known Itself and the fact, nor could the fact, know itself and the Being from its own knowledge. The Being cognizes Itself through the primary law of the Spirit through which the fact cognizes also. Thus the primary law of the Spirit of the absolute Being is the law of the fact, that is, it is also being revealed in the fact—in man. But it is being revealed in an imperfect cognitive spirit, in proportion to the cognitive ability of man. For we cognize the Being according to Its beingness, but according to Its essence and nature we know This imperfectly. With the development of our spirit, however, and of our cognitive perfection we cognize the Being more fully and more perfectly. But our finite cognitive nature being ignorant at the beginning, or not applying in all its activities the primary law of cognition, is being deceived, and for this it is in need of an infallible, impeccable, and undeceived guide, which is capable of guiding us to the cognition of the Being and the Truth, to the doing of the good, and the realization of justice. And this guide can not be a man subject to error and sin, just as we are, but the very same infallible and impeccable by nature and from the beginning primary law of cognition — the Logos of God — Which revealed Himself to mankind and to the moral world through the i n c a r n a t i o n in the perfect nature of man. This then is the Godman, our Lord Jesus Christ, our Professor and Teacher in theory as well as in deed, the perfect moral example of our life, the Lord and Legislator and King of human society. Christ is the ontological Law of the Spirit, the self — existing Logos of God, and the undeceived guide of the intellectual spirits to the cognition of the Being and of the first cause. Christ is the road leading to the knowledge and perfect knowledge of the Being, even as He Himself says, «I am the way and the truth and the life» (John 14. 6), and it is through Christ that the Being — God — is cognized, and through Him is the Being revealed to men, and unto them that Christ wills will He reveal Him, as He says, «And no man knoweth the Son, but the Father; neither knoweth any man the Father, save the Son, and He to whomsoever the Son will reveal Him» (Matt. 11. 27). God cognizes perfectly the primary law of cognition therefore it is both known and cognized by Him. Whereupon inasmuch as God is a person, so is His Law a person. Therefore God's Law is the eternal offspring of His cognition and His volition, the Logos Which was eternally and timelessly born from His eternal Essence, Which was personified and dwelt in us full of grace and truth. This eternal Law, then Which became incarnate in order to teach truth, God did manifest in both Jordan and Mt. Tabor, saying, «This is my beloved Son, in Whom I am well pleased; hear ye

Him» (Matt. 17. 5). It is Him therefore that we all must necessarily hearken to, and to cognize, to will, to act and to do according to Him, if we yearn for the bliss and blessedness lying in the cognizing acting, and doing according to Christ, the perpetual Law of God's cognition, action and doing, and of the rational and moral beings. In Christ, as the primary Law of the Spirit, is founded, as upon a foundation, the physical and rational and moral and social world, and which abides perpetually firm and unshaken. And every being not founded in Christ is illegal and rejected by the eternal rational and moral class of beings, it is a moral monster, worthy of the everlasting fire and the everlasting damnation. Now such a being is Satan and the demons, and all they that have violated the eternal law of the Spirit, and which have defied the perfect Volition of the Being — Jesus Christ — Whom God has made a law and a foundation and the Authority of His God — established society. All these constitute the illegal and anti — social order, being therefore predestined for the everlasting perdition and affliction. Such is the primary Law of the Spirit and the consequences of Its keeping and transgression or violation. Its keeping forms the social order, while Its violation forms the anti — social disorder and impropriety, and produces the privation of the eternal good of bliss and Blessedness, which is being enjoyed by those that stand in the social order being founded on Christ, the universal Legislator and Lord of society.

THE POSSIBLE AND THE NECESSARY

That is possible which is under some moral cause capable of being done, and whose conception in its mind exists before the thing done. And that is necessary which is possible to be done as being in harmony with and agreeing with right reason. Everything that is possible to be done, it is not for this that it ought to be done. And that which is necessary is also possible to be done. That which is possible to be done presupposes a free efficient force and action ; and that which is necessary presupposes a correctly cognizing cause according to reason and the law, and not voluntarily. It presupposes a force acting intentionally and according to some deliberate plan. God is the supreme and principal moral cause, being creative and effective of all things. Being as it is a moral cause It acts and does freely, having an infinite ability, capable of doing all things without any hindrance of limitation. Anything whatsoever God cognizes that He can also do. Now He cognizes both the good and the evil, therefore He can in His omnipotence make both good and evil. He cognizes the being and the nonbeing; therefore He can make a being out of the nonbeing, and to annihilate the being. Whatsoever He cognizes infinitely that He can also cause to exist infinitely. Before the ability of God the being becomes nonbeing, and the nonbeing becomes being. But the ability in God is not spontaneous, because it follows right reason, according to which God judges and wills and acts and does. God's omnipotence can not effectuate anything without the Logos, but acts and works always according to the Logos. Had God acted spontaneously, He would have also then judged and willed spontaneously, not conforming with any law, nor regulating His action according to that which is right and just ; then God's spontaneous action would have been unjust, injurious unto others, egotistic, selfish, and a tyrannical one. God's power follows His volition, which follows His cognition. God's cognition cognizes the perfect good and its opposing evil ; it cognizes the Being and the nonbeing. The being, on the one hand, as an absolute thesis, as a perfect good, the nonbeing, on the other hand, as an absolute privation, as the negation of the being, of the perfect good, and as an absolute evil. Consequently He entertains in His cognition ; a) the Idea of the Being, of the perfect good ; b) the idea of the evil. But because God cognizes the evil and is able of doing this spontaneously, yet for this He is not doing it, because He is being hindered by His own Law and His most perfect and most impeccable nature and volition. God, as a Being, can not according to reason act and make the nonbeing, He can not act against the being and on behalf of the nonbeing, because His volition always remains orderly in connection with the law of the perfect good judging and willing and deciding for ever the perfect good. The work of God, therefore, which is done according to judgement and volition and reason, this is that which is necessary, which is in harmony with His Logos. God cognizes all beings and nonbeings, the good as well as the evil. By cognizing the truth He also cognizes its negation. By cognizing the thesis He also cognizes its antithesis, but never judges according to falsehood and opposition, but always according to truth. And as He judges, even so does He decide and acts, and God's action and doing bears not only the seal of that which is possible to be done, but even that of that which ought to be done. In being able to do evil God does not will this, because this opposes His most perfect and most good and most wise volition, which is followed by His perfect ability. The doing of evil results either from an imperfect cognition being ignorant of that which is right, or from an ill — natured and envious volition. And if God was to do evil, even as He is capable and willing to do good, He would have been, either imperfect and finite in cognition, being ignorant of what is good and evil, or would have moved to His action through envy and ill will. But a God that is ignorant or envious, is not then a perfect and good and just God, working and doing according to some deliberate and excellent plan. Whereupon God, being wise and good He can not do anything against His Logos, because every action opposing His Logos is the denial of His own nature, which thing is absurd. For this we say that God can not deny Himself nor destroy Himself through the making of the absolute nonbeing, nor can He make beings out of the nonbeing contrary to His volition, nor can He annihilate and destroy and lead the beings which he made to nonbeings. Consequently the evil can not have as its cause the good will of God, but a will that is contrary to God's will, a wicked and perverted will, acting against and contrary to the good will of God, an envious and ill-natured will. The evil, although not accomplished by God's good volition nor created by it, yet because it contributes to the accomplishment of God's volition due to action and counter-action, to the fulfillment of Creation and being done by some moral and free being, is that which is necessary, and for this, although God detests and persecutes evil, yet He permits this to come to be, to exist, and to resist His Volition to Its accomplishment. And He has predestined this after the accomplishement of His volition to its everlasting condemnation and destruction. Else the perfecting of the imperfect creatures is not done without the action and counter-action of good and evil and it is for this that evil is from amongst things that ought to be done, therefore it came to be and exists and shall exist until God's volition be fulfilled, namely, man's perfect resemblance to God. God is able to do evil, but it does not befit Him since He is good and perfect. But as for me, I do that which is evil with the intention of frustrating God's volition. Consequently for myself I do that which ought not to be done. Yet this doing of mine can not frustrate God's volition, but it even establishes and serves this against my will. In this case the evil done by me is that which is necessary, it was necessary that it should be done, because, though having become the cause of profit for others, yet the cause to my own condemnation, for no rational being should under any reason do evil.

That which is necessary is also possible to be done. And the nonbeing is that which to be done into a being according to the Idea of the perfect Being, and according to some deliberate and excellent plan. Creation is that which ought to be done from the nonbeing; and the world to be made according to the perfection of the omniscient Creator, descriptive of His ability, wisdom, and goodness. And this is possible to be done, for God has the ability of accomplishing all things whatsoever His omniscient will approves, and which judges these things as being good and excellent. And God knows that it is good. Inasmuch then as He made the Creation with the intention of perfecting things, for this then He used suitable means for the accomplishment of His volition. And these are the things which are necessary. He revealed His perfect volition a) in an imperfect work; b) in a most perfect work. His imperfect work is man, who yearns for perfection. And the perfect work of God is Jesus Christ, the Godman. Now He perfects His imperfect work through the perfect one, for through the Godman He creates and forms and rec reates and regenerates the imperfect man, leading unto perfection. In God's recreation of the imperfect man, however, counteracts the moral evil which takes place without God, the Devil, and through this action and counteraction is the imperfect one being perfected, and becomes similar to God. Whereupon the making of the world and of man, the origin of the moral evil, the Devil, and the incarnation and manifestation of the Logos in the person of the Godman, is that which is necessary and possible to be done. God wills that all things should be done according to His volition, and that all Creation should be perfected through Christ : for Christ is the efficient and final volition of God. Therefore He permits every suitable means for the accomplishment of His final volition, which is also that which is necessary to be done. The evil is that which ought to be done, inasmuch as it contributes to the involuntary service of God's volition, but the doer of evil, which intents the frustration of God's volition, is condemned by divine justice as having swerved from His primary nature. And it is for this that Christ said, «it must needs be that offences come ; but woe to that man by whom the offence cometh» (Matt. 18. 7). He that is the cause of the offence is being condemned by divine justice not because he was able to frustate God's volition, but because he was moved against God's law and displayed a wicked and envious intetion, having swerved from his own nature and acted against the divine volition. This wicked doing of his, however, is that which ought to be done, which, though being involuntary by the doer, yet it serves God's plan, because God knows perfectly and from evil is able to bring forth excellent and good things, and from darkness a most brilliant and most clean light.

PROOF OF THAT WHICH IS POSSIBLE AND NECESSARY FOR THE REVELATION OF THE SPIRIT'S PRIMARY LAW

The primary law of the Spirit whereby is known the Being and Truth, and the moral good and justice is executed and accomplished within the society, is a suitable means for understanding the Being and that which is possible to be done and exist, and toward the doing of that which is good and just. And its analogy toward the Being and the Truth is its equality. For without the equality of the means toward the end and the purpose of knowing and doing the knowledge of Truth and the doing of that which is good and just is impossible. God, as the perfect Spirit, as the Very Spirit, for «God is a Spirit» (John. 4. 24), cognizes the Truth, that is, Himself, as ever being, and ever living, and ever cognizing, He does that which is good, and for ever executes perfectly and exactly that which is just. He cognizes the Truth through the primary Law of cognition, but does and accomplishes that which is good and just through the primary Law of volition and activity. But He cognizes that which is outside Him, namely, the nonbeing and the possible being, which He entifies in time through His entifying ability. From His entification He perfects the imperfect and the possible being, He leads this toward the equality with Himself, and to its apotheosis by the primary law of cognition and activity. God's cognition of the nonbeing and the possible being is the cognition according to to the same law of cognition whereby God cognizes Himself. Because, if God cognizes Himself by the same equal Law of cognition, and has a perfect Idea of Himself, and if God cognizes the Being, Himself, by a perfect law, then He cognizes the nonbeing and the possible being and the fact through the same Law of cognition, because the more imperfect is permitted within the more perfect, even as the content to the container, and is cognized by the more perfect. Consequently the Law of God's cognition of the Being and the cognition of the nonbeing and the fact is one and the same, according to which is known the absolute Truth. But man too aims at the same end, because he yearns to know the Being and the Truth, and to do the moral good and that which is just in his intercourse with the rational and moral beings of his kind. In having an imperfect mind, however, he can not satisfy his yearning, nor can he know the truth of the Being and of the fact according to the requirement of its nature. And the primary law of cognition is lawfully perfect in the perfect Spirit, whereby and wherein is perfectly known the Being and the fact. Now if God made man to yearn after the Truth, He also made him receptive of the perfect Spirit and of the perfect law of cognition, whereby is known the Being and the Truth ; but we are not to think that God made man to yearn only for the Truth and not be capable of attaining it, because this is an unbecoming contradiction against God, Wisdom, and Justice. The yearning for the Truth introduces also the possibility to cognize the Truth necessarily, and herein lies that which is necessary for the revelation of the primary Law of cognition, which is also possible, because God Who is able to make beings from the nonbeing, is also able to perfect them, and to manifest to them His Law and His volition. The yearning for the Truth necessarily requires also the means of cognizing this, and the one yearning — for must have the means whereby his yearning is being accomplished. But we ask, Can there be any other means toward the satisfaction of an infinite yearning, than the infinite and perfect Law according to which God cognizes? Impossible. Therefore man also, as does God, in order to cognize the Being and the fact perfectly, must be able to cognize according to the same Law of cognition. But the primary Law of cognition in God is equal to Himself, for by It is known the Being. Wherefore It has a beinghood and a hypostasis; It is a Being distinguished from the first Being, the absolute Nous, and the absolute Spirit, Which emanates from the absolute Nous; the Law of cognition in God is a rational, moral, free, and perfect person; and this person cognizes the Being and the fact, and it is by This person that the intellectual man is able to cognize the Truth and to do that which is good and just. But in order for this to be cognized of man it is necessary for him to yield to Its perception and knowledge, and to become the subject of Its cognition. It is necessary that It should be revealed before man's intellect in a perfect manner and a perfect Spirit. And that which is necessary for the revelation of the primary Law of cognition is the demanding of human yearning to know all Truth, and to know the Being and the fact. Whence it is necessary for the primary Law of cognition to appear upon the stage of the rational and moral world in order to become the unerring teacher and guide of men, guiding unto all Truth, and introducing to the knowledge of the Being and the fact, to the accomplishment of the moral good, and the realization of justice. This self - existing and personal Law of the perfect Being and the perfect Spirit must be revealed in a perfect moral and rational form in the moral world in order to be known and perceived. And the moral and rational form in the world is that of the perfect man, whose nature must be the self - existing primary Law of cognition and volition receive. Therefore it is necessary that It should become incarnate and be made a perfect man. The hypostasis of the Law, according to the natural law of birth, ought to be conceived in the womb of a Virgin woman and to assume a human nature within this and to be born with a human form and to be perfected according to the assumed human nature in time. And this is the work of history, to show whether or not this has ever occcured and when. Now this incarnation and manifestation of the primary Law of cognition did indeed occur about 1882 years ago, as is witnessed by true history, in the person of the Godman Saviour and our Lord Jesus Christ. The Godman therefore is the Law of God's perfect cognition, whereby is known the fact, and is accomplished that which is good and just. And the union of man with God in the Godman is their union with the primary Law of cognition and volition, having as its effect the c o n c o r d of God with man through Truth, their s a m e n e s s o f c h a r a c t e r through the perfect moral Good, and the s y m p a t h y through the identity of feelings in the internal and external application and execution of the Law, in one word, the spiritualization and deification of man. In this rational and moral and social union of man with God, through the primary Law of cognition and volition and action, lies man's eternal benefit, his blessedness and happiness. For, by the union of God with men through this Law, lies the intercourse of the perfect good, the inefable and untold joy which never ends, but for ever vivifying man. And for this did the Godman define the eternal life in the theoritical as well as the practical knowledge, by saying, «And this is life eternal, that they might know Thee the only true God, and Jesus Christ, Whom Thou hast sent» (John 17. 3). And really ; unto this end are all things being directed, for irretional and rational and moral nature is being led to its universal center, to its connection and regular union and contact with the primary Law of cognition and volition, in Which God acts and works, and upon Which is the entire Creation being established as upon an unshaken and perpetual foundation. All minds, and all volitions look upon as the rational and eternal moral Law. Upon Him looks the entire society as the perfect social Law, through Which is secured the peace and everlasting harmony of the social body, animosities and disputes and wars are being abolished, ugly wickedness vanishes and righteousness triumphs with peace and truth and virtue, and man is being united to God by the relation of morality and reasonableness.

THEORY OF METHOD

EXPERIMENTAL METHOD

To the cognition of the absolute principal of identity, of causality, and of purposefulnes we are being led from things given through experimentation, from the knowledge of conscience and perception, and from the internal observation. The thing given through experimentation is known, being correlated with the Idea of the necessary Being according to the principal of identity, of causality, and of purposefulness; which form the gist of right reason, which binds together the fact with the Being, nature with its scope, and the imperfect with the perfect. The method is distinguished in the experimental and the logical or metaphysical. The experimental, on the one hand, is founded upon experience and the facts of conscience and perception, the logical and metaphysical, on the other hand, is founded upon reason. For this the experimental one is called a posteriori method, while the logical one a priory method. And both together form the philosophical method, concerning which we must now start an investigation.

The experimental method has as its foundation the experimentation resulting from conscience and perception, upon which it is being founded as upon two pillars. For this it is a method applied for the cognition of the finite, of the ego, and of the world. Observation affords us the cognition of the existence of the ego and the world ; of the one as a cognizable essence, of the other as a non - cognizable essence. And this cognition is the beginning of the experimental method, or its s t a r t i n g p o i n t. Conscience and perception are its i n t e r m e d i a t e p o i n t ; and the f i n a l p o i n t is the reason of the existence of the ego and the world, from which starts the logical method, and in which ends the experimental one. I am ; — The world is —. These two propositions form the beginning of the empirical method, because they are the thing given by experimentation. What am I? What is the world ? These propositions can in no way be explained without right reason, and it is for this that they constitute the end of the experimental method. Experimentation affords us the matterial for the knowledge of the ego and the world, but without generality, and unity, and bond. It is for this that experimentation without any beginning generalizing and binding the individual and particular knowledges of conscience and perception is in no way advantageous in the building - up of the experimental sciences. Consequently the experimental method becomes useful to right reason whereupon is erected the scientific structure of experience. Because it generalizes all the particular consciences and perceptions through reason by way of induction, extending the cognition upon all things that are the same, identical, and analogous. Induction is established upon experimentation, and, beginning therefrom, it reaches the cognition of the generality of knowledge resulting from reason. Induction infers from the part to the whole, from the particular to the general, but according to the conditions of, a) identity, b) similarity, c) and analogy. Induction becomes true when the observation established thereupon becomes also true, and when this takes place upon things that are similar, identical, and analogous. Else it is false. And this relies upon the principals of identity, and purposefulness. I observe myself through conscience, therefore I cognize my beinghood. I know my identi-

ty immediately and straightway, that I cognize and will and
sence, and that I am a being distinguished from other beings.
This cognition of my identity, as being judged in accordance with
the law of contradiction, is a particular and individual one. And
inasmuch as I cognize my existence then I have the conscience of
some individual and particular knowledge, which I can extend
through the principal of reason wherein is generalized and united
the knowledge of all the individual and particular existences, as
many as they be, and which are in noway being essentially distinguished from each other ; whereupon the ability of generalizing knowledge is possible with reason, and knowledge becomes
true when this is being done according to the principals of reason.
Now the induction of identity is as follows.

I am a being that cognizes, wills, and sences.
And so every being identical to me, is likewise
one that cognizes, wills, and senses.

All beings of the same essence and nature have the same essence and nature. All bodies fall according to the same law. These
general inferences of induction proceed from the observation
resulting from the individual essences and the particular fall of
the bodies. But the foundation of this generalization is the principal of identity. Paul's essence and Peter's essence is cognitive,
volitive, and passive. But Paul and Peter are equally men. Therefore every man is also cognitive, volitive, and passive. Stone,
lead, cotton, all these fall to the center of the earth according to
the law of gravitation. But these are bodies. Therefore all the
bodies also fall according to the same law of gravitation. The
induction of experimentation is true not necessarily, but according
to that which is possible and contingent, because experimentation
is also that which is possible and contingent. The identity of
contingency contains also knowledge analogous to its nature.
And since the fact is established upon the will of the Being, and
Its will being logical, It does that which is logical and never
destroys, but perfects the fact, we are then being convinced that
the deductions resulting from induction are true when they are
based upon the firm principles and laws of the fact, whose foundation is the will of the Being. And induction, which is based
upon the everlasting and necessary and invariable laws of the
Spirit, i. e., of contradiction, of causality, and of purposefulness,
possesses certainty for ever. The experimental sciences are based
upon the induction which extends cognition upon all things that
are the similar, idendical, and analogous, according to the allmigh-
ty law of contradiction, of the cause and purpose of every being
and every phenomenon. The apple tree, the fig tree, the orange
tree are planted on the earth. But these are plants. Therefore all

plants are also planted upon the earth. This inference is based upon the principle of identity. Man and woman are begotten of seed. But these are people. Therefore all people are likewise begotten of seed. James and George are begotten of Anthony their father. But they that are begotten as well as he that begot are people. Therefore every man is likewise begotten of a father. This inference is based upon the principle of identity. A is the cause of B and B the cause of C. But A B C are letters. Therefore every letter is the cause of another letter. This is the principle of causality : A certain white marble is useful for the making of a statue ; therefore every white marble is useful for this also. The stone, the plant, the dog, the cat, they all have a certain goal toward which they were made. But these are beings. Therefore every being has a like purpose toward which it aims. This inductive inference, according to the principle of the general order and the universal purpose, extends the cognition from the particular purpose of the stone, the plant, and the dog, as beings, and of every being whereunto belongs the species of stones, of the plants, and of the dogs, as the content to the container. The identity of the species, and the identity of the genus, is the general principle of reason, whereupon is induction based. Induction extends the particular cognition from the individuals to the species, and from these to the genera, according, to the principles of identity, of similarity, and of analogy. Thus, for instance, the general cognition of identity is this : I am a being distinguished from another being. An identical being. But every being that is also identical to me, is distinguished from another being. I am a being having a hypostasis, nature, relativity, duration, and extention. But every being also, identical to me, has the same. D and K and L have A as their cause. But D K L are beings. Therefore every being also has a like cause. This cognition is of the general causality, according to which we cognize that all beings have a cause. The sheep, the cow, and the cat have a certain purpose. But these are beings. Therefore every being has also a certain purpose. This cognition of the general purposefulness, according to which, through the observation of some particular purpose, we extend the cognition also upon every purpose of the being.

Induction is based upon the principle of purposefulness and the general order of all things according to which every being exists and can not at the same time be inexistent, having an analogous cause of its nature, and, pursuing some end, on account of which it was made. Being therefore convinced from before concerning the general order, based upon the principles of reason, we extend our particular cognition upon all things that are similar, identical, and analogous, beginning with the individual and particular cognition. Induction depends a) upon the right observation of the particular cognitions ; b) upon the principles of reason. Right observation is the activity of conscience, of perception, and of logical cognition. And induction is the activity of reason. Right reason shows us the generality and universality, the causality, and the end of beings and the phenomena, and through reason we generalize and universalize the ideas according to its principles and the necessary laws of the Spirit. Nor can we ascend to the cognition of the general and universal conceptions without the observation of the particular conceptions, nor again to descend to the extention of the cognition of the particular conceptions without the cognition of the general and universal ones. Conscience and perception, or experimentation, is the seat of the individual and particular knowledge, while reason is that of the general and universal one. But the principle which generalizes and universalizes the particular conceptions constitutes the gist of reason, and this is the universal and necessary law of the spirit. T h a t w h i c h i s c a n n o t a t t h e s a m e n o t b e, a n d t h a t w h i c h i s d o n e h a s a c a u s e. T h a t w h i c h i s, i s f o r s o m e e n d. The logical principle of contradiction is implied in the inductive syllogism as follows : We seek to know, for instance, as to whether or not this piece of gold possesses the attribute of solubility, that is, if among the other elements of the conception of this piece we can also add the element of solubility. Thereupon we multiply, we vary, and criss - cross the experiments. And after having been convinced of this atribute as being common in all the pieces suggested by our experiment, we infer that all the pieces of gold also possess the attribute of solubility after having been tested. But how is this done ? This is done according to the conception of the general order whereunto belong the pieces of gold that we have dissolved, which, although being few, yet they indicate the identity of all the pieces of gold which have not dissolved. The solubility, therefore, of the few pieces of gold whereupon the experiment was made, is also the solubility of all the pieces of gold in the world, and whereupon there was no experiment ever made. Why ? Because the dissolution of the pieces of gold of the same genus is by nature impossible, as is also the indissolubleness of the pieces oft he same genus. For their dissolubleness and indissolubleness is contradictory, therefore it is impossible. Thereupon there is no need for melting all the gold in the world in order to see as to whether or not this possesses the new attribute of dissolution which we have discovered in its few pieces. And if these possess identity, it is necessary that they should all also possess identity ; otherwise the gold was both in its identity and with their identity and it was not, which thing however opposes the principle of contradiction which is the implied foundation of syllogism. Accordingly then we observe that induction depends on deduction and the a priori general principles, on right reason, for had we not general and universal principles, we would not be capable of making syllogisms according to the inductive method ; thus reason is the sign according to which our conceptions are being cognized and generalized, the seat of generalizations and universality.

Induction being founded upon the principle of purposefulness and the firm and general order infers from the past and the present to the future, but always according to the conditions of identity, of similarity, and of analogy, therefore its inferences are true. I am today ; therefore I will also be tomorrow. This inference becomes true if it is supposed that the same circumstances that exist today will also exist tomorrow. For should these be altered the inference is not true. The alteration and change of the circumstances alters the conditions according to which induction is made, and then the inference is also altered. The conditions and the circumstances depend on the will of God, and for this the inductive syllogisms are based on the supposition that the will of God is unalterable, firm, and unchangeable. And the change is phenomenical and not essential, because it is not being changed or essentially altered. For the will of God is unchangeable. Therefore so are its works. The essence of beings is for ever the same, unchangeable and unalterable. But their phenomenon is changed, as is also the external nature. And this change supposes progress, because God's will is progressive in its works, and from the more imperfect it proceeds to the more perfect works. The change therefore is an impulse and tendency leading from worse to better, and for this the beings are changed externally, and not in their internal essence which is unalterable. The inference therefore, that in the future I will be a living and cognizing and willing being, immortal and incorruptible and perfect in my essence, is true and certain, because it is based a) upon my progressive nature which requires perfection, namely, immortality, and b) upon my logical conviction in the supreme Providence and Will which works progressively leading the Universe unto some final purpose. Thus induction is incontrovertible.

THE LOGICAL AND METAPHYSICAL METHOD

Induction is the activity of the mind, according to which we generalize through reason the particular conceptions. For by ascending unto reason from the particular observations, we extend this cognition upon all the identical, the similar, and the analogous phenomena. Thus then we construct the experimental sciences concerning which we can say that there is nothing in reason, unless formerly in experimentation. Because without observation and experimentation we are unable to generalize. But the principles of reason is the law of the spirit. Yet how is it that we possess the conception of the absolute, the infinite, and the necessary, since through experimentation we observe but relativity, finiteness, and contingency? How is it that we possess the conception of eternity since all things are the products of time? Is it through induction? No. For it infers from the identical to the identical, and from similar to similar. And the thing witnessed by experimentation is not identical, but different and dissimilar to the conception of the absolute, the necessary, and the infinite. The relative and the finite is different and dissimilar to the absolute and the infinite. But how is it that we possess the conception of the absolute and the infinite through observation and induction not having acquired this? Then it is through a different cognitive work which is called reduction. Reduction is founded upon what is given by experimentation, that is, on conscience, perception, and induction, upon whose general inferences it is founded. Being thus founded upon these, it seeks through reason the cause of that which is relative, finite, and contingent, which cannot be the same but dissimilar to that, as also absolute, infinite, and necessary. Reason, through the given inferences of induction from experimentation, reveals the conception of the absolute and universal being as the cause and the purpose of all the contingent and finite beings. And conscience and perception, or the entire phenomenon of cognition, is so suitably bound together in reason, so that the finite is bound with the infinite, the contingent and the fact with the Being, the relative with the absolute, and the possible with the necessary Being. For their bond is reason. But without experiment we can not cognize the infinite. And for this we can say that nothing is possessed by reason unless formerly by conscience and perception. Nor can induction or reduction without observation. Reason fulfills and unifies and perfects the experimental knowledge, and it reveals the idea of the Being, and opens us the examination and theory of a new infinite and universal world. When founded on the conception of the finite it guides us to the infinite opened therefrom before us. When founded on the temporary, the contingent and the fact, it leads us to the world of eternity and presents us before the absolute and necessary Being. Therefore, had we not reason, we would not have had the conception of the absolute and eternal and infinite Being. We would not have had the unity of knowledge, but would have been as the irrational animals. But conscience and perception without reason would have been impossible with us. Because the spirit cognizes according to some law. For conscience and perception being of the same spirit, how could they be without the spirit? The reason of experimentation is the reason of induction. The reason of experimentation is the reason of reduction. The first work of reason of induction is clearly experimental, for generality exists in experimentation, but we are not capable of cognizing this unless ascending to reason, as upon some hill whereupon we observe the plain of the particular conceptions and knowledges. Therefore the generalization of induction can be called an experimental observation through reason. But the work of reason at reduction is clearly theoretical and metaphysical, because the infinite, the universal, the absolute, the necessary and eternal do not exist within the finite, the general, the fact, and the contingent being, but in the eternal Being, which cognizes that it exists distinguishably from the fact. For this then the reductive mode of reason must be called metaphysical and theoretical, according to which ascending to reason from the generalization of experimentation through induction we observe the eternal Being, which is outside the finite, the fact and the relative, and which also possesses eternity. This then is the clearly metaphysical aspect of reason. Hence in reason meets the infinite with the finite, the fact with the eternal Being; by means of reason the contingent takes place, and it is through reason that it is being furthered and perfected. In our reason (word) meet the conceptions of the infinite with the finite, and in the ontological Reason (Logos) the infinite Being with the finite. i. e., God with man. And thus as the right reason in us aids a) to the birth of the ideas; b) to the progress and perfection of their science, even so does the ontological Reason (Logos) aid a) to the making of the fact ; b) to the progress and consummation of Creation, as the efficient and final Reason. And as the right reason in us it has two aspects, the experimental at induction, and the metaphysical at reduction, and according to the first, manifesting itself at the experimentation as being a unifying and binding agent of things given thereby, while according to the second elevating us above every experimentation to the metaphysical theory of the Logos (Reason), even so does the ontological Logos has two aspects, that of the theological and the ontological, and the anthropological. According to the first it is the eternal image and Idea of the Being, and according to the second it is the image of the fact, a perfect man. According to the first it unites in itself all the ideas of the contingent being, thus being the bond between the Being and that which is contingent ; and according to the second it unites in itself all beings thus making itself the ontological criterion between them, after which these are being judged. In the first it reveals God eternally in God; while in the second it reveals God as being in time within man. These two aspects of the Logos, i. e., the metaphysical and the experimental, indicate His incarnation, according to which the Logos is called Godman. Reduction relies on the principle of causality. The reductive cognition elevates us to the idea of the eternal, the absolute, the unalterable and necessary Being, to the absolute principle of identity, of causality and purposefulness. And by means of this we cognize the absolute Being according to its essence and nature. This idea then is the absolute idea of the Being, wherein is found that which is universal and necessary and perfect, and when the intellect is raised thereupon it observes the Universe, because this is being contained therein. Now our intellect ascends to the idea of the Being after its journey to the fact, by the observation and generalization through induction. And its first ascent to the idea of the Being has as a consequence in itself the immediate and clear revelation and manifestation of the Being. Now this first manifestation is imperfect at first, and analogous to the first perception of the eyes of the ego. The more the cognition is being strengthened, the more the revelation of the Being becomes also more complete in us, and our knowledge of God more perfect. And this first and imperfect theory of the Being by means of reason, is the first sign, the starting point, of the logical and metaphysical method. It is an absolute Being. But what is this Being? This proposition constitutes the end of the logical method; and right reason is the law whereby we know the existence of the Being, and its unknown we shall know, for this is the intermediate point of the method. When ascending to reason, we already cognize the absolute Being concerning which experimentation gives the occassion and the suggestion for its pursuit and discovery, namely, the relative and the fact. And just as when ascending from experimentation to reason we become the possessors of the fact in the intellect, through the inductive generalization concerning its knowledge, even so when beginning with the things given through induction we ascend by way of reduction through the law of causality, unto reason and become the possessors of the idea of the Being in the intellect. When the intellect ascends to the general conception of the fact, it ascends to the general principles of reason, and thence it observes the universal, the absolute, and the eternal Being. And after having ascended to the universal Idea of the Being it descends to the idea of the fact, and, by means of the Idea of the Being, it observes the fact as a being united to the Being, from the conception of the infinite it descends to the finite, just as from the general principle of induction cognition descends to the individual and particular conceptions. Upon ascending to the Idea of the Being the mind enters the infinite, and thereby it descends to the finite and thus cognizes both as being bound together to the Idea of the Being. And the cognition of the finite resulting from the conception of the infinite, the cognition of the relative and the fact resulting from the conception of the universal and eternal Being, is a deductive cognition, from the principles to the consequences. Hence by way of reduction we ascend to the Idea of the eternal Being, from the idea of the fact, and from deduction we descend from the Idea of the eternal Being to the idea of the fact. These two logical activities are formulated as follows.

> I and the world are a fact.
> therefore the eternal Being exists necessarily.
> Every fact is finite and in time.
> Therefore the eternal Being is infinite and perpetual.

The reductive mode of thinking is not a syllogism nor a proof, because we do not seek the demonstration of some unknown through another mode. The idea of the fact introduces together also the idea of the Being necessarily. The cognition of the fact has the cognition of the Being as a necessary consequence ; so inasmuch as the existence of the fact is self-evident, even so is the existence of the Being self-evident. Just as there is a cognition of the fact, even so there is a cognition of the Being ; and for the self-evident and things originally known there is no proof.

> God is the cause of all existence
> But I and the world exist
> Therefore our cause is God.
> God is the cause of life and cognition
> But I live and cognize
> Therefore God is the cause of my life and my cognition.

The deductive syllogism deducts a general and particular truth from some universal truth, for they are contained within the latter. And for this it is being called deductive. Now this syllogism relies upon the principle of identity and contradiction according to which that which is universally true can by no means not be true also in a general and particular manner, when being of the same nature and of the same order. Deduction is valid not only upon the metaphysical conceptions, but also upon the physical and empiric, but according to the law of identity. From the general principle that, every piece of gold happens to be dissolvable, I descend to the particular idea, that, even any piece of gold then happens to be dissolvable. Or every phenomenon is directed according to some natural law. But the fall of bodies is a phenomenon ; therefore this is being directed according to natural law. Even so from the universal principle every attribute of the Being is infinite. But justice is an attribute of the Being; therefore it is infinite. When deduction occurs from the general idea of the contingent, that is, of induction, it possesses the contingency of induction. And when relying on the necessary and the universal, it possesses the necessary and the universal, for it comes to be from the idea of the universal to the idea of the particular.

> Every cognitive being knowing itself through itself is necessary a trinity.
> But God knows Himself through Himself and not through any other means.
> Therefore God is a trinity.
> Every being cognizing itself through itself is the cause of its own cognition.
> But God cognizes Himself through Himself.
> Therefore God is the cause of His own cognition.

That which exists and cognizes and lives through itself is self - causative, self - existent, and self - cognizing, and that which has its existence and cognition and life in some other, is the cause of the self - existent, the self - living, and the self - cognizing Being. Therefore it exists through the first and in the first Being. The fact exists through the Being and in the Being as a contingency. And deduction deduces the contingent from the necessary Being, the particular from the general, the general from the universal, the finite and the relative from the infinite and the absolute, wherein it exists virtually, and through which it possesses the contingent beinghood, for it relies upon this.

THE ENTIRE PHILOSOPHICAL METHOD

The entire philosophical method comprises three definitions; a) the definition s t a r t i n g   p o i n t, b) the definition i n t e r m e d i a t e   p o i n t, c) the definition f i n a l   p o i n t. The definition s t a r t i n g   p o i n t is the thing known at first by conscience, perception, and reason, concerning the ego, the world, and God ; the definition i n t e r m e d i a t e   p o i n t is conscience, perception, and reason, by which we know whatever we know ; and the definition f i n a l   p o i n t is the unknown of the ego, the world, and God, which is made known to us through the spirit and reason. Experimentation and reason constitute the philosophical method. The beginning of the method is knowledge and ignorance, because the one philosophizing knows and knows not, and commencing from knowledge he is led to the

understanding of scientific knowledge. Scientific knowledge is th e
eternal Being, and unto this we ascend when proceeding from the
fact through reason. And when ascending to the fact through
right reason, we consider the Being and possess its Idea as the
foundation of the science of the Being, and as the object of Philosophy. But the viewing of the Idea of the Being through right
reason, being imperfect at the beginning, is completed through
the revelation of the ontological Logos (Reason), and in the incarnate Logos we cognize the Being perfectly, even as it is, because it is by means of this that we receive the perfect Spirit of
cognition. In the ontological Logos God reveals Himself perfectly,
for that which is perfect is revealed through the perfect by giving
us the perfect Spirit of cognition in order that we may cognize
and consider this. Hence the revelation of the ontological Logos
is not the removal of the right reason in us, but its fulfillment
and completion. For this then, the right reason in us leads directly to the evidence of the ontological Logos, as the universal
center whereunto Philosophy aims, about which all sciences appear
as maids. The ontological Logos is the final center of the Uni.
verse, about which revolve the beings, God, the world, and
man. Upon commencing to philosophize from the three signs of
knowledge, we proceed through the spirit and reason to the uni.
versal Cause of beings, and their final Logos. After having observed this through experimentation and reason in the fact, we view
it from the metaphysical light of reason in the Being, and get
to know this in the incarnation, in the person of the perfect Man ,
of our Lord Jesus Christ. We consider this in the Godman. And
through the Godman we consider the Being and the fact in the
hypostasis of the ontological Logos as being united together in
an inseparable and unchangeable and unmixed manner, in one
person, but of two natures. Accordingly then from the viewing
of the ego and the world through the spirit, and of God through
reason, we discover the efficient and final cause of beings, and by
means of this we explain all things. Therefore this Cause is an
absolute Truth, explaining all things to us absolutely ; it is a
Logos expressive of the nature and essence of the Being, its identity and perfection. It is to this absolute Truth, upon which all
truths rely, that Philosophy aims at, for this Truth explains all
things and mainly the necessary and absolute Being, which we
can learn by no other science. And this Truth is the Idea of the
Being, and the universal Law of the Spirit, of the absolute contradiction, causation, and purposefulness. Through this Idea we
cognize the Being, and construct the theological science. This
Idea of the Being then is the absolute ideality toward which our

nature aims and is being led to until it be perfected, to the end
that it might pragmatize this.

Experimentation, that is, observation and reason, are the
two principles of our knowledge, by means of which we know the
fact and the Being, for without these we can not receive any such
knowledge concerning the truth of the Being as well as of the
fact. Observation together with reason fulfills our knowledge, for
it furthers our cognitive faculty through the viewing of the absolute Truth to the knowledge of the eternal Being and of all beings. Upon observing the ego and the nonego by means of conscience and perception, and through reason we ascend to the idea
of the Being, we embrace in our mind the entire scientific object,
and in the Idea of the absolute we consider the Being and the
fact. When deliberating according to the principle of contradiction,
of causality, and purposefulness, we form the method of
induction, being founded upon the principle of purposefulness,
the method of deduction, relying on the principle of contradiction, and the method of reduction, being founded upon the
principle of causality. Thus, by being induced and ascended,
and by deducing from the principle the false consequence, we
then enforce in the mind the three principles of reason, i. e.,
that of contradiction, of causality, and of purposefulness.
Induction is the extending of the cognition from things in
particular to things in general, in accordance with the conditions of identity, of similarity, and of analogy. Reduction is the
cognizing of the cause from the effect, the principle from the
consequence. And the deducing something from something, is the
cognizing of the false consequence from the principle, and its deducing according to the laws and regulations of syllogism.

Every attempt for the separation of reason from observation, is the attempt for the breaching of the logical nature and
the denial of the principles of knowledge, leading to the most
pernicious delusion, namely, to the negative skepticism. Observation is the knowledge of the individual and the particular element, and reason is the knowledge of the general and the universal element, according to its principles of contradiction, of
causation, and purposefulness. For anything that we know proceeds either from observation, as an individual and particular
knowledge, or from observation and reason, as a general and universal knowledge. And all our knowledge emanates from observation and reason, through the immediate consideration of every
being, through induction, reduction, and deduction according to
the principles of right reason. For without these we possess no
knowledge. And for this when undertaking to prove or confirm
some truth we employ the inductive, or reductive, or the deductive

method. The past and the future we know through induction, while the present through the immediate observation. That which is eternal and perpetual and infinite we know through reduction, while the false consequences in the principles we know through deduction and syllogism. Therefore, within these modes of the philosophical method is contained every knowledge, for we have no other mode of knowledge for proving the truth.

Principle of contradiction	deductive mode of cognition
Principle of causality	reductive mode of cognition
Principle of purposefulness	inductive mode of cognition

THE GODMAN

The Idea of the Being from what preceded was proven to possess the following characteristics ; a) it is cognitive of the possible and contingent beings ; b) it is volitive of granting a hypostasis to the nonbeing ; c) it is capable according to its ability of performing its will. Therefore this is the creative instrumentality and the bringing - into - the - world and the preserving of the fact. This then is the revelation of the Idea of the Being ; among things that exist ; b) among things than live ; c) in man. Now the revelation thereof is more perfect in man that among things that exist and live simply. The revelation of the Idea of the Being in man, through mind and reason, is imperfect at first, but susceptible to perfection. However, the imperfect revelation of the Idea of the Being, does not express itself, nor does it explain the perfect nature of the Being and the final purpose of Creation. In order for this then to become manifest, there is need for the revelation thereof through a perfect work. Because otherwise Creation would be for ever imperfect, and its purpose obscure. Wherefore the need for the revelation of the Idea of the Being in the fact through a perfect work introduces the idea of the incarnation of the Idea of the Being. But is this possible? If by the Idea of the Being were all things made, why is not this possible to be done when this is expected by the perfection of all things, and its incarnation ; If the Idea of the Being in the more imperfect beings was revealed in their own form and kind, why can not this be also revealed in the more perfect Being? Is it perhaps that the revelation of the Idea of the Being through a perfect work contradicts its own perfect nature? The thing perfect can participate with the thing perfect, when the scope of such a participation be the perfection of that which is imperfect. Hence the revelation of the

Idea of the Being in the fact is also possible. But by what means can this be done? By incarnation. Because the perfect revelation of the Being requires the manifestation of its B e i n g n e s s, which is impossible by nature without the incarnation. The Idea of the Being in being infinite and eternal comes into the finite and perishable world without departing from its infinite and eternal element, because divinity is indiscribable and unlimited, therefore it receives a human nature from a Virgin woman, and thus is born according to the natural law of birth, as a perfect man. The incarnation of the Idea of the Being in the fact is its humanization, for the Idea of the Being, as being represented in the fact more perfect than any other work by man, becomes man, assumes the perfect nature of man, this being essentially unaltered, and is born in a human visible form, at the beginning as an imperfect man, being made perfect in time, according to the general law of progress and perfection. Hence the Idea of the Being appears in Creation under the following aspects ; a) as a law in nature — Natural law — ; b) as a law in cognition — Rational law — ; c) as a law in volition — Moral law — ; d) as a law in the sense — Sensible law — ; e) as an ontological law in the order of the moral and free beings, uniting and joining to itself the perfect God with the perfect Man — Ontological law. The ontological law is the perfect revelation of the perfect nature of God and man, and without the viewing of the Godman, the viewing of God and man is impossible, because in the Idea of the Godman meets and harmoniously is united the perfect God with the perfect man, so that, in the same manner as we view the Godman, we also view the perfect God and the perfect man. The Godman is the perfect Idea of God and man, He is the law according to which we cognize what is God and what man. For this then in the Godman is recapitulated every natural, moral, rational, and sensible law, and in Him we consider the sum total of laws, according to which we cognize the Being and the fact according to their beingness and kind, and according to which are directed the phenomena of nature, of cognition, of volition, and of art, and is known the truth, that which is excellent, and the good.

The idea of the Godman is composite from the idea of the Being and the idea of the actual man, of which, the former is an eternal idea existing necessarily, an hypostatical Idea in God, the latter is an eternal idea in God nonhypostatical, having its beingness made contingent outside of God and in the fact. These two eternal ideas, of which the one in God is hypostatical, while the other nonhypostatical in Him, are related in such a manner that the Idea of the Being contains in itself the idea of man, and God cognizes through His Idea or in His perfect idea of man. In His hypostatical Idea He cognizes the idea of man as harmonizing and being in concert therewith. He cognizes the possibility of the entification of man's perfect idea in His hypostatical Idea. Therefore He cognizes the possibility of the incarnation of His perfect Idea. The perfect Idea of God in assuming in its hypostasis the perfect nature of man, takes on flesh and becomes man in time, yet at the same time being God eternal. In this Idea of the Being then is united a) that which is perfect with that which is imperfect; b) that which is eternal with that which is in time; c) the Being with the fact; d) God with man. When God cognizes the perfect man in His Idea as His image in the Creation, He cognizes him as being equal to His idea, He cognizes the Godman in him. And this cognition is in the Idea of the Being, occuring in time and done in its revelation, that is, in the person of the Godman. The idea of the Godman, therefore, is a logical possibility, and not a chimerical and imaginary one, as the enemies of right reason believe. For if God can logically cognize the idea of the Godman in Himself, then He can also create and materialize this externally. The perfect idea of man in the Spirit of God is equal to the perfect Idea of God, for in the perfect idea of man only can the perfect existence and cognition and the life of God's hypostatical Idea be cognized and made manifest. The perfect Idea of God possess a perfect beingness, life, cognition, and ability. But the perfect idea of man can also assume beingness, life, and awareness that are just as perfect. Therefore it can be equal to the perfect Idea of God. The Idea of God possesses the necessary beingness, life, and awareness, while the idea of man possesses the possibility and contingency of perfection. Hence the perfect man is equal to the Idea of God, he is the image and likeness of God; and the perfect work of God in Creation is equal to the Idea and His perfect Volition. And this is the Godman, or the incarnation and humanization of the Idea of the Being in the fact. The Godman, as the ontological law which unites in Himself God with man, reveals a) the perfect Nature of the Being, i. e., of God; b) and the perfect nature of man. In this revelation, therefore, we see the cognition of man by the Cognition of God; and the volition and sense of man by the Volition and Sense of God. We view the common law of cognition, of volition, and of action. In the revelation of the Godman consider the manifestation and divulgance a) of the everlasting laws, and relations, and principles of cognition the eternal Truth; b) of the everlasting relations and laws of volition — the eternal moral Good; c) of the everlasting laws and relations of our external action — the eternal Righteousness and the principle of social unity, and equality, and concord;

d) of the everlasting laws and relations of balance and concord and analogy in the consideration of the truth with that which is good and just, in concord with the action—the eternal Beauty. Hence the Godman as the Idea of the Being, is the Truth, the Good and Righteousness; and in respect to the concord of God's nature with man's nature in the incarnation of the Logos He is the m o r a l B e a u t y. Whereupon, the Godman is the source of the eternal and everlasting laws and through which we are being mentally and morally and socially united to God, He is the apotheosis of human nature through the Idea of the Being; and these eternal laws are a) religious, regulating the relations of the people's sinful nature with the sinless Nature of God. In connection with this relation then the Godman is a Guarantor and Mediator and an High Priest; b) logical and moral, that is educational and philosophical, regulating the relations of our imperfect nature with the perfect Nature of God. In connection with this relation then the Godman is a Guide and Master, and Teacher, guiding unto truth and goodness; c) political, regulating our relations with each other and with the perfect Being, God, in order to do that which is right and lawfull. In connection with this relation the Godman is a Legislator, Magistrate, Judge, and King, legislating, and judging, and governing the society, and directing it to its supreme goal. It is for this then that the Godman's teaching is religious, educational, and a political one, accordant with our nature, and in general, a political one aiming at the social goal of mankind. This then is the most perfect teaching, which fulfills the teaching of the imperfect man, and judges and purges the teaching of our sinful nature by separating and making known thereto the truth from falsehood. Such then did we, according to reason which reflects on that which is possible and contingent, consider the Godman to be: as the logical mixture and blend of the perfect Idea of God and man, as the perfect representation of the Being; a) in Itself; and b) in Creation, that is, in the fact. But as concerning this possible Idea and conception of the Godman being eternal in the cognition of God, let us now see as to whether or not it has been fulfilled and received existence in time.

JESUS CHRIST AS THE PERFECT MAN

The fulfillment of God's perfect will, which is the revelation and the incarnation of the Idea of the Being in the fact, in the duty to show it to us, as being the witness of the past, if this did indeed take place in the past. And firstly this most great of God's works we find being prophesied of God to the protoplasts during their banishment from Paradise, and the condemnation for their disobedience to the word and law of God. In connection with the legislation of the protoplasts we observe the Idea of the Being as the law of their free activity by the affirmative law, «eat» from all the fruit of Paradise, and by the negative, «eat not» from the forbidden fruit of the tree of knowledge. «And the Lord God gave a charge to Adam, saying, of every tree which is in the garden thou mayeet freely eat, but of the tree of the knowledge of good and evil—of it ye shall not eat, but in whatsoever day ye eat of it, ye shall surely die (Gen. 2. 16, 17)). Unto the violators of the moral law, namely, the protoplasts, which were for this account condemned, God manifested the restoration of their fall, the rise of the penalty, and their return to the obedience of the divine law by means of the incarnation and revelation of that very same law against which the violation was made. And He did prophetically reveal to them the fulfillment of this great work in the world for the salvation and perfection of mankind. Upon cursing the author and introducer of sin for the seduction of the infant and imperfect protoplasts, God declared beforehand by the following words the overthrow of his dominion, through the man that was to be born of an only Woman, of the seed of a woman, that is, of a Virgin, for the salvation and instruction and perfection of mankind: «And the Lord God said unto the serpent, Because thou hast done this thou art cursed above all cattle and all the brutes of the earth, on thy breast and belly thou shalt go, and thou shalt eat earth all the days of thy life. And I will put enmity between thee and the woman and between thy seed and her seed, he shall watch against thy head, and thou shalt watch against his heel» (Gen 15, 16). The woman. which was to beget the Logos of God from her own seed, and not from the seed of a man, was to hate Satan with an implacable enmity, and Satan was likewise to hate her; so that there would be an irreconcilable hatred which results from the contrary nature of the Woman and Satan. And by means of this enmity God foretells as to what this Woman is, which was to beget the Saviour of makind. But that there would also be an irreconcilable hatred between her seed and Satan's because of the contrary element resulting from the nature of the two seeds. The seed of the Woman is her offspring, which she was to beget, He is the Saviour of the people; but as for the seed of Satan, are his moral children which possess his wicked nature. The woman's seed shall watch against Satan's head, and he, on the other hand, shall watch against His heel. This signifies that He that was to be born of the Woman, will reflect upon Satan's thoughts, and will watch to disperse and frustrate his wicked schemes; while Satan will reflect upon the Saviour's heel, i. e., His undermost part — the part opposite the head — His corporal and material life, and he will watch to hurt his enemy with a bodily injury, and to inflict a wound and suffering in His body. The head is the uppermost part of the body, the most essential and most important and ruling in the body; while the heel is the undermost, the lowest and basest, whose infliction does not destroy the head, while the infliction of the head does indeed destroy the heel. It therefore signifies that the Woman's seed will wound Satan in the head and shall destroy him utterly, and he will wound his enemy in the heel, and shall hurt Him temporarily; notwithstanding Satan will not be able to divert and frustrate the design and intent of the Woman's seed. From this prophecy of God given to the protoplasts it becomes evident a) that the Woman has been sealed for this end, being foreordained in the plan of Creation that it will be born in the world not having voluntarily tasted of sin. Therefore she is very virtuous; b) that this Woman shall beget a son without the seed of a man, inexperienced of man; c) that the seed to be begotten of her shall watch against Satan's head and shall be thereby watched against the heel; d) that there shall be a struggle and war between the two until the Woman's seed will disperse Satan's head, and he will wound His heel. The birth of this seed from the Woman is the birth of a Man. But how is He to be born without a man? What is His hypostasis had this not been in the seed and from the seed of man? Whence then could His hypostasis be? The Woman that begot Him only gives Him the body and the flesh, that is the human nature, but not the hypostasis also, which is in the seed of man, in the begetting element of the male sex. Whence this then, since it has been prophesied that the Woman was to give birth without a man, that is being a Virgin? This is not to be found in the Woman, for the Woman gave birth by having conceived without a man. Therefore is it not evident that this is with God? And if the hypostasis of the Woman's seed is with God, it would not then be human, because it is not being born of man, but it is divine and of God. This then is the hypostatical Idea of the Being, the ontological law in God, which, while being an eternal God, receives the form and nature of man in the womb of the Virgin, and is born of her in the world according to the laws of nature. The Hypostasis of the Logos in having entered the Virgin's womb, and assumed within her humanity, was born in a human form. And this is the first prophecy given to the protoplasts of God concerning the Godman that was to be born of a Virgin. Wherefore before the real outcome of things we observe their prophetical proclamation, after which follows also the realization of things prophecied. This prophecy is the fundamental one amogst the other prophecies, it is the Gospel of God's promises concerning the Saviour; and all the other prophecies are, as if to say, an unfolding and explaining of this sublime prophecy, wherein is the entire drama of the Godman's incarnation being prophetically revealed. For instanse, in the prohecy, «A n d   I   w i l l   p u t   e n m i t y   b e t w e e n   t h e e   a n d   t h e   w o m a n   a n d   b e t w e e n   t h y   s e e d   a n d   h e r   s e e d», is revealed the Godman's incarnation and His perfect virtue, which is opposed to and wars against Satan's perfect vice; it is the enmity and war between the two contrary natures of virtue and vice. On the other hand, in the prophecy, «H e   s h a l l   w a t c h   a g a i n s t   t h y   h e a d,   a n d   t h o u   s h a l t   w a t c h   a g a i n s t   h i s   h e e l», is revealed the purpose of the incarnation of the God Logos, and the means whereby He will pursue His fulfillment. Herein is also revealed the achievement of His intent against vice, the defeat and fall of Satan, his ruin and destruction, and finally His sufferings in the world, and His death at His departure from the body. Nevertheless this wound is curable, but Satan's, which was to be of the head, is incurable. Therefore the one, of the Godman, is able of being cured, while that of Satan remains incurable for ever. It is therefore being prophecied that after the Godman is to endure sufferings and shall die bodily in the struggle against Satan, He shall be again resurrected, and shall live eternally, the same as God, even in a human form, dispassionate and invulnerable in the future. Whereupon, as concerning what the nature of the Godman, and what His war against the contrary nature of Satan, what the purpose of His incarnation and what the means leading thereto, what His life in general and His death and resurrection, and His triumph against Satan, all these are contained in this prophecy, wherein is contained the sum-total of prophecies concerning the Saviour.

This admirable prophecy given to the protoplasts by God as the Gospel of the coming of the Saviour that was to free them from the hands of Satan, and having been unfolded specifically by the prophets of God's Old Testament, is in harmony with both the nature and requirement of man, and the nature of Creation in general; it was necessary that this should come to pass, and its completion should be witnessed to us by history, if it actually came to pass. During the years of Caesar Augustus, the Roman monarch, about 1882 years ago, there appeared in the country of Judaea a man named Jesus Christ, preaching himself as the son of the living God, and alleging that He was sent of God in the world in order to establish and do the work and intent of God. He speaks of himself as of God and man, as the son of God, and as the son of man, and His e g o He proclaims as being eternal. He invites all to the faith and knowledge of Him, that He is the son of God made human, even as was said by the prophets, that He is the promised Messiah, the Emmanuel, the Godman, the mysterious meaning of Jehovah, of the Being. He speaks and enjoins as a God. He teaches the unfeigned and true virtue, and seeks to draw and raise man to God. He shrilly declares to the world that He is the truth and the light of the world, the eternal One, the beginning and the end of beings, the perfect work of God's perfect volition, the moral sun of the moral and spiritual world, and the universal center of Creation. He explains the nature of God and Himself, and shows His equality to God, and admits His consubstantiality to God before all. He speaks of Himself as being wholly sinless, and challenges officially the Pharisees of the congregation of Israel to reprove Him of sin, if they can. He maintains that He speaks as He knows, and that He can not speak other than what He knows and has heard, than the testimony of His own conscience, and that He can not speak falsehood as did the Pharisees. He confirms and ratifies the logical law of cognition by judging according to conscience, perception, and the testimony of reason, in an inductive and reductive and deductive manner, and attest the principle of contradiction, of causality, and of purposefulness. He confirms and ratifies the moral law of volition by willing and doing the perfect good on account of the good, and by not willing nor doing the thing that is evil on account of the evil. He confirms the prize of virtue springing from God, the eternal life, and the punishment of vice, the eternal damnation. He confirms and ratifies the political law of action, by keeping Himself first His duties to God and unto others and observing His ordinances perfectly even to the last tittle, by living, and cognizing, and acting, and conducting Himself in the law of God, for the sake of which He even died in order to sanction this by means of His most holy example. He publicly preaches contrition and conversion from evil - doings, and promises pardon unto those that repent and are being converted from the way of unrighteousness. He preaches the law of penitence and pardon as the forerunner of the law of ethics and its perfection in Him. He confirms that through Him is the salvation of the sinner, and through Him is the perfection of the one saved and has received remission of sins. He preannounces the judgement and righteousness of God as impending against those that disbelieve Him and spurn the law of God. He promises that He was sent of God not to judge the world, but that the world might be saved through Him. He proclaims His everlasting judicial coming according to which he shall come to judge and not to save the world. He reveals to us that time was given for our perfection, and when this is ended then will the everlasting kingdom of God come to earth as a perpetual and eternal one. He bases His teaching a) on the Old Testament prophecies ; b) on His most moral and most perfect life ; and c) on the power of His miracles. He refers to the prophecies concerning Himself in order to prove His identity, that He is the Messiah sent of God. He makes mention of His most sinless life in order to confirm His divine descent. He refers to His miracles in order to prove His divinity. He assails unbelief through three witnesses and considers this as a guilty and unpardonable aphasia. He draws the logical people's faith in Him through three witnesses, and only through His life He astonishes all Creation, because, as the prophet says, «His excellence covered the heavens, and the earth was full of His praise» (Hab. 3. 3). The virtuous and most sinless life of the Godman is the greatest of all miracles. He raises the dead from the graves, He heals those that were blind from birth and those that were inflicted with incurable diseases; and in general, «He heals all manner of disease and sickness among the people» (Latt. 4.23), thus proving Himself a benefactor over the healing of the sick; He does good by means of both kinds of beneficence, the bodily and the spiritual, and the bodily He uses as a means to benefit the soul, whose immortality He preaches and whose eternal personality He confirms by declaring the straight - forwardness thereof. He inexorably attacks the vice of Satan; He wars and struggles against him when tempted by him in the wilderness, thus defeating and casting him far away from Him. He fights against him in the society, and finally on the Cross, whereat He also destroys him completely, because through His death on the Cross He very methodically and skilfully overthrows Satan's darkness over the dominion of the people. And after this glorius and unique victory He cries out, « b e o f g o o d c h e e r » all ye that believe in me, « f o r I h a v e o v e r - c o m e t h e w o r l d » (John 19. 33); while from the Cross He shouts, « i t i s f i n i s h e d » (John 19. 30). Satan, through his instruments, accomplishes the bodily death of Him that crushed his head to pieces, but is caught in His trap after having risen fron the dead and having established upon the earth His everlasting dominion. This event is the fulfillment of the prophecy given to the protoplasts by God, it is the Gospel of salvation and history. Therefore between the Gospel of the ideal Godman, the Gospel of the prophecy concerning Him, and the Gospel of the Godman's revelation, there is an identity and a perfect concord; and this is because the ideal Godman is the One prophecied by the prophets, and Which revealed Himself in the

country of Israel 1882 years ago. Since, therefore, the Virgin
Mary was holy and blameless and from childhood being dedicated to God, after having received the good news from the angel
Gabriel concerning the conception of the Logos from the Holy
Spirit, and the birth of Emanuel, she conceived Him in her
womb, and begot Him in the den at Bethlehem, and nourished
Him as a Mother does with her only begotten, and rejoiced
greatly at the sight of Him as her beloved son. Therefore when
seeing Him suffering unjustly upon the Cross, as the guileless
Lamb of God, her maternal bowels were shocked and greatly
pained, until seeing Him resurrected and rejoiced so greatly that
no one can take the joy away from her, for it is eternal, even as
He said of this, «And ye now therefore have sorrow: but I will
see you again, and your heart shall rejoice, a n d   y o u r   j o y
n o   m a n   t a k e t h   f r o m   y o u» (John 16. 22).

THE IDENTITY OF JESUS CHRIST
IN RELATION TO THE PERFECT IDEA OF THE BEING

That is called identical which is the same in relation to
another, as having the same essence and the same peculiarities,
as a being of the same essence and nature. And that which is
essentially different, but partakes of another nature, is similar
and not identical. The essence of the Being is not the same with
the essence of the fact, because this is distinguished by certain
essential peculiarities of the other essence, a) of the eternal beinghood ; b) of the necessary beinghood ; c) and of the perfect beinghood. But the essence of the fact possesses the beinghood in time,
and the contingent and original imperfect beinghood ; and since
this partakes of the attributes of the Being's essence, i.e, of beinghood, of life, and of cognition, for this then we say that it is
similar, and not the same as the essence of the eternal Being. The
Idea of the Being is a perpetual Hypostasis in God, being complete and perfect as God. Therefore this is the same with God ;
but the deed also done thereby in Creation is identical with it, as
a being of the same essence, since its foundation and hypostasis
is the perfect Idea of the Being. It has been aforesaid that the
perfect action of God requires the incarnation of His perfect Idea,
and that it is impossible for this to be fulfilled without it ; because
what is the perfect action of God ? the perfect action of God is the
realization of His perfect Idea and Volition, which is one and only,
complete and perfect, entire and undivided. And the realization of
God's perfect Idea in Creation is the representation and depiction
of God by means of a perfect action. But the depiction of the
Being by Its Idea is possible ; consequently then the realization of

God's Volition by means of a perfect action is the incarnation and revelation of Its Idea in the world. Therefore the perfect action of God in the world has the very same perfect Idea of the Being as its hypostasis, otherwise it is unable of presenting God perfectly in the world. And if God knows Himself perfectly by a perfect hypostatical Idea, how will He be able to reveal Himself in the world by an imperfect action not having His Idea as the hypostasis? If God could know Himself by means other than His perfect Idea, how can His perfect knowledge in the world be possible without His perfect Idea? But how could the Idea of the Being make God known to the world unless having become incarnate and fell to our perception? It is for this then that we accept the fact that, if God intented to reveal Himself to the world, He could by no other means reveal Himself, than the incarnation of His perfect and eternal and self - existing Idea, Which for this reason is also called the Logos. This being already acknowledged it is also being acknowledged that the most perfect action of God in the world becomes identical to the perfect Idea of the Being, and this is identical to and of the same essence, because it has the very same Idea of the Being as its hypostasis, and this is the image of the Being in the Creation, for it represents God perfectly. But the perfect action is a moral and spiritual one, and it receives a hypostasis in the moral world, because the moral world is incomparably superior to the physical one. Therefore among the moral world of men there is no action more perfect than that of Jesus Christ, as this is being witnessed by history and the experience of the ages, and as is proven by things themselves. Christ's coming was foretold by the prophets, was proclaimed by Christ Himself, as He also confirmed this by His life and miracles, and finally ratified this by His resurrection and the permutation which His word exercised upon human affairs, having thus become the cause for the better by the permutation of the world. Jesus morality is equal to God's morality. He speaks of God as one having seen Him, and explains of things concerning God as one that knows Him and understands Him perfectly. He says that He has things in His hand, whatsoever belong to His Father, God, and that He is coessential to Him, «All things are delivered unto me of my Father: and no man knoweth the Son, but the Father; neither knoweth any man the Father, save the Son, and he to whomsoever the Son will reveal Him» (Matt. 11. 27). «I and the Father are one» (John 10. 30). If God then represents Himself perfectly in the world by a perfect action, and the perfect action is Jesus Christ, it is to be inferred that the Idea of God, whereby He knows Himself, is made identical with Jesus Christ, as the perfect action of God; therefore

Jesus Christ is the incarnation of the perfect Idea in God, and the perfect revelation. If God cognizes Himself through Himself, He can also represent Himself outside Himself, and He can explain Himself perfectly to the people by means of the incarnation of His Logos. God therefore spoke and speaks to the world through Jesus Christ, Which is the perfect God and perfect man. «This is my beloved Son, in whom I am well pleased; hear ye Him» (Matt. 17. 5). Since then Christ is identical to the Idea of the Being, and the Idea of the Being being the criterion of every idea and every being, it is to be inferred that Christ also is the criterion of every work and every action and every deed, and the law and the rule of every cognition and knowledge, and of every volition and sensation. Christ is the image of God, the Truth, the object of Philosophy, the Principle of the most perfect Morality, and in general, the social Principle of religion, of education, and of right conduct. Christ, in being identical to the Idea of the absolute Being, is the Mediator between us and God, the Master and Teacher, and Legislator, and the wise and just and eternal King. It is Him therefore that Philosophy, the highest of all sciences, seeks to learn as the ontological truth, and it is through Him and in Him that it seeks to discover the logical solution of the efficient and final reason of the beings, and to know the nature of the Universe. To the question then of the philosophical spirit, W h a t i s t h e U n i v e r s e? Jesus Christ replies, I a m t h e U n i v e r s e — «I a m t h e T r u t h» (John 14.6). For he that knows Christ knows the w h o l e (all things); and he that ignores Him ignores the w h o l e, because he ignores the ontological Truth itself, the Idea of the Being. In the Idea of the Being is the knowledge of the Universe; Christ, as being the Idea of the Being, promises the knowledge of the Universe, for in Him is the Universe, i. e., God, the world, and man. The being and the fact is cognized through the Idea of the Being; therefore through Christ also we know God, the world, and man, and the relations existing between them. «No man hath seen God at any time; the only begotten Son, which is in the bosom of the Father, he hath declared Him» (John I. 18); for Christ is the incarnation of the perfect Idea of the Being. In Christ we know the Godman, the perfect God, and the perfect man. Thus then we perceive the identity existing between Christ, as the most perfect work of God, and the most perfect Idea and Volition of God, as in the person of Christ we also perceive the incarnation of God's perfect Idea, and its revelation through the perfect man. And the perfect work of God is the Godman.

THE INCARNATION AND SPIRITUALIZATION

The accomplishment of the most perfect Volition of God is man's deification, or his spiritualization. And the means for this is the incarnation and humanization of God's perfect Idea, His Logos, a means that is analogous for the accomplishment of the Creator's chiefest will and of the purpose of Creation. Because, if man aims for deification and aspires God's perfection, then the incarnation of the Logos is the requirement of human nature, which, being sinful, deserves its sanctification and purification by such a sacrifice that requites divine justice and brings God's infinite commiseration upon the sinner, and as for perfection, seeing that it is by nature progressive, it deserves an analogous means for the perfection thereof, the law of its own activity and a social principle that is both infallible and impeccable. And for this the incarnation of the Logos has a twofold nature; a) a salutary one; b) and a perfective and a deific one. It is the duty of the incarnate Logos to save man from the hands of the Devil; to lead him away from sin, to sanctify him by granting him forgiveness for his doings upon the condition of true repentance, and to guide him through the road of truth to his perfection and deification. So if our salvation and deification comes through the incarnation of the Logos, is it not evident that without this it is impossible? Therefore the incarnation of the Logos is indispensable for our salvation and perfection, and they that deny this deny the salvation and deification of man, and oppose the soul's intimate desire and the logical demand of the means leading to our salvation and deification. Because by acknowledging and accepting our aspiration for the deliverance of evil, and that of our perfection, they acknowledge and accept and are being reluctant of embracing the logical demand of the Logos' incarnation, for the accomplishment thereof. Therefore the idea and the logical incarnation of the Logos is incontrovertible, for this idea reconciles the creation with the Creator, and produces the moral, order in the world.

When the Logos of God reveals Himself to the world in a perceptible manner, He receives the body and the soul of man, whereupon is laid the substance and the hypostasis. And this assumption of the body and soul is the assumption of the fact with the eternal and perfect Hypostasis of the Logos, wherefore the words, «the Logos was made flesh» do not signify that the Logos fell into flesh by having changed its essence, which thing is absurd and impossible by nature, but that the Logos, being eternal and remaining unchangeable, assumed a human soul and body according to divine providence, both being holy straightly from the beginning, for He kept their peculiarities and attributes in an unchangeable condition, and made them both incorruptible and immortal. This action of the Logos is called incarnation and humanization, because according to this the Logos assumes the human nature in a sound state both physically and morally, and deifies it, by making it equal to divine nature, and granting it its attributes, i.e., omniscience, omnipotence, goodness, incorruptibility and immortality. Human nature, on the other hand, receives spiritualization and deification, because it assumes the attributes of God, and becomes the participant of divine nature, not being changed at all, nor does it become a divine nature and essence. The Logos when made incarnate becomes man, that is, It assumes spirit from God and becomes the participant of divine nature. Now if the incarnation of the Logos is possible and according to reasson, why is the spiritualization of man impossible and contrary to reason? If the Logos when made incarnate did assume man's soul and body in order to accomplish the Will of God, why is it that when man becomes spiritualized he can not receive spirit from the essence of God, in the same manner as the Logos received soul and body from the essence of man? Why is it that the Logos, when made man, became the son of man, and man, not being the son of God, can not become God through the spirit of God? Let them give us an account which deny spiritualization, which, although acknowledging the essential incarnation of the Logos, yet do they neglectingly deny the essential spiritualization of man through the assumption of the essence of the divine Spirit, and not of Its hypostasis. If it be true that when the Logos became incarnate It received man's essence, and became perfect man by essence and nature, it is also true according to the same reason that man too, when received deification, he assumed God's essence through regeneration, and became a perfect God in essence. The incarnation of the Logos is unhypostatical, because the Logos did not assume man's hypostasis therein, nor was He born of the seed of man, but He was joined to human nature as an hypostasis whereupon the soul and the body are established. But man's spiritualization and deification are also unhypostatical, for the one deified does not assume the Hypostasis of the Spirit, i.e.. of God, nor is he immediately begotten of the Father's eternal Hypostasis, as is the eternal Logos of God, nor does he emanate therefrom as does the eternal Spirit, but is joined to divine nature as a subject, which (divine nature) it assumes as an hypostasis and a center of the body and of the spirit at the same time. So then, body and soul and spirit, these three, constitute the deified man. And just as the body and the soul of the incarnate Logos, Christ, became the components of

His hypostasis in time, although not being formerly when eternally He was the Logos without the flesh, even so do the body and the divine spirit become the components of man's hypostasis in time, although not being formerly joined thereto before this was sown in the female womb according to the matrimonial law and came into the world, and became incarnate and spiritualized in accordance with the physical and spiritual laws of generation and regeneration, as these were unfolded in my book entitled «The human Nature» wherein I would refer any one that desires to know the birth, growth, progress and the consummation of human nature. For before man's hypostasis became incarnate and spiritualized, it was formless, and invisible, and fleshless, and spiritless, as also unaware and unconscious, existing somehow simply amongst all the hypostases as a simple molecule of matter, as a B e i n g h o o d without perception and awareness. Before our hypostasis receives flesh and spirit it is susceptible to becoming incarnate and spiritualized, capable of assuming a perceptible body, and an intellectual spirit, of which, the former is of the matter pertaining to the world, and the latter of the matter pertaining to God. But they which deny spiritualization characterize this truth as a pantheistic idea, not knowing the nature of Pantheism, and not being able to comprehend this truth of man's tricompositeness, who was created according to the image and likeness of God. Pantheism confounds and does not distinguish God from the world, the Being from the fact, and teaches that the whole is identical to the essence, — to God' s hypostasis —, or that the eternal essence of God — the hypostasis — is identical to the essence — to the hypostasis — of the world. But the incarnate Logos is not identical to man's hypostasis, nor does the deified and spiritualized man become identical to the eternal hypostasis of the Spirit, that is to the hypostasis of the Godhead. We must therefore distinguish the hypostatical confusion of Pantheism concernig the Being and the fact, from the union of the fact with the Being, i.e., God, which is according to essence and nature and not according to the hypostasis, with man, which union is an ontological one. For just as our hypostasis becomes united with the corruptible body, but does not fall into corruptibility, nor to the hypostasis of the matterial and complicated body, but remains simple and incorruptible, even so when united with the divine spirit it does not fall into its hypostasis, nor does it become deified hypostatically and identical to the eternal Spirit of God. But from the essence of the world it assumes the body, and from God's essence the Spirit, the former being complicated and corruptible, while the latter simple and incorruptible. And because our hypostasis is by nature incorruptible, the union thereof with the incorruptible Spirit of God is much more harmonius than its union with a corruptible body, for when this is incorruptible the Spirit of God also becomes related much more with man's hypostasis than does the matterial body. And when the body shall become incorruptible and made new, our hyposta-sis shall be between the incorruptible body and the incorruptible Spirit, and, through the body and the Spirit, it will be enjoying the life of incorruptibility, of immortality, and of bliss. And if the Logos became man and partook of our essence and nature, even so can man become God by partaking of the nature and essence of God. But they which deny man's compositeness resul-ting from three essences, they deny his deification, they deny the incarnation of the Logos, for they ignorantly understand this fundamental truth of Christianism to be a pantheistic doc-trine, they deny the purpose of the Logos' incarnation, and contradict themselves, because, though accepting the Logos' incarnation, they foolishly deny man's spiritualization, which is the purpose of the incarnation of the Logos. If this truth, viz., that man is essentially deified by partaking of the Spirit of God, is indeed a pantheistic doctrine, as the uninstructed ones say, then the truth also, viz., that the Logos became essentially incar-nate by partaking of man's essence and becoming a man, is li-kewise a pantheistic doctrine. Accordingly then Christianism is a pantheistic system, as is also its foundation. And thus they which repel and deny the truth that the divine spirit is an essential component of man, fall into the denial of the fundamental truth of Christianism, i.e, to the denial of the Logos' incarnation, whose purpose is the spiritualization of man, this being the second fundamental truth of Christianism. Because if man does not par-take of God's essence, neither would the Logos partake essentially of man's essence. And if He actually partakes of man's essence, by becoming man, then man too necessarily partakes of God's essence, by becoming God. The Logos became man to the end that man may become God, after having been taught the law according to which he receives deification, and to conform in accordance therewith. The humanization of the Logos is a my-sterious union of God with man, and a very close relationship between the two. It is the exaltation of human nature, and its equalization with the divine Nature. And the spiritualization and deification of man is the mysterious union thereof with God, and the closest relationship with Him. In His incarnation, the Logos assumes man's essence by dispensation and condescention for the sake of mankind, while Himself being perfect and not in want, and man, in his spiritualization, assumes the Spirit from the essence of God according to the Law of progress and perfection for his fulfillment of his destination, while himself being imperfect and in want of perfection, which he can accomplish only through the acquisition of the divine Spirit. Accordingly then our spiritualization is the consequence of the Logos' incarnation.

THE GOSPEL

The Gospel is the word expressed by the incarnation of the perfect Idea of the Being, which occured at some definite place and time, and which is a historical fact. The Gospel is the fulfillment of the prophecy given to the protoplasts by God, as we have above mentioned, and the revelation of man's ideality in Christ, the perfect man, and perfect God. This word, as being the good and excellent messenger of the revelation of the only good amonst the people, has deservingly received the appellation fit its nature and purpose, that of G o s p e l (or Good Tidings; from eu -- , good, and angellein, to proclaim. Translator's note). By means of this are made known to us the life and teaching of the Godman, our predestination, and the means whereby this is accomplished, God and man, and the relations existing between them. In the Gospel are contained the sentiments, the meanings, the feelings, the wishes, and the actions of the perfect man, of Christ, and is clearly manifested the relation existing between him and God, as of the representation to the thing represented. And since the account herein is concerning the Idea of the Being, the principles and the laws of the Spirit, under their theoretical sence, for this then the Gospel must be examined under its theoretical and philosophical aspect.

THE FUNDAMENTAL IDEA OF THE GOSPEL

The fundamental idea of the Gospel is the incarnation and the revelation of the Idea of the Being in Christ, the perfect God and perfect man, and the spiritualization of man, which is the purpose of the Logos' incarnation, and its deification. Christ is, the subject of two natures in one Hypostasis of God's eternal Idea, namely, the divine and the human one, of which the former is the eternal nature of the Idea of the Being, while the latter is the assumption in time by the incarnation. Christ as the incarnation of the Idea of the Being, is the image of the Being, that is, His real Truth, as He says of Himself, «I am the way and the truth and the life» (John 14. 6). Wherefore He is the object of the principal science, of Philosophy. Christ, as being the chief Truth that reveals the first Being, God, and manifests every truth, as being the source of every truth, He is the efficient and final cause of the Being's existence, even as He Himself says. «I am the Alpha and the Omega, the Beginning and the end» (Rev. 1.8). «For by Him were all things created, that are in heaven, and that are in earth, visible and invisible . . . And He is before all things, and by Him all things consist . . . . For it pleased the Father that in Him should all the fulness of the Godhead dwell . . . . Who is the image of the invisible God, the firstborn of every creature» (Col, 1. 15 - 19). Christ is the image of God and man, manifesting equally both the Being and the fact in perfection. He is the son of God, and the son of man. As the son of God He is God, and as the son of man He is man. No one comes to God, but by Christ (John 9. 6). Christ is equal with God, «I and my Father are one». Christ as the Truth is the light of the world, «I am the light of the world» (John 8. 12). He is the idea and the image of God, «If ye had known me, ye should have known my Father also» (John 8. 19). Christ as the son of God knows God perfectly, and He alone reveals the things concerning God as one that knows them. «No man hath seen God at any time ; the only begotten Son, which is in the bosom of the Father, He hath declared Him» (John 1. 18). «No man knoweth the Son, but the Father ; neither knoweth any man the Father, save the Son, and he to whomsoever the Son will reveal Him» (Matt. 11.27). God's revelation through Christ witnesses the perfect knowledge of Christ concerning God. And if Christ knows God perfectly, then He is His Idea, whereby God knows Himself. Because the perfect Being is known by a perfect Idea. The fundamental idea of the Gospel is the idea of Christ as a being of the perfect Idea of God in a human form, the idea of the Godman in the eternal Hypostasis of the Logos, the idea of the perfect man in its equality with God by means of its granting of the God-equal Spirit, that is, his deification. In Christ are both the perfect God and the perfect man united together, but without the attributes of each nature to be confused, because both natures remain unchanged and unalterable in the Logos. And thus when God and man are become united in the Logos, they exist together eternally and in a perfect harmony, for this is the ultimate purpose of the Logos, incarnation : the spiritualization and deification of man.

THE PHILOSOPHICAL PRINCIPLES OF THE GOSPEL

Jesus Christ by being perfect in respect to the knowledge of the Being, as the Very Truth, He knows the method of the science, and knows thoroughly the laws of cognition ; therefore He is the infallible Master and Teacher of Philosophy, even as He says of Himself, «But be not ye called Rabbi : for one is your Master, even Christ.... Neither be ye called masters : for one is your Master, even Christ» (Matt. 23. 8 - 10). We must therefore know as to what principles and what laws of cognizing did Christ confirm and validate, in order that we too, in cognizing in accordance with them, may also cognize correctly and not to be deceived, as to those that philosophize without a criterion and a discreet cognitive faculty. The Gospel, as the revelation of the word of truth and the declaration of the Idea of the Being in the incarnation of the Logos, contains also all the ideas which form Philosophy, and explain the efficient and final cause of the beings. It then contains both the logical laws of cognition and the philosophical method whereby we know the truth and comprehend the Idea of the Being ; in other words, the Gospel contaits the efficient and final cause of the beings, and gives us the key to the knowledge and the science of the Being and the fact, so that by means thereof we may open the door to the first science, and receive an exact conception of the first and primary and absolute Idea of the Being and of the primary law of the Spirit, according to which we cognize the Being and the Truth, and establish Philosophy and the science of the Being.

The philosophical principles are : a) that of contradiction ; b) that of cause and effect ; and c) that of the principal end and purpose. The first is a l o g i c a l principle, for by means thereof we can not at the same time cognize two principles or two ideas contrary to and excluding each other as being equally true. And without this principle of the spirit it would have been impossible for us to philosophize and to instruct. For this then it is merely called a logical principle. The second principle is i n v e n t i v e of the being, which the spirit seeks by the phenomenon through its observation, because by the principle of causality we discover the causes of the beings and the phenomena, and the efficient cause of the Universe. And without this principle the science of the Being would have been impossible. It is for this then that Philosophy depends on this principle, and by means thereof is the science of the Being established. Whence it is called an inventive principle, in so far as it discovers the cause of the phenomenon and reveals it. The third principle, that of purposefulness, is a legal one, because, from the observation of the nature of the beings, it raises us to the conception of their purpose, which is also their law. By means of this principle we cognize the universal purpose of Creation and its final cause, when beginning from the observation of the particular purposes and particular principal ends. We thereby cognize the necessary existence of a universal Law aiding to the completion of Creation and its equality with the eternal Being. Without this principle we could have no conception of the law and of the termination of the beings, and no idea regarding the order existing in the universe. Upon the logical principle of contradiction is based syllogism and the a p r i o r i method of reduction. Upon the inventive principle of causality is based the method of reduction, which raises us from the phenomenon to the cognition of the being, and which by means of the phenomenon knows the being and the truth. And upon the legal principle of purposefulness is based the inductive syllogism and the inductive method, whereby we cognize the general from the particular in accordance with the conditions of identity, of similarity, and of analogy. The three philosophical principles and methods, of deduction, of reduction, and of induction, which are based on these, are the principles and laws of the spirit whereby we cognize the being and the truth, and upon which we establish the sciences, and chiefly the science of the Spirit. Philosophy. Now observation and right reason are the witnesses of every knowledge and every truth ; that is, consciousness, perception, and reason, upon which is erected the structure of every knowledge and science as upon three unshaken pillars. The principles, the methods, and the sources of knowledge, are being fully attested, and confirmed, and sanctioned by the Gospel, as shall be thus made evident.

THE LOGICAL PRINCIPLE OF CONTRADICTION

The Gospel bears testimony of the logical principle of contradiction whereby it is impossible for us to embrace at the same time two ideas or two principles contrary to the same place and in the same manner as being, equally true, for the following reasons. «No man can serve two masters : for either he will hate the one, and love the other, or else he will cling to the one, and despise the other. Ye cannot serve God and mammon» (Matt. 6.24). That which in action is good or evil, the same is also true or false in theory. Servitude is an impossible action with two masters of a contrary nature. Because, either it will hate one of its masters, and love the other, or else it will cling to the one, and despise the other. And if the act of serving two masters of a contrary nature is impossible, the conception also of two contrary ideas and principles as being equally true or false is likewise impossible. God and mammon (avarice) are two masters of a contrary nature which is impossible both to serve and despise at the same time. For either we will serve God or mammon. Our will can not at the same submit to both, for God excludes mammon, and mammon God. And two masteries of a contrary nature concur in identity. Therefore it is impossible to serve God and mammon. And · ·

if this is impossible, it is also by nature impossible to cognize both as one, that is, God and mammon. Whence the principle of contradiction leads to the distinction of the contrary ideas, principles, and natures, and without it logical science can not exist. When the Gospel sanctions the principle of contradiction in action, it also sanctions this in the cognition and science. When it sanctions this in the practice of action it sanctions this in the practice of ethics and politics. It sanctions this in the ontological science, in Philosophy, and in the sciences whose instrument is the logical science. That which is impossible in practice is also impossible in logic, and that which is possible in practice is likewise possible in logic. And if we can not serve two masters of a contrary nature, nor can we cognize two principles or two ideas of a contrary nature as being equally true or false. This almighty law of contradiction, which has been misunderstood by those that philosophize dogmatically up to now, was excellently enforced by Christ in the Gospel and in the life of the Godman. Therefore the Gospel, from its beginning to the end, possesses this logical principle and in nowhere does it contain not even the least contradiction. It is therefore the infallible codex of the Logical science, wherein every one learns correctly the logical laws and becomes the possessor of the Logical science.

THE INVENTIVE PRINCIPLE OF CAUSALITY

The Gospel as possessing the logical principle of contradiction upon which is established the Logical science, this common instrument of all sciences, possesses also the inventive principle of causality, whereby, from the observation of the phenomena, we seek and find out their cause, that is, the truth. And this chief principle is a philosophical and scientific one, according to which it is impossible to cognize the phenomenon without some cause corresponding therewith. The cause of the phenomenon is the truth thereof. Thus then its principle is being confirmed by the Gospel in the saying, «Beware of the false prophets, which come to you in sheep's clothing, but inwardly they are ravening wolves. From their fruit shall ye know them. Do men ever gather grapes out of thorns, or figs out of thistles? Even so doth every good tree produce good fruit; but the rotten tree produceth evil fruit. A good tree cannot produce evil fruit, neither can a rotten tree produce good fruit. Every tree that produceth not good fruit is hewn down, and cast into the fire. Wherefore from their fruit shall ye know them» (Matt. 7. 15 - 20). The false prophet, who appears to be a true prophet, mistakes our observation, for he appears to be of the same peculiarity as of the true prophet; whereupon we gave need of the criterion in order to judge concerning him, viz., as to whether or not he is a true prophet, and for such a criterion we have his life and actions, which things are his fruit. The sheep is beneficial, for it affords fruit advantageous to us. So is the prophet true, if he affords fruit advantageous to us; else he is false. But if the wolf, whose nature is evil, shall put on sheep's clothing and stand in the midst of us as a sheep, which by nature is good, how shall we be able to know his nature? How is it possible for us to know that he is a wolf and not a sheep? Assuredly from his fruit. Because when seeing him snatching and teering the sheep to pieces we will then be able to judge that he is a wolf and not a sheep, as he appears to be. And thus from the phenomenon we ascend to the being and the truth. For it is impossible for us to assume the snatching wolf, in sheep's clothing, as a guileless sheep. The good and the evil tree are revealed by their good and evil fruit, because the fruit is the effect of the tree, which is the productive cause thereof. Consequently the tree is known by its fruit and we can not cognize an effect contrary to its cause or greater than that. From the works and sayings of the prophet we ascend to the cognition of his nature, to the cause of the works and sayings, which are its (nature's) cause, and from the snatching and murderous nature of the sheep - formed wolf, we ascend to the cognition of the wolf, and from the nature of the fruit of the tree we cognize the nature of the tree. Thus we ascend from effects to the cognition of the causes, from the phenomena to the beings, from the fact to the eternal Being, from conjecture to truth and to the Idea of the Being. And when cognizing the cause from the effect, we cognize an unchanged relation between them and a necessary law whereby is associated the phenomenon together with the being, and the effect with the cause. By cognizing this relationship between them, we cognize the analogy existing in them, according to which the effect can not be greater and superior to its cause, but analogous thereto. Judging then in accordance with this principle of causality, we cognize that negation can never result from thesis, or from negation thesis, from truth falsehood, or from falsehood truth, from good evil, or from evil good, or from justice injustice and from injustice justice. We cognize that the being produces being, the animal produces animal, and cognition produces cognition; that the being produced can not come to existence without the Being, but it receives its existence from the Being, and that all phenomena possess a first and superior cause, which, by reason of its perfection and infinity, is self - existent and causeless, or self - causative, possessing in itself the efficient and final cause of its existence. We cognize the absolute cause of existence, of life, of cognition, the eternal Being, God, and the dependence resulting therefrom of all existence, life, and cognition. And this cognition, according to the principle of causality is a universal one, for it is extended everywhere, and by means thereof we cognize the cause of every phenomenon to the cognition of the absolute Cause of the Universe. Now the Gospel from its beginning to the end possesses this chief philosophical principle of causality, and everywhere amonst all its phenomena we are able to find its efficient cause. Thus then the Gospel by confirming this principle unerringly and enforcing this everywhere, proves itself to be the infallible codex of Philosophy, wherein every man learns thoroughly the science of the Logos and becomes the possessor of true Philosophy, having as its object the personified Logos, Jesus Christ.

THE LEGAL PRINCIPLE OF PURPOSEFULNESS

The Gospel as possessing the logical philosophical principle of contradiction and of causality, possesses also the legal principle of purposefulness, according to which we cognize by every being and analogous purpose and end after which this has a nature in the general and universal order of the beings. The principle of purposefulness is witnessed of Christ by the following, «Be ye therefore perfect, even as your Father which is in heaven is perfect» (Matt. 5. 48). But to the young aspirer also asking for what good thing must he do in order to inherit the eternal life, Christ answered, «If thou wilt be perfect, go and sell thy possessions, and give to the poor, and thou shalt have treasure in heaven : and come and follow me» (Matt. 19. 21). Perfection is the additional acquisition of necessity ; for every being aims at the acquisition of those qualities which it must possess in order for it to become perfect in respect to its order. Now perfection is relative and absolute. After the being is made perfect it neither assumes nor rejects anything because it possesses all things required, and is in need of none, nor does it superabound ; it therefore has neither deficiency nor superabundance, but is perfect. The bound of perfection is God, the infinite and eternal and ever living Being, whereon aims the perfect aspiration, that of man's perfection. Now in proportion to the perfection and purpose where every being aims at there are analogous means provided by which this accomplishes its predestination and becomes perfect. And these means are the laws ; and it is for this reason that this principle is called a legal and legislative one. Between the nature of the being and its end lies a law that is analogous to both its nature and its purpose. In longing for perfection, or to become equal with God, the young man receives a law analogous to his aspiration and to the final purpose whereunto he aimed ; and this law is that of our self - denial and departure from everything that is vain and superfluous. It is the law of temperance, whereby, the nearer we are to God, the more do we become unneedy of the things appearing good to the world, and self - sufficient unto God Which himself is the real Good. This is the law of freedom and simplicity. But the young man who loved riches more than God, and was addicted more to the thing appearing good than to the being, through ignorance, did not resolve to reform through the word suggested him by the Lord, but foolishly repudiated the wise law of perfection ; and thus he swerved from his desire. When judging in accordance with this common principle of purposefulness, we cognize the progressive nature of the Creation of the beings, we find out the laws of their progress, and ascend to the conception of the idea of the universal purpose of the beings and of the universal end whereunto Creation is directed, by natural and logical and moral laws, as by suitable means. When observing the innate tendency and inclination of the beings toward progress, we ascend to the cognition of their end, and we seek to learn not if there is a universal end of Creation, which is obvious through the principle of purposefulness, but as to what is the universal end of Creation, and by means of what laws is Creation being led thereunto. Now the Gospel which explains what the end of the beings is, it also interpretes their nature, and lays down the suitable law for its accomplishment, which is perfect and leading toward that which is perfect. It is therefore the infallible codex of nomology, the perfect law of Ethics and of the social science of justice, whereby every one learns perfectly the universal end of the beings, and the perfect law leading thereunto. Thus the Gospel confirms the principle of purposefulness, possessing this from its beginning to the end, by revealing the final cause of the Universe, and legislating the means by which Creation is safely being led thereto. Therefore the Gospel can justly be called the R e v e l a t i o n   o f   t h e   e f f i c i e n t   a n d   f i n a l   c a u s e   o f   t h e   b e i n g s   a n d   t h e   l a w ,   w h i c h   l e a d s   u n t o   p e r f e c t i o n ,   n a m e l y ,   i n c o r r u p t i o n   a n d   i m m o r t a l i t y ,   o r   d e i f i c a t i o n. After this cognition of causes, and means, and ends, which we received from the Gospel's contents, and after the knowledge of the three universal principles, of contradiction, of causality, and of purposefulness, let us also look into the logical actions and methods, by means of which we know the truth, as these being confirmed and declared by the Godwritten Gospel.

THE INDUCTION

The method of induction is the transmission of the spirit from the particular to the general, and from the general to the universal, in accordance with the principle of identity, of similarity, and of analogy. And without this method we could in no way ascend to the conception of the general and the universal from the individual and particular perceptions and representations. And this method is being confirmed and sanctioned by the Gospel as follows, «Therefore whosoever heareth these sayings of mine, and doeth them, I will liken him unto a wise man, which built his house upon a rock : and the rain descended, and the rivers came, and the winds blew, and fell upon that house, and it fell not ; for it was founded upon the rock. And every one that heareth these sayings of mine. and doeth them not, shall be likened unto a foolish man, which built his house upon the sand : the rain descended, and the rivers came, and the winds blew, and dashed against that house, and it fell : and the fall thereof was great» (Matt. 7. 24 - 28). The induction here is made from things physical to things ethical according to the principle, that the physical world corresponds in similarity to the ethical and spiritual world, and that the phenomena in the ethical and spiritual world are being deducted according to such laws that have a similarity with the laws of the physical world. And this induction is according to analogy and similarity. The cognition here, according to the principle of universal order, extends, its power from the phenomena of the physical world to those of the ethical and spiritual, by deducting an inference that is similar and analogous from a similar and analogous comparison resulting from two similar and analogous representations. From the physical observation of induction, that every one who builts his house upon the sand is a fool, not knowing its peril from the mutation of the weather, cognition is being transmitted to the idea that in the same manner also is every one foofish that builts the ethical and spiritual house of the soul upon the alogy and unbelief in the word of God, not knowing that from the enemy's assaults he will be in danger of perishing and falling morally. And from the observation that every one who builts upon the rock is wise and fears not the peril resulting from the weather's mutations, cognition is being led to the idea that in the same manner also will not he that builts his house upon the word of God fear any moral danger, for he is wise. «Another parable put he forth unto them, saying, The kingdom of heaven is like to a grain of mustard seed, which a man took, and sowed in his field : which indeed is the least of all seeds : but when it is grown, it is the greatest among herbs, and becometh a tree, so that the birds of the air

come and lodge in the branches thereof» (Matt. 13. 31 - 32). The
observation here is made on the grain of the mustard seed of the field
and of its sprouting and growing to a big tree wherein lodge the
birds of the air. And from this observation of the physical phenomenon we induce our cognition to the ethical phenomena also,
which is similar to and analogous with the physical ones. Hence
from the grain of mustard seed we cognize that which at the beginning is occult and invisible in the soul regarding faith in the
divine word. By the field we cognize the moral field, i.e., our
soul, wherein is sown the divine word and is planted and sprouts
and becomes a big tree, that is, it produces in us works of virtue
which benefit others, just as the trees benefit the birds and the
animals. For virtue is the ethical tree whereby all people are
being nourished. So the kingdom of the heavens, the kingdom of the ethical law and virtue, is occult in the world
at the beginning, but in due time it becomes manifest and then
all they which soar lodge therein and are being nourished by its
fruit. But we also receive another exemple from the Gospel pertaining to induction, «And in the same day went Jesus out of the
house, and sat by the sea side. And there were gathered unto him
many multitudes together, so he went into the ship and sat ; and
the whole multitude stood on the shore. And he spake many
things unto them in parables, saying, Behold, a sower went forth
to sow ; and when he sowed, some seeds fell by the way side,
and the fouls came and devoured them up ; and others fell
upon stony places, where they had not much earth ; and forthwith they sprung up, because they had no deepness of earth :
and when the Sun rose, they were scorched ; and because
they had no root, they withered away. And some fell among
thorns ; and the thorns came up, and choked them ; but other
fell into the good earth, and gave fruit some an hundredfold, some
sixtyfold, some thirtyfold. He that hath ears to hear, let him
hear» (Matt. 13. 1 - 9). In connection with this parable the Lord
gave the following interpretation, «When any one heareth the
word of the kingdom, and understandeth it not, then cometh the
wicked one, and catcheth away that which was sown in his heart.
This is he which was sown by the way side. But he that was
sown into stony places, the same is he that heareth the word, and
anon with joy receiveth it ; yet hath he not root in himself, but
is ephemeral : for when tribulation or persecution ariseth because
of the word, he is straightway offended. And he that was sown
among the thorns is he that heareth the word ; and the care of
this world, and the deceitfulness of riches, choke the word, and
he becometh unfruitful. But he that was sown into the good earth
is he that heareth the word, and understandeth it ; which also

fruiteneth, and bringeth forth, some an hundredfold, some sixty, some thirty» (Matt. 13. 19 - 23). By this parable, from the conception of the seed and the earth wherein the seed is sown and planted under the infuence of the physical circumstances, cognition is transmitted to the conception of the divine word and of the souls in which this is being sown when taught by God, and the conception of the law according to which this is being planted and grows after the infuence of moral circumstances. It must be noted that this ethical induction is based upon the physical induction, and when the Gospel confirms the ethical induction it also confirms the physical one at the same time, which is the foundation of the other. And when it sanctions the two kinds of induction it confirms the principle of identity and of universal order, and acknowledges the principle that the physical world is the image and phenomenon of the ethical and spiritual world, and that whatsover is true pertaining to the image is also true by analogy and similarity pertaining to the thing represented. Now this truth is being recorded and enforced to perfection by the Gospel from its beginning to the end, but unfortunately it is being slighted up to the present by the unskillful dead philosophers.

THE REDUCTION

Reduction is the mode according to which cognition cognizes from the relative, i. e., the contingent and the causative, the absolute, the eternal Being, and the cause. And the relation existing between the relative and the absolute, that is, between the contingent and the necessary, and the causative and cause, is the necessary law of reduction. Now this is being induced according to the principle of causality, by which we cognize the being from the phenomenon, and the cause from the effect. The Gospel admits God's existence and His perfection whereunto it also exhorts us, His perpetuality and eternal life, and by means thereof it suspends man and the world as the works of His free volition. «Of his own will begat he us with the word of truth, that we should be a kind of firstfruits of his creatures» (Jas 1. 18). «Be ye therefore perfect, even as your Father which is in the heavens is perfect» (Matt. 5. 48). This admitting is at the same time the admitting of the law of reduction and the validity of the reductive method. When the Gospel declares to us the rule of knowing perfectly the tree's nature from the nature of its fruit, the character of the true teacher from his good works and actions, it forms the method of reduction according to which we cognize reality and the nature of every cause from the reality and nature of its effects ; «Beware of the false prophets, which come to you in sheep's clothing, but inwardly they are ravening wolves. From their fruits shall ye know them» (Matt. 7. 15). The character of the false prophet is invisible and occult to us, and we can not see this directly through observation ; but we can see it indirectly by its effects, namely, by the exoteric actions that fall into our perception. A false prophet is a moral cause known by the moral actions produced thereby. And if the works thereof are good, it is indeed good, and so is the cause whereby these resulted ; but if vile, so is their cause also vile. But the nature of the effect and the nature of its cause presupposes the reality of both, for had these not existed we could have neither seen the nature of the nonbeing. When the Gospel, therefore, validates the reductive method in the quality of the cause, from the nature of the effect, it validates this in accordance with the reality of the cause from the reality of its effect. Does the effect exist ? If so, it therefore has a cause analogous therewith, and which we seek to know as to what this is through reduction in accordance with the principle of causality. When Christ said, «Be ye therefore perfect, even as your Father which is in the heavens is perfect», He distinguished the imperfect from the perfect, and from the imperfect idea concerning us He ascended to the idea of God's perfection where our imperfect nature aims at by employing the reductive law. For the imperfect presupposes the perfect ; and the perfect Being is infinite, eternal, and immutable. But from the imperfectibility of our nature we can not infer that God Which made us is also imperfect, for He did not make us with the intent of having us imperfect for ever, but that we might proceed and advance until we be perfected, as this is evident from our progressive nature. And by observing our progressive aspiration we ascend to the cognition of the existence of a perfect Being whereby we have received the beginning and the imperfect beinghood, and where we are being led to, and progressing thereunto until we be perfected in this and become perfect. The Gospel therefore teaches us the law of our practical reduction leading us from imperfection to perfection, which presupposes the logical and theoritical reduction, which is being acted upon by the logical faith in God deeming Him as a perfect and eternal Being. And the faith in God is the reduction of the soul from the effect to the cause, from its reality to the reality of the eternal Being, and from its own living and cognition to the living and cognizing eternally and perfectly in God. To believe in God is to ascend to God through the law of cognition as unto an absolute cause from the observation of the effects. For the faith in God is the immediate manifestation of the cause resulting from its effect, and not a proof, for we have no need for such means as to prove the existence of God which is self - evident and self - proven. And as regards the first principles, as being self evident, not even the slightest doubt can penetrate, but faith unhesitating, that is, scientific certitude. Therefore when the question arises concerning these, as to whether or not t h e s e e x- i s t, it is said to be an absurd and inconsistent one. Hence the question laid by the modern philosophers i f t h e r e i s a G o d, reproves their ignorance and absurdity, and proves their nescience concerning the nature of cognition and of the principles and laws of the Spirit. It is for this that the accepted first principles in the Gospel are self - proven, being known from their effects and the method of reduction, which is a philosophical method, according to the principle of causality.

THE DEDUCTION

Deductive is called the syllogistic method by means of which we deduce its erroneous consequences from some given principle. The Gospel confirms the validity and application of this method, which is based on the principle of identity, by the following, «Then was brought unto him one possessed with a devil, blind, and dumb: and he healed him, insomuch that the blind and dumb both spake and saw. And all the people were amazed and said, Is not this the son of David? But when the Pharisees heard it, they said, This fellow doth not cast out devils, but by Beelzebub the ruler of the devils. And Jesus knowing their thoughts He said unto them, Every kingdom divided against itself is made desolate ; and every city or house divided against itself shall not stand : and if Satan cast out Satan, he is divided against himself ; how shall then his kingdom stand ? and if I by Beelzebub cast out devils, by whom do your children cast them out ? therefore they shall be your judges. But if I cast out devils by the Spirit of God, then the kingdom of God is come unto you. Or else how can one enter into the strong man's house, and plun- der his utensils, except he first bind the strong man ? and then he will plunder his house. He that is not with me is against me ; and he that gathereth not with me scattereth abroad. Wherefore I say unto you, All manner of sin and blasphemy shall be forg- iven unto men : but the blasphemy against the Holy Spirit shall not be forgiven unto men. And whosoever shall speak a word against the Son of man, it shall be forgiven him : but whosoever shall speak against the Holy Spirit, it shall not be forgiven him, neither in this world, neither in the world to come. Either make the tree good, and its fruit good ; or else make the tree rotten, and its fruit rotten : for the tree is known by its fruit» (Matt. 12. 22 - 33). When Christ was attacked by the Pharisees that He casts

out the devils by the ruler of the devils, that Christ's beneficent
curing to those that were possessed with devils had Satan as its
cause, He used syllogism according to the law of deduction in
order to defend the truth attacked and to muzzle his enemies by
laying down this principle, «Every kingdom divided against itself
is made desolate; and every city or house divided against itself
shall not stand». And to this principle He compared the proposition of the Pharisees, «Satan really casts out Satan», and saw if
this proposition is included in the principle as its consequence
and then He inferred that Satan's kingdom is really overthrown
by Satan himself. Therefore Satan was divided against himself.
«How shall then his kingdom stand?» Notwithstanding since it is
not true at all that a kingdom or house or city should be divided
against itself, it is also not true then that Satan should be divided
against himself. And consequently the proposition made by the
Pharisees, that Satan is cast out by Satan, is false. But if Satan
is expelled by the Spirit of God, then the kingdom of God is at
hand, being the expeller of devils. It is then one of the two; either confess that the Spirit of God is evil and wicked and Its
works are evil and wicked, or else that It is good and beneficent
and the works thereof good and advantageous. And thus Christ
proved through syllogism that the consequence resulting from the
principle cannot be contrary to it, and if the principle is false, so
is its consequence also false; and if this is true, so is the consequence thereof necessarily true. The proposition of the Pharisees,
that Satan expells Satan, was a consequence resulting from a false
principle, that every kingdom wars against itself
and destroys itself, but the proposition that He drives
out Satan by the Spirit of God, was a consequence resulting from a true principle, that it is impossible for every kingdom to war against
itself, and that it should pursue his own
abolishment, it was a consequence resulting from the principle that every kingdom wars against its ini-
mical kingdom, and never against itself. Hence the inference is derived that God's salutary kingdom
is therefore come by the expelling of Sa-
tan from the people through the Holy Spi-
rit. In being by nature evil, Satan performs also evil works;
and Christ acting through the Holy Spirit, acts and performs good
and excellent works. Christ therefore says, either make the tree
rotten and its fruit rotten, or else make the tree good and its
fruit good. For it is by nature impossible that from a false principle should a true consequence result, or that from a true principle should a false consequence arise; the inference corresponds

to the principle whereon it is dependent, and the principle is analogous to the inference resulting therefrom, and is never contradictory thereto. In this manner did Christ validate the principle
of contradiction and confirmed the method of deduction and of
syllogism, according to which (deduction), we deduce, from a
given true principle, a true consequence, and from a given false
principle we deduce a false consequence. And thus is the tree
known from its fruit, and the principle from its consequences. For
between the consequences and their principle there exists a perfect consonance and analogy.

THE SOURCES OF KNOWLEDGE

After we have learned according to the Gospel the principles
and the laws of the spirit and their enforcement by means of the
inductive, reductive, and deductive method, we now also proceed
to the knowledge of the sources of knowledge. The sources of knowledge are a) observation, or conscience and perception; b) and
right reason. And firstly let us ponder on conscience, and of how
does the Gospel speak concerning this. Conscience is the source
of the knowledge of the ego, and the witness of the truth of the
ego. And the testimony of conscience is unerring and indisputable
with the cognition taking place according to the criterion of truth
and according to the primary judgement I exist as a relative and dependent being. The truth ascribed to
conscience is being validated and confirmed by the Gospel in the
following manner; Jesus Christ, Who was conscious of Himself,
did speak according to the conscience He had of Himself, by demanding an unhesitating faith for the testimony of His own conscience according to which He spoke the truth. In being conscious that He came out of God and goes back to God, and that He
was not come of Himself but was sent of God, Christ censured
the Jews for their unbelief in His testimony, and from this unbelief He characterized them as the children of Satan, who from
the beginning is a homicide and abode not in the truth, because
there is no truth in him, and speaks a lie of his own, being the
father of lies (John 8. 42 - 44). Therefore when Christ demanded
faith from the Jews, unto which He spoke concerning Himself,
He demanded the recognition of truth, and confirmed the validity of conscience, and condemned as the sons of Satan those
which disbelieved the testimony of conscience and spoke against
this. Upon the validity of the testimony of conscience, Christ founded every truth concerning Himself, that He is the Son of God,
and the Son of man, or the Godman. «Before Abraham was I am.
I am the light of the world. I am the way and the truth and the

life. I am the good shepherd. I am the door of the sheep. I am the vineyard. I am the resurrection and the life. Ye calle me, Master and Lord; and ye say well: for I am so. I and the Father are one. I came forth from God and I am here. I am the bread that came down from heaven. I am the bread of life». In being aware of Himself, Christ had a perfect and profound conscience of Himself. And when He spoke of Himself according to the consience He had, He was worthy of being believed for the things He spoke of Himself. Faith, in His speech, He judged as an honor attributed to His conscientiousness, while, on the contrary, the unfaithfulness of others toward Him He judged as impudence attributed to His conscientiousness wherewith He spoke of Himself, and by so much did He judge the unbelievers as being responsible before divine Justice and worthy of eternal demnation for their unbelief, as much as He judged those worthy of eternal honors and prizes which believed in Him for their faith. For faith, to those which Christ spoke of Himself, is the recognition of His conscientiousness, and unbelief in them is the assault against His veracity. It is then an insult to the spirit of conscience by which Christ spoke as He knew Himself, an insult to the Holy Spirit speaking through Christ, and for this unbelief is a blasphemy thereto and an unpardonable sin. And thus Christ validated and confirmed the principle of conscience as the primary principle of knowledge and the source of knowledge concerning the ego and His nature.

In confirming the cognitive source of conscience, the Gospel also confirms the woven and inseparable cognitive source of perception resulting therefrom in the following manner. Perception is the witness of the outside world, of the nonego, a true and indisputable witness respecting the primary cognition of the world's existence, as a r e l a t i v e a n d f i n i t e b e i n g d e p e n d i n g o n G o d. In the same manner as He confirmed the validity of conscience, Jesus Christ also confirmed the validity of perception, for He spoke concerning the people and to the people, and His teachings were based on worldly experiences when He spoke by means of parables, and examples, and likenings, and comparisons from the physical and ethical world. And with such a conviction did He speak to the people concerning their nature and the perceptive objects, as the certainty that He had concerning their existence. And this certainty of those that He spoke to and concerning the perceptive objects that He spoke of, is the product of the perception whereby we cognize that which is outside of us, the nonbeing. «Ye», said He to the Jews which disbelieved Him, «are of your father the devil, and the lusts of your father ye will do. He was a homicide from the beginning, and abode not in the truth, because there is no truth in him. When he speaketh a lie, he speaketh of his own: for he is a liar, and the father of it. But as for me, besause I speak the truth, ye believe me not» (John 8. 44 - 45). The unbelieving Jews and their father the devil were the object of Christ's perception, and Himself being the subject thereof and the object of His own conscience. And elsewhere He says when confirming the phenomenon of perception, «The world cannot hate you ; but me it hateth, because I testify of it, that the works thereof are evil» (John 7. 7). And by the words, «If I do not the works of my Father, believe me not. But if I do, though ye believe not me, believe the works : that ye may know and believe, that the Father is me, and I in Him» (John 10. 37,38) He manifested the clarity of the perception resulting from His works, and therefrom He raised those that disbelieved the testimony of His own conscience to the faith of His own conscientiousness, that He speaks true of Himself, and that He is indeed in the Father and the Father in Him. And by reproving the faithlessness of the Jews He said unto them, «I told you, and ye believed not : the works that I do in my Farher's name, they bear witness of me. But ye believed not, because ye are not of my sheep, as I said unto you» (John 10. 25,26). And when the Jews took stones to stone Him because He said that He was the Son of God, equal with God, He said to them, «Many good works have I shewed you from my Father ; for which of those works do you stone me» (John 10 32) ? So He referred them to His works and miracles, which they themselves had seen, and which they perceived, and therefore they could not deny the fact thereof, but they did very insanely ascribed them to the work of Satan and for the satiation of their own envy, which they supported against Christ, and from the perception resulting from facts He challenged them to declare for which work they stone Him. Not being able, however, on account of the activity of perception, to deny neither the facts nor even to characterize them as hurtful and evil, although characterizing them as good, they answered Him in an impertinent manner, «For a good work we stone thee not ; but for blasphemy ; and because that thou, being a man, makest thyself God» (John 10. 33).

When the Gospel validates the testimony of perception with conscience it validates the experimental principle of knowledge, namely, observation, and it also validates and confirms the testimony of right reason. Through right reason we discover the causes from their effects, the principles from their consequences, and the beings from their phenomenon. When Christ said that none comes to the Father except by Him, He heard from Philip, «Shew us the Father, and it sufficeth us» (John 14. 8) ; and the Lord said to him, «Have I been so long time with you, and yet hast thou not known me, Philip? He that hath seen me hath seen the Father; and how sayest thou then, Shew us the Father» (John 14. 9)? Here then, by the things which Christ said to Philip, He manifested the law of reason by means of which we ascend from the phenomenon to the cognition of its cause, and from the representation to the thing represented. What was Christ before the eyes of Philip? A great ethical phenomenon, and a worthy product of some great ethical cause. But Philip, who was infinite in consideration in accordance with the law of cognition, and having heard that if the Lord's disciples knew Christ they would have known God, and that from thenceforth they both know and see Him, he presumed that Christ speaks of the sensual visibleness of God, and therefore said unto Him, «Shew us the Father, and it sufficeth us». But by His reply, Christ declared that the present saying is not concerning the perceptive and sensual visibleness, but concerning the vision made by reason, viz., concerning the purely spiritual sight, which begins from the conscious and perceptive beholding of Christ as the perfect work of God, and ascends to the cognition of the absolute cause of all beings, to the knowledge of the absolute Nous. «He that hath seen me», says Christ, «hath seen the Father; and how sayest thou, Philip, Shew us the Father»? and thus Christ, from the thing manifest and visible, raised Philip's cognition to the knowledge of the thing cognized and of the Being, Whose likeness and perfect work is Christ. But even when speaking concerning God as He perceived Him, Christ also confirmed the validity of right reason. «If I», said He, «honour myself my honour is nothing: it is my Father that honoureth me; of Whom ye say, that He is your God; yet ye have not known Him; but I know Him: and if I should say, I know Him not, I shall be a liar like unto you: but I know Him, and keep His saying» (John 8. 54). Whereas Christ knew God according to the entire profundity of His nature He could not say that He did not know Him, for He would have thus been accused of lie, and then would have been like unto the Jews which spoke against conscience and against right reason, saying that Christ expells the demons by Beelzebub. Not being able therefore to lie, Christ confirmed the invincible validity of right reason, whereby God is known, and thus proved His respect for right reason. I know myself, as being the truth, and the light of the world; I know the world, whose light I am; I know God. These three judgements explain every mystery of knowledge in Christ, and confirm the everlasting validity of conscience, of perception, and of right reason, the validity of the spirit and its primary law of cognition. In knowing Himself — Knowing the world — Knowing God, Christ cognized, spoke, willed, and acted in accordance with the testimony of conscience, of perception, and of right reason, and it is for this that His entire life is, in theory, the foundation and the rule of the right and perfect Logic, while in action the rule of perfect Ethics. For this then we must think and do according to the logical and ethical laws and rules of the perfect man, and to philosophize both theoritically and practically after the invariable logical and ethical principles of the Gospel, by recognizing Christ as our omniscient Professor and Teacher Who knows all things, namely, God, the world, man, and the relations existing between them. Christ Who knows God perfectly and represents Him perfectly, is the incarnation of the Idea of God, the Wisdom and the Logos of God by Whom are all things known and made, and consequently He is the absolute Truth of the Being, and the object of Philosophy, the efficient and final Logos of the beings, Whom Philosophy is required to comprehend as the science of the efficient and final Logos of the beings, and as the science of the primary and universal Truth. Our School in Christ seeks the perfect knowledge of the Universe and investigates the explanation to the mysterious problem w h a t i s t h e U n i-v e r s e. It also promises to all the conscientious believers the understanding that it possesses the key of all knowledge and science, the incarnate Logos of God, our infallible Professor and Lord Jesus Christ.

THE THREE ONTOLOGICAL PRINCIPLES

Existence, life, and cognition are three absolute principles, whereby emanate the existing, the living, and the cognitive faculty of every being, of both those that live and cognize. Experience shows us not only their existence and coexistence, but their distinction also, which thing convinces us that these things do not result from one cause, but from three causes and principles, which exist in a united and distinct manner. This coexistence forms the most perfect amongst the beings in the world, and for this, man, in that he centralizes in himself the existence, the life, and the cognition, is then the most perfect amongst the beings upon the earth, the sum of Creation. Observation shows us three orders of beings, of which some have beinghood without life and cognition, and some have beinghood with life, but without cognition, and others have beinghood together with life and cognition. The inorganic order of beings is existential, while the cognitive order of beings is the most perfect and most complete, for it contains in itself the existential and the animal order and the superior and most perfect among their attributes, that of cognition. Hence man is a being, animal, and possessed with awareness, and this being the most perfect amongst the beings in the world. However, neither his life, nor his cognition, and consequently neither his existence are perfect ; for he lives not as he wills and wishes, nor does he cognize according to the will he possesses, and therefore he does not exist as he desires to exist. And consequently the perfect existence, the perfect life, and the perfect cognition, is not within him, but outside of him, and within the most perfect Being whereby he has received them and possesses them. The cause of the imperfect existence is the perfect existence of the Being, and the cause of the imperfect life and cognition is the perfect life and cognition of the Being, and inexistence and imperfect existence can not be the cause of imperfect existence, nor can mortification and lifelessness and incognizance be the cause of life and cognition ; consequently man, as an animate and cognitive essence, is by nature impossible to result from the nonbeing, or from an inferior being to itself and wanting of life and cognition. For man's efficient cause must be superior to him altogether the same with himself. He must have beinghood, life, and awareness, for how else could he impart that which he does not have ? Accordingly then, the Darwinian theory, which supposes man to be derived from apes, and from animals inferior to his nature, is false for it makes the effect better and superior to its efficient cause, which is utterly absurd, and is logically confuted as an insanity and a great deceit. Logic declares that the effect cannot be superior to its cause, but either inferior or equal thereto. And observation confirms that similars are caused and produced by similars, that the inferior is made from the superior, and the more imperfect from the more perfect. And the law of progress depends on this, In the perfection of the imperfect by the influence acted thereupon from the more perfect Being. For if the more perfect Being does not exercise any influence upon the progress of the less perfect, progress would be unachievable. And how can one that is ignorant become wise unless the influence of the wise teacher be exercised upon his cognition? How can the nonbeing become a being without the influence of the Being? How can the nonliving become a living being, without the efficacy of the living being acted thereupon? How can the noncognitive being become one that is cognitive, unless the influence of the cognitive being be exercised thereupon? How can man become an animate and volitive and cognitive essence, without the influence of an animate and volitive and cognitive essence be acted thereupon? Or can this be perfected in the way to its progress without the efficacy of a most perfect Being acted thereupon, and centralizing in it a perfect existence, life, and cognition? Accordingly then, our efficient cause is a perfect existence, life, and cognition. For it created us imperfect at the beginning, not that we should always be as such, but that we should become perfect by contributing to our progress our willingness and free choice, and God granting us both the strength and power and the enlightenment for the journey to the road of perfection. God, Who is perfect, made us imperfect, not that He could not made us perfect from the beginning, because such a thought contravenes His omnipotence, but because He desired to work together with us in our perfection, by working willingly and moving voluntarily in the road to virtue and duty, and accepting freely God's influence acting upon us for the sake of our own perfection. Our perfection therefore is o u r l i k e n e s s t o G o d, our Maker and Father. And our likeness to God is the acquisition of His perfect nature and His perfect attributes towards our own perfection, and the eternal possessiveness of the beinghood, life, and perfect awareness, the same as God. To be in the beinghood of God ; to live in His perfect livingness ; and to cognize in His perfect cognittance, is for us to be perfect in the essence of the perfect Being, and having a perfect existence, life, and cognition. And our beingness in the essence of God as rational and free and Godequal persons, excludes and spurns every pantheistic and ungodly and blasphemous idea and notion.

The three principles of beingness, of life, and of cognition, whereby emanates every existence, and life and cognition that is both relative and finite, are ontological and absolute principles existing together and forming the perfect Being, God, the Creator of the Universe and our Father. Life without beingness does not exist ; but cognition also without beingness does not exist. Whereupon life and cognition presuppose beingness. Life and cognition in man are peculiarities and attributes of his existence which cannot exist without beinghood. Accordingly then beingness precedes life and awareness. B e i n g n e s s, l i f e, a w a r e n e s s, this is man's gradual formation. But whence is beinghood? whence life? whence awareness? Necessarily from an existing and living and cognizing principle, or from ontological principles resulting from beinghood, life, and cognition. And there is one principle and principles that is essentially and hypostatically, that is, triadic in person, it is the Nous, the Logos, and the Spirit, viz., the Father, the Son, and the Holy Spirit, the God of Science and the Gospel T h e B e i n g, t h e L i v i n g O n e, a n d t h e O n e A w a r e o f a l l t h i n g s. The Being is eternal, as He says, I a m t h e B e i n g (Ex. 3. 14), the efficient and productive of life and cognition, of the Logos and the Spirit, because It is a perfect existence, one that is both cognitive and animate. And from this is begotten the principle of awareness, the Logos, the perfect principle, having a perfect beingness, and distinguished from the absolute principle of existence. From this proceeds or emanates the principle of Life, the Spirit, a perfect principle, having a perfect beingness distinguished from the absolute of existence and from the principle of awareness. B e i n g h o o d, L i f e, A w a r e n e s s, these are the three ontological and personal principles in God, and these three principles are being revealed to us by the Gospel. The principle of beingness is absolute. An absolute Principle is also that of awareness and the Principle of life. But there is one absolute Principle of existence ; one of life ; and one of awareness. Now all beings are caused by God's perfect existence, they were made by the Principle of life. Hence Creation is the work of the One and Triadic Godhead.

The Gospel has revealed to us the idea of the One and trihypostatical Godhead, the absolute Principle of beinghood, of life, and of awareness, the three Principles of existence, of life, and of knowledge. As the Godman sent His disciples to preach, He bade them both to teach and baptize the nation in the name of the trihypostatical Godhead, saying, «Go ye therefore, and teach all nations, baptizing them in the name of the Father, and of the Son, and of the Holy Spirit» (Matt. 28. 19). And John the Theologue also says in his epistle, «For there are three that bear witness in heaven, the Father, the Logos, and the Holy Spirit : and these three are one» (John 5. 7). And in the Revelation God says of Himself, «I am the Alpha and the Omega, the beginning and the ending, saith the Lord, Which is, and Which was, and Which is to come, the Almighty» (Rev. 1. 8). John the Evangelist again says at the beginning of his Gospel, «In the beginning was the Logos, and the Logos was with God, and the Logos was God... In Him was life, and the life was the light of men» (John 1. 1, 4). God the Father, the Logos, and the Life in the Father and the Logos, viz., the Spirit, these three are persons of the one Godhead. Moreover the Triadic God did reveal Himself when Christ was being baptized in Jordan. For while the Logos and Son of God was being baptized, the Father from heaven exclaimed and testified of His Son, saying, «This is my beloved Son, in Whom I am well pleased» (Matt. 3. 17), and the Holy Spirit came down from heaven like a dove and sat upon the head of the Godman that was being baptized. And thus the mystery of the Holy Trinity was even manifested perceptibly according to the divine and unfeigned historical testimony of the Gospels. Though Christ distinguished Himself from His Father as a person and being similar with, yet He again united Himself essentially with the Father, saying, «I and the Father are one» (Iohn 10. 30). Two I's-Ego persons in one Essence; and when He had promised His disciples that He will sent unto them another Paraclete, the Spirit of truth, He distinguished this Paraclete from Himself and the Father as a similar person and Being, in the one indivisible Essence of the Godhead. There are three I's in one Essence of the Godhead. «And I will pray the Father, and He shall give you another Paraclete, that He may abide with you forever; even the Spirit of truth; Whom the world cannot receive, because it seeth Him not, neither knoweth Him: but ye know Him; for He dwelleth with you, and shall be in you» (John 14. 16,17). The I of the Christ God, the I of the Father God, the I of the Spirit God, not three heterousian Gods, but one God according to the Essence in three hypostases or persons. Three I's with one immovable and unchangeable perfect Nature. «Howbeit when He, the Spirit of truth, is come, He will guide you into all truth... He shall glorify me: for He shall receive of mine, and shall shew it unto you» (John 16. 13.14). And elsewhere Christ, says «But when the Paraclete is come, Whom I will send unto you from the Spirit of truth, Which proceedeth from the Father, He shall testify of me» (John 15. 26). The I of Christ, the I of the Father, and the I of the Spirit, are the three I's of the Godhead, three persons, three Beings, three Hypostases, but in One perfect Essence.

common attribute	God Father God Son God Spirit	identical attributes	Nous Or Logos Spirit	Or	Being Truth Cognition

One God : three persons. One God : three Beings. One and three.

Principle of beingness	God
Principle of livingness	God
Principle of awareness	God

three Principles. One God

And thus the Gospel reveals, testifies, and confirms fully the three absolute ontological Principles and their essential unity, by means of which (Principles) emerges every existence, life, and cognition. For this then the God of science is also the God of the

Scripture, and the God of the Scripture is the God of science, He is the God Who, by His power and wisdom, created all things in His good will, and Which established Creation from the nonbeing, and Who formed and made the order of the beings through His Logos, and Which maintains and orders and holds this together by His perfect Spirit, by His two spiritual hands. This is the God therefore Which is known and worshipped by them which through Christ were regenerated by water and spirit, and are become the children of God, created in the image and likeness of God.

THE NATURE OF TRUTH

When speaking of thruth in this case we mean the absolute and primary and universal one whereon depends every truth and in relation to which harmonize all the truths of the numerous beings. The absolute Truth is the faithful and perfect image and representation of the absolute Being, equal therewith and coeternal, and the product of the Being's perfect existence and cognition. Hence the absolute Essence is a) the absolute Being, its absolute Truth, and the absolute cognition. As the image of the Being the absolute Truth shows the absolute Being a) that it is an eternal Being and possessing eternity also ; b) that it has in itself the cause of its own existence, that it is a self—existent and self—causative Being ; c) that it is a Being having in itself its final cause of existence ; that it is self - sufficient. Therefore in the absolute Truth we distinguish the three principles of the spirit, that of contradiction, of causality, and of purposefulness, which constitute the essence of right reason with the Idea of the Being, or with the matter of cognitiveness. The laws and principles of contradiction, of causality, and of purposefulness are found to be inseparably united together with the conception of the primary Truth, because inasmuch as God cognizes Himself eternally He therefore cognizes His identity, causality, and purposefulness. When, therefore, He intents to make beings outside of Himself, He makes them in accordance with these three eternal principles of His, which He also reveals amongst His works ; a) He gives them beingness ; b) He makes them depend on Himself as causal beings ; c) He makes them susseptible of perfection. And the revelation of these principles is the manifestation of right reason a) in the part of nature as a physical law and as a physical principle ; b) in the part of the ego — I — as a logical law and a logical principle ; c) in Christ, as a social law and a social principle. With nature the revelation of the Logos' principles with the beinghood of the beings is imperfect, it is also the means of some more perfect revelation. With the ego, the revelation of the Logos' principles with beinghood and the ego and the spirit, is more perfect than the physical revelation and the forerunner of a more perfect revelation in Christ. The revelation in Christ resulting from the principles of the Logos is the revelation of the Logos' essence, of the Being's absolute contradiction, and its absolute causality and purposefulness. The revelation of the Logos in Christ is the revelation of the perfect beingness, livingness, and awareness of the Being, the Being's image, manifesting the perfection of His essence with its identity, causality, and purposefulness. The revelation of the Being was made in Christ ; and it is complete and perfect ; and for this everyone that sees Christ sees God, for Christ is the image and the Truth of God, «he that hath seen me hath seen the Father» (John 14. 9). «No man hath seen God at any time ; the only begotten Son, which is in the bosom of the Father, He hath declared Him» (John 1. 18) : «I am the way, and the truth, and the life» (John 14. 6). Accordingly then Christ, as the revelation of the Being, is called the primary Truth; and as the declaration and manifestation of the Spirit's eternal law, of its eternal Principles, He is the Way and the philosophical method leading to the cognition of the Being ; and as the revelation of the Being's perfection and its immortality, He is the life everlasting. Christ is the revelation of the Truth of the Being and of the essence of the Logos, of the everlasting Law of the Spirit, containing the three Principles of the Logos, viz., that of contradiction, causality, and purposefulness. He is the revelation of a social Principle and a social Law binding and controling the society for its own sake and for the sake of God, and regulating its affairs a) religiously, through the religious intercession of Christ as the High Priest between the society and God ; b) educationally and philosophically, through Christ's logical and ethical and philosophical teaching between the society and the beings ; c) politically, through the legislation and the possession of equal rights of Christ the King, the Ruler, and Legislator of the God-ordained society that conducts itself religiously and philosophically and politically according to the perfect social Law of the Gospel. The society is being kept, progresses, and perfected in Christ the social Principle, it also knows its beginning and ending, and the means whereby this is being led thereunto. In brief, it becomes the image and likeness of God, and knowing thoroughly its beingness, cause and final purpose. It represents in its life the threefold nature of Truth, and through discipline and its legal activity it pictures the eternal law of the Spirit, which has thus been revealed therein, to its Principle, Christ. Therefore, in seeing the Truth in its perfect revelation through Christ as the revelation of the Logos' essence, and as the perfect representation of the Being, we see God in

Christ, and Christ's identity to God, the identity of the absolute Truth to Christ, and the revelation in Christ of the eternal laws of the Spirit, that is, of the essence of the eternal Logos in God. From this identity then results the unobjectionable truth that Jesus Christ is the object of the first science, Philosophy, and the perfect and eternal Law of the Spirit, and unto Him, as unto the absolute Truth, aims the aspiration of knowing which is also being perfected and cured through Him. When cognizing Christ, we cognize God, Whose image He is, and we cognize the perfect man made equal to God ; we cognize the Being and the fact, the Universe, and are ignorant of nothing. But in order to cognize the truth in Christ we have need of much study. Commencing from the faith that Christ is the absolute Truth, this being witnessed by Logic, Ethics, prophecy, and history, we result to its understanding wherein lies the knowledge of all things. And if all knowledge is in Christ, then Christ is the universe. He that ignores Christ ignores all things and departs to the darkness of ignorance. Such then is the nature of Truth.

THE UNITY IN CHRIST

Since Christ is the absolute and universal social Principle, the unity in Him then is the consequence of this Principle. And the purpose of society is its unity with Christ in one moral body. The social unity in Christ is one that is complete and perfect, logical, moral and political, through the truth of the good and the just, having as its effect the birth of science, virtue, and justice. Such things as wisdom, morality, virtue, and justice, spring forth from the unity of society with Christ Who is its legal and natural Principle. Christ, as the social Principle, draws society to Himself, for He is both the efficient and final cause thereof, and society depends on Him as a consequence. The existence of society depends on the existence of Christ. Accordingly then its preservation, salvation, progress, and perfection depend on Christ, and they must be pursued by Christ. For should they be pursued without Christ, they are being pursued amiss, and contrary to truth, morality, and justice, and a society that is being legislated and ruled without Christ goes in the way that is contrary to justice, truth, and morality, neglecting and overlooking its social end. Society without Christ is like unto psychic forces without reason, for Christ is Himself the Right Reason. And just as the soul without right reason cannot unify its forces, because it lacks a unifying force, i.e., reason, neither could it ascend to generalizations and general ideas, even so could neither society unify its forces, accomplish social unity, and succeed to its final purpose, without its legal Principle, without Christ the ontological Logos (Reason). The unification of moral forces is accomplished by some moral Principle capable of centralizing in itself all the moral forces, and that this should serve as an unshaken and firm reason. And the moral and social unity is possible and accomplishable only in the Logos and through the Logos. In Christ is united the society as the body to the head, and constitutes an excellent and perfect body, upon which is observed the moral comeliness and glitters the order, harmony, justice, and truth. The social unity in Christ is moral, scientific, and political. For Christ, as the universal and absolute Truth, is a scientific Principle. He is a moral Principle in that that He is the moral Good. He is a political Principle in that that He is the image of God's perfect righteousness, as the Principle of justice and the laws. He is the legislative, judicial, executive, and the absolute Principle. Christ is the universal Law of activity for all the logical, moral, and free beings, and the society founded on Christ is founded upon the Law and Justice, and upon Truth and Morality. A society, therefore, that is founded upon such an unshaken and everlasting Principle can never be overthrown and crumble, or that it should not accomplish its goal. Would then that all mankind be established on Christ the sooner that it might reap its social fruit, and first of all the Greek nation which retains this Principle of almost 18 centuries, but unfortunately does in no way appreciate the value of this treasure that is in Christ, but aspires to the false wisdom of the West, which denies and nulifies the eternal validity of this divine Principle that is in many and various ways being witnessed of and proven to be a divine and universal and eternal Principle.

The social unity in Christ is a union with the Logos of God, and the society founded on Christ is founded on the Logos of God Which is indistructible and eternal. Therefore it is for ever undiminishing and unshaken. Accordingly then no one force can prevail against it, for there is nothing mightier than the Logos of God. Such establishments as the Church, the School, the Tribunal are found to be united together and distinguished and in harmony with each other, and in no way do they ever conflict with each other. The Church is the school of reverance and of ethical reformation, the clinic for the souls, and the baptismal font for the social regeneration in Christ. The School is the delight and the fireplace of the logical and moral education of the society, the cast and the form of the scientific instruction for the youth, the study of truth and of the pursuit and discovery of the efficient and cause of every phenomenon. The Tribunal is the school of political wisdom, of virtue and justice, the study of knowledge and of the enforcement of the principles of the social and political righteousness, and the workshop of the practical enforcement of the law and justice. In the Church the logical shepherd and guardian of the souls' conduct performs his duty in accordance with the religious and moral commandments delivered him by Christ the Chief Shepherd and eternal High Priest. In the School the tutor and educator and the teacher of truth performs his duty in accordance with the logical and scientific and moral commandment delivered him by Christ the Chief Teacher and Professor. In the Tribunal the governor, the judge, the senator, the mayor perform their duties in accordance with the political commandments delivered by Christ the Legislator and King, by legislating, and governing, and judging after the invariable principles of Righteousness whose source is Christ. And thus, in the performing of the duties of every social order, lies the harmony and prosperity of the entire society, the peace and the progress and the perfection thereof. This then is the social justice and peace and harmony; and society is being led to Christ by the influence of the shepherds, the teachers, and the rulers, it assumes His nature, and fulfills its needs, and thus becomes unneedy; it becomes abundant in wisdom and science, in moral and political virtue, and in righteousness; it is made rich in material and moral power, and is mighty both materially and morally. The physical and moral life therein proceed in such a way that the physical one serves as a means for the accomplishment of the moral life, and both together contribute to the accomplishment of political goal of justices wherein meets the moral virtue with the political virtue, goodness with righteousness, ethics with politics, and are being harmoniously united together and pursued as the supreme social moral goal.

RECAPITULATION

The matter treated in this book is concerning the nature of the absolute Idea and the first principles of Philosophy. That there is an absolute Idea and a first Principle that is likewise absolute, this is known from the beginning, and no one can logically dispute this. But what is this Idea and Principle? Here lies the question whose solution is a great conflict to the spiritual world. For the materialists, on the one hand, take the idea of matter as an absolute Idea and first Principle, while the idealists, on the other hand, the idea of the ego or the abstract general conception of the being by panegotism, criticism, and eclecticism. The improper solution results from the improper thesis of the question and from the ignorance of the philosophical method. For we ask, Whence do we know the beingness of the abso-

lute Idea and Principle? By what means do we possess in our
mind the idea of their existence? Is it not from the observation
of the relative ideas entering our mind through consciousness and
perception, and through the logical cognition whereby we ascend
to the cognition of the absolute Idea and Principle? If then it is
through the spirit and reason that we cognize the Idea and the
Principle of the absolute after their beingness, should we not
through the same method also cognize their nature? And when
by this means we cognize the world and man as relative beings,
as a finite nature, how can it be possible for us to cognize the
world and man as their cause? How we be able to cognize the
same being as relative and absolute at the same time? We must
therefore do one of the two : either to suppose the world and man
as relative beings and to seek their analogous cause, the Being,
or to suppose them as absolute to the testimony of conscience and
perception, and then we must seek the relative causal being. But
such an opinion is erroneous and false, and for this materialism
is false. And by cognizing the abstract idea of the being, or the
idea of the ego, as the absolute Idea, we then by imagining cognize
the abstract before the concrete, the indefinite and obscure, not
cognizing according to reason. For what else is the abstract idea
of the being other than the idea of the finite which we abstract
thereby? And what else is the idea of the ego other than the idea
of the relative and the finite? Accordingly then idealism, with its
manifold branches, is just as false as materialism. The solution
of the question requires the enforcement of the method according
to which we proceed from the known to the unknown after the
testimony of the spirit and reason. Observation refers to reason,
and from reason we descend to the field of observation. And thus
we solve the philosophical question : What is the absolute Idea
and Principle of cognition that satisfies the yearning of knowing.
We therefore solve this in the following manner. From the observation of the fact we conceive the idea of the absolute Being as
the law of cognition, this being both a cognitive and volitive
being ; and by cognizing the perfect Being, we possess its perfect
Idea in accordance with the perfect law of cognition, and this
Idea is the principle of causality. We therefore possess the first
Idea and Principle of Philosophy whose thorough knowledge and
understanding makes us just as wise as God. But the Idea of the
Being, as the image of the perfect Being, is an ontological and
hypostatical Idea, being cognized by a perfect Spirit and perfect
cognition, in accordance with the principles of contradiction, causality, and purposefulness, as the idea of self - causativeness, self -
beingness, and self - perfectiveness. And since God, Who cognizes
Himself through a perfect Idea, can also represent Himself out-

side of Himself through His Idea, He reveals by the incarnation of His Idea in the person of Jesus Christ, Who is the object and the first ontological Principle of Philosophy. Therefore, the laws and the principles of cognizing are being set forth in the words of Christ and Philosophy is contained in the Gospel. And after the present work has logically proven the first Idea and Principle of Philosophy, it has also proven this ontologically by the hypostatical Idea of the Being and by its revelation in the person of Christ. It has explained the nature of Christ and of the Gospel, as a social Principle and as a social Law, and has also described the social unity in Christ which shall be the result of the future, the ideal of society which is being realized in the present and perfected in the future. Such then in brief is the recapitulation of the contents in the present work. And now let us proceed to the conclusion.

CONCLUSION

The conclusion derived from the entire work is this: That Jesus Christ is the absolute Idea and the first ontological Principle of cognition, whereunto man's philosophical spirit aims as unto the object of Philosophy, for He is the Godman, the incarnation and the revelation of the Idea and of the hypostatical Logos of God. The human mind seeks to comprehend Christ, the object of Philosophy and the first and universal and absolute Truth, and the philosophical yearning of knowledge has from the beginning of its birth aimed at this Truth, and the understanding and apprehention thereof did it desire. And it was indeed necessary that it should aim and desire this, for only this Truth ensures the satisfaction of the yearning for knowledge, the solution of the propounded questions in man's mind. It is only this Truth revealed in Christ, which is infinite by nature and essence and universal, as being the sum of all truth, and absolute and superior to all, that responds to man's infinite, primary, universal, and absolute yearning for knowledge, and is very harmoniously conjoined and adapted thereto; and from this link of identicals, from the yearning for knowledge in man with the knowledge and Truth in the Idea of the Being, in the Logos of God — Christ — , and their application, generates forth the perfect knowledge, the perfect awareness in us, the knowing of all things.

Yearning	absolute
Law of cognition	Truth
Awareness	

When cognizing according to the Principle and principles of cognition we find the truth in Christ, we know and understand this, and make this our own possession. We therefore possess this inalienably. Accordingly then the yearning for knowing has Christ as its object, Who possesses perfect knowledge. And when we have cognized Christ, in accordance with the law of cognition, we cognize the perfect knowledge in Him, the Truth of His words, «The word of God is truth» (John 17. 17), and get to know the beings and the phenomena, even as does Christ the Very Truth. It was necessary that there should be an absolute knowing for the absolute yearning for knowledge, an absolute Truth to respond as a corresponding agent, and such a Truth is Christ, Who said, «I am the Truth» (John 14. 6), that is, the first and universal Truth Which the human mind sought from the very beginning, and which, because of ignorance in the method and deceit, it ignored and rejected. «I am the Truth»; this is the Truth whose eternal existence we feel and also know as being incarnated in Christ, and before us, calling us to its recognition. «I am the Truth»; the Truth, the beginning and the ending of knowledge, the one ignored and slighted and rejected by the people, for they have been deceived in connection with its philosophical inquiry and search because of being ignorant of the right method, of the right observation and consideration, the Truth testified by the spirit and reason, and of prophecy as well as history. «I am the Truth»; the Truth Which Satan's delusion has slighted and Whose attributes it ascribed to matter and the fact, and thus having characterized the thing in time and the finite as everlasting and infinite, and the relative as absolute. «I am the Truth»; Which materialism sought in matter and in the material world by ignorance of the right method, idealism in the general and abstract idea of the finite, panegotism in the finite essence of man, and pantheism in the chimerical identity of the Being with the fact, namely, in the deification of matter.

We turn to those that philosophize and seek the Truth, and prove to them that Christ is the sought - for Truth, and Which grants every ensurance concerning its credibility. In Christ we find beingness, causativeness, and the final purpose in their absolute meaning, the principles and the eternal laws of cognition. And by cognizing Christ we cognize the absolute

Beingness of the Being, Whose image He (Christ) is, we cognize the absolute cause and the absolute Purpose of the beings. We cognize the Being in connection with the fact, the perfect God in the Logos in relation and union with the perfect man. We cognize in Christ God's perfection and the apotheosis of human nature in its union with the Logos. Since therefore it is in Christ that we find the Truth Which we relish and seek, why should we not take advantage of it now? Why not forsake delusion in order to embrace the Truth revealed in Christ? Why is it that, by slighting the revelation of Truth, we feign that we seek that which has already been revealed and cries out, «I am the Truth»? What more do we seek for since that which is sought - for has already been made known, and is come to seek us which are deceived and not able to find it. But now, since Truth was made known in Christ, the searched - for Truth has ceased, and the time has been appointed for its recognition and perfect knowledge in Christ. To the conscientious voice of Christ, «I am the Truth» we are by right reason obligated to answer, «Yea, Lord, Thou art indeed the Truth! and we have learned and believed that Thou art Christ the Son of the living God. Moreover, Thou art the absolute Idea of God, the universal Logos of God, and the absolute Entification and Causation and Puprosefulness. Thou art the first and absolute Principle of cognition, Thou art the perfect God and perfect man, and the union and bond to both in Thine eternal and divine Hypostasis». Now by recognizing Christ as the Truth and as the absolute Principle of cognition, we must necessarily study Him and to understand perfectly His sayings for solving all the problems presented to our minds. For, by possessing the first Truth, we are then able, and only then, to sail through the sea of knowledge fearlessly as well as firmly, by being enlightened and led to our philosophical journey from the light of the first Truth, and by means of the right philosophical method we proceed to the perfect understanding of all knowledge, namely, all the Truth in Christ. Our School possesses this eternal renown: that it does not seek, as do the other schools of illogicalness, as to whether or not there is a first Truth and a first Principle of cognition, or what is the so - called first Truth and first Principle, but as to what is the revealed Truth and Principle in Christ, and as to how will we be able to understand this perfectly and to enforce this in our practical life. It is being convinced through right reason, and both prophecy and history, through experience and logic, that Christ indeed is the incarnation of the Idea of the Being, the revelation of the Logos of God, and the manifestation of His perfect Volition. And thus our School turn out to be one that is progressive for the sake of mankind and not stagnant or retrogressive, as the schools which do not recognize yet the revelation of Truth in Christ, and which deny this directly as well as indirectly without reasons and proofs, but by sophisms and absurdities, and by ill esteem for the beings and the facts. In being progressive and conflicting with the retrogressive and stagnant schools, our School is at the same one that teaches and proves the truth and reproves falsehood. It does not only prove the eternal Truth in Christ, but also reproves the delusion and fatuity resulting from the schools of materialism, of pantheism, of panegotism, and eclecticism, by proving their falsity. It also invites the lovers of Truth to the recognition of the ontological Truth in Christ, and propounds to them the right and true method of Philosophy by means of which they would become wise and the possessors of knowledge; it shows them the true principles of Philosophy by which our mind discovers and knows thoroughly the Truth desired and sought - for. In knowing Christ as the ontological Truth, being everlastingly and eternally as the first and supreme and universal One, it knows its logical and moral and natural truths, and deduces every truth contained in this ontological Truth, Which is the sum of all truth. In knowing Christ as the ontological Law of the Spirit, as the primary Law of the Being's Cognition, the absolute and universal One, it gets to know the logical, moral, and natural laws in Him by means of which is governed and directed the scientific, the moral, and the physical world ; it learns the logical, physical, and social principles existing in the ontological Principle of the Logos through which are conducted the sciences, the moral and practical and social life, and the occurent events and phenomena in nature. Our School therefore is indeed one that is philosophical, and natural, and social, having the pure knowledge of sciences, of the nature and organization of the entire society, of its efficient and final cause, of its purpose, and of the means leading thereunto. And being as such it is also a civilizing one by reason of possessing the true and pure civilization, pledging thereto the impartation of a holy and true religion to the society, of a right and true philosophy and education, of a government that is just as true and righteous, of a Chist-governed social system, whose speedy and excellent and successful preponderance do we wish for to the advantage of society, and to the glory of the Godman our Saviour the founder and establisher thereof. Amen.

THE END

CONTENTS

THE DECALOGUE AND THE GOSPEL

by Dr. Sotirios D. Philaretos

A Review by Dr. Floyd A. Keeling, D.D., LL.D., TH.D.,

Only through the enlightenment afforded by the Gospel can human society be reconstructed and be changed into a society of rational and moral beings. Accordingly, it is the duty of those of us who have been enlightened to enlighten the rest of society, and to strengthen society as a whole in connection with what is good for its salvation.

OUR GREATEST DUTY TO SOCIETY IS TO TELL IT : Thou wilt be wretched as long as thou art ignorant of the cause of thy welfare and wretchedness. As long as thou goest on thinking that thou canst satisfy thyneeds with what thou deemest to be good things, but which are bad. Thou wilt emerge from thy woes if thou seek out, if thou succeed in discovering that which is good and which can satisfy thy needs, and which exists before thine eyes. Jesus Christ and His Gospel are the good agent which will enable thee to fulfill thy needs.

Believe Him. Love Him. Obey Him submissively. Give Him thy heart and thine intellect.

Keep His Laws and commandments, and thou shalt feel within the omnipotent power competent to liberate thee from thy woes and to rid thee of thy misfortunes.

THOSE ARE THE WORDS WHICH EVERY EN-LIGHTENED CHRISTIAN OUGHT TO SPEAK CONTI-NUALLY TO HUMAN SOCIETY, OUT OF CONVICTION AND WITH MARTYRLIKE SELF-ABNEGATION Page 54-55.

In this 62 page book by Dr. Philaretos, are to be found Heaven Inspired, Holy Spirit Anointed statements of profound truths covering such subjects as God Exists, Man Exists, Human Life The Divine Law Exists because God Exists. The Decalogue and the Gospel, then follows an Exposition of Each Command-ment by a Spiritual, Concecrated, dedicated Expositor, Philoso-pher, Sociologist, Political Economist, Theologian and Educator.

You Fathers and Mothers of Orthodoxie read this book so that you can teach your children rightly and «Bring them up in the admonition of the Lord».

Young Men and Women of Orthodoxie especially College

and High School Students who will be instructed by Pseudo Scientists and Philosophers read this book for within its 62 pages You will find the words mentioned by the Psalmist David in the 9th verse of the 119th Psalm when he answers the question «Wherewith shall a young man direct his way? by keeping thy words». Surely all young people are included in this advice, Yes read this book «The Decalogue and the Gospel» take heed to the words found therein, for as Dr. Philaretos so truly stated «Jesus Christ and His Gospel are the good Agent which will enable thee fulfill thy needs. Read again the opening citation found on pages 54 and 55 of this wonderful book translated from the Greek into sublimely beautiful Englich by an anointed translator.

Reverend Fathers in God, Clergyman and Educators, those who are not members of the Orthodox Church but who have read this book wonder that this book has not been introduced to every member of the Orthodox Church, for as one widely known Evangelist stated «The Author of that Book knew the meaning of Holiness, Evangelism & true Christian Living. In proof he cited the following statement found on page 43 under the caption «The Gospel Way of Life» «If I want to be a true Christian, and if I am working with the Aim of accomplishing this end, it is plain that I love myself. If I want all men to become followers of Jesus Christ, and am contributing my best efforts to bringing about this condition, it is plain that I also love all other human beings. But if I neither entertain any desire nor make any efforts in this direction, it is evident that I love neither myself nor others».

A Professor of a Theological Seminary stated that «Not only does this book contain a way out of the worlds dilemma a message for our troubled times, dut every page has some of the most wonderful statements to underscore». Oh? Orthodox Christians see that a copy of this book is in your home. Heed its teachings and your home will be truly ORTHODOX.